After a career in journalism spanning a decade from 1974, Sandi Logan joined the Australian foreign service and undertook postings to Papua New Guinea (Port Moresby), Germany (Bonn) and the United States (Washington, DC) before returning to Canberra as a senior executive and spokesman for various federal departments, agencies and government ministers. He has been consulting privately in communications strategy since 2014.

Sandi was first alerted to the story of Americans Vera Todd Hays (Toddie) and Florice Bessire (Beezie), who became known as the 'Drug Grannies', as a 21-year-old journalist, before taking up an active role fighting what he perceived to be the injustice of their case.

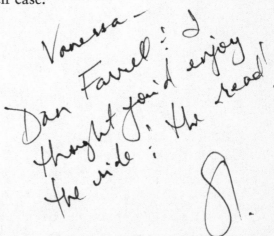

Vanessa –
Dan Farrell : I
thought you'd enjoy
the ride : the read!

S.

BETRAYED

THE INCREDIBLE UNTOLD INSIDE STORY OF THE TWO MOST UNLIKELY DRUG-RUNNING GRANNIES IN AUSTRALIAN HISTORY

SANDI LOGAN

hachette
AUSTRALIA

Quote on page 207 reproduced with permission from *The Bend Bulletin*.
Quote on page 208 reproduced with permission from *The Oregonian*.
Quote on pages 254–256 from *City Extra* reproduced with permission.
Quote on page 268 from 'Drug penalties and politics', 23–24 January 1982, reproduced with permission from *The Australian*.
Quote on page 271 from David Halpin's 'OUT Notorious drug-smuggler goes free after sentence cut short', 16 May 1982, reproduced with permission from the *Sun-Herald*.
Quote on page 325 from 'Balance Needed', 4 May 1978, reproduced with permission from *The Daily Telegraph*.
Quote on page 325 from 'Drug Penalties', 4 May 1978, reproduced with permission from *The Sun*.
Quote on page 329 from 1 July 1979 article reproduced with permission from the *Sun-Herald*.

hachette
AUSTRALIA

Published in Australia and New Zealand in 2022
by Hachette Australia
(an imprint of Hachette Australia Pty Limited)
Gadigal Country, Level 17, 207 Kent Street, Sydney, NSW 2000
www.hachette.com.au

Hachette Australia acknowledges and pays our respects to the past, present and future Traditional Owners and Custodians of Country throughout Australia and recognises the continuation of cultural, spiritual and educational practices of Aboriginal and Torres Strait Islander peoples. Our head office is located on the lands of the Gadigal people of the Eora Nation.

NATIONAL
LIBRARY
OF AUSTRALIA

A catalogue record for this
book is available from the
National Library of Australia

ISBN: 978 0 7336 4860 1 (paperback)

Cover design by Luke Causby, Blue Cork Designs
Cover and internal images courtesy of Sandi Logan unless otherwise credited
Author photograph courtesy Andrew Parsons
Typeset in Sabon by Kirby Jones
Printed and bound in Australia by McPherson's Printing Group

MIX
Paper from
responsible sources
FSC
www.fsc.org   FSC® C001695

The paper this book is printed on is certified against the Forest Stewardship Council® Standards. McPherson's Printing Group holds FSC® chain of custody certification SA-COC-005379. FSC® promotes environmentally responsible, socially beneficial and economically viable management of the world's forests.

For two wonderful women –
Toddie (Vera Todd Hays) and Beezie (Florice Marie Bessire) –
who proved there was life after near-death.

CONTENTS

INTRODUCTION by Michele 'Miche' Khoury, former Federal
Bureau of Narcotics agent   ix

FOREWORD   xi

PART ONE THE TRIP   1
CHAPTER ONE All in the family   3
CHAPTER TWO Home by Christmas   16
CHAPTER THREE Bathed in opportunity   19
CHAPTER FOUR The Hippie Trail awaits   27
CHAPTER FIVE Negotiating an Indian passage   45
CHAPTER SIX Carnet or bust   65

PART TWO OPERATION GENIUS   73
CHAPTER SEVEN You know the drill   75
CHAPTER EIGHT This was no holiday   83
CHAPTER NINE Your cake and you're stuck with it   93
CHAPTER TEN Don't 'Aunty' me   113

PART THREE BUSTED AND COURTSIDE   123
CHAPTER ELEVEN You look familiar   125
CHAPTER TWELVE Only a 'little illegal'   147
CHAPTER THIRTEEN Hashish and old lace   176
CHAPTER FOURTEEN Kill those damned Yanks   203

PART FOUR THE FIGHT FOR FREEDOM 221

CHAPTER FIFTEEN An eye for an eye and a Queen's amnesty? 223

CHAPTER SIXTEEN Beaten not bowed – US support grows 243

CHAPTER SEVENTEEN Damn their politics and injustice 263

CHAPTER EIGHTEEN This is for real, right? 290

EPILOGUE 307

POSTSCRIPT 311

APPENDIX 1 313

APPENDIX 2 321

ACKNOWLEDGEMENTS 333

INTRODUCTION

By Michele 'Miche' Khoury,
former Federal Bureau of Narcotics agent

The case of what's commonly referred to as the 'Drug Grannies' was for me one of the biggest operations and take-downs in my career as a former Federal Bureau of Narcotics agent. Vera Hays and Florice Bessire and their drug-laden campervan presented a challenge in undercover narcotics detection, the likes of which we'd rarely seen in Australia. I knew that, depending on the success of the team of agents (which I was a part of) assigned to track and eventually arrest the two women, drug enforcement could conceivably earn greater respect from the nation's politicians who were essentially our paymasters and commanders in proxy.

On the morning of the Operation Genius briefing in the bureau's Melbourne office, there was a cross between excitement and apprehension among my fellow agents. We knew of this particular West German–based syndicate, but we hardly expected our suspects to be two elderly women in a campervan.

For once, we weren't told *not* to work overtime. Staff was made available from every crack and crevice in the department; there was bugging equipment and even an army helicopter helping our surveillance, rarities in the oft problematic relations between law enforcement and the armed forces.

As the days of surveillance grew into weeks, I couldn't help but notice a certain friendship, a certain understanding develop between me and the two targets. While I had a job to do, I found myself admiring these two old gals for their gall, their spunk and the sheer chutzpah of it all. Still, from my perspective based on everything I saw, heard and read, they were breaking the law – to the tune of importing almost two tonnes of cannabis resin.

When we arrested Florice Bessire and then Vera Hays, the shock on their faces and the tremble in their voices was quite pitiful. Most people when apprehended by law enforcement display this same shock, but for these two elderly women in a foreign country, it was very sad. Both women were willing to cooperate with me and my senior partner.

From time to time during their incarceration, I received updates from various sources on the Drug Grannies in prison, and each time I was reminded I had helped to put them there, condemned them to a long stretch in prison unless someone took on their case and argued for an early release. Fortunately that 'someone' – Sandi Logan – did fight for them, and though my views on their complicity in the case did not change – they had pleaded guilty after all – I was relieved to see how their lengthy sentence was ultimately resolved.

FOREWORD

Little did I anticipate, when checking the newswires one night as a 21-year-old police rounds reporter at the *Toronto Sun* newspaper in my homeland of Canada in early 1978, to read a story that would later end up leading me into a near four-year fight for justice for two elderly American women languishing in an Australian prison. As a teenager, I'd lived Down Under at various times between 1968 and 1975 so I was familiar with its people, places and politics. The short report about these American women, then aged fifty-nine and sixty-one, being sentenced to fourteen years' imprisonment for importing their campervan loaded with 1.9 tonnes of hashish was too good a yarn to ignore. I ripped the telex paper from the machine, stuffed it into my shirt pocket and then filed it away, making a mental note to follow it up when I returned to Australia in late 1978. Once there, I made contact with the two women prisoners – Vera Todd 'Toddie' Hays and Florice 'Beezie' Bessire – and over several months, I earned their trust, and them mine, such that we would go on to meet almost weekly for the next near-four years, to plan and advocate for their freedom.

This is their – and our – story. A story about how two gullible women, close companions for almost twenty years, accepted a nephew's offer of the 'trip of a lifetime' and found themselves duped and betrayed, then intimidated and eventually threatened into unknowingly importing Australia's then-biggest drug haul in history, secreted in the base of a 26-foot campervan they drove from Stuttgart to Bombay (Mumbai), and then trans-shipped to Australia. Their subsequent fight for justice would challenge the anti-American bias in their sentencing, an Australian government seemingly hell-bent on appearing to be 'tough on drugs', and a systemic inequality discriminating against federal prisoners incarcerated in state prisons. It challenged the political resolve of Australia's government of the day and tested the bilateral relationship between two close allies.

Throughout their ordeal, the women kept diaries. At first, thoughts, reminders and queries were scribbles – often on scraps of notepaper during their trip. They then progressed to single-spaced typewritten foolscap pages before taking to recording events in their own handwriting within day-to-a-page bound diaries while in prison. They pinned letters and cards – and filed newspaper clippings of relevance – they'd received to a specific day's page. Most of the women's entries were contemporaneous, though it appears in some instances that accounts were recorded at a later time.

In this book, conversations and quotations attributed to the women, and the network of people associated with their case and their lives, are predominantly based on these documents. Accounts from my weekly visits at the prison, and the interviews I recorded for broadcast and publication, have also been drawn upon to tell this story.

This is the story of the Drug Grannies, and how and why they were made to pay such a high price for their crime.

PART ONE

THE TRIP

CHAPTER ONE

ALL IN THE FAMILY

It was the summer of 1976. The 200th anniversary of the American Declaration of Independence was being celebrated with bicentennial enthusiasm across the USA. Earlier in the year, the Pittsburgh Steelers had defeated the Dallas Cowboys 21–17 to win the Super Bowl in Miami; the UN Security Council had voted 11–1 to offer the Palestine Liberation Organization a seat at the table; George H W Bush was named the eleventh director of the Central Intelligence Agency, and New Zealand Prime Minister Robert Muldoon was one of the last world leaders to meet Chinese leader Chairman Mao Zedong when he visited him in Beijing. Mao died in September.

The year was also remarkable for other reasons: the US Supreme Court ruled the death penalty was constitutionally valid; Legionnaires' disease was the name given to the mystery disease which claimed twenty-nine lives at an American Legion convention in Philadelphia; both Air France and British Airways began trans-Atlantic passenger flights on the supersonic Concorde from London and Paris; and NASA's spacecraft *Viking 1* landed on Mars.

In an otherwise unremarkable event in July of that same year, Oregon residents and retirees 58-year-old Vera Todd 'Toddie' Hays and her long-time companion 60-year-old Florice 'Beezie' Bessire had driven their motorhome from the small community in which they lived in the state's north-west to visit Vernon Sr, Toddie's brother, 776 miles (1250 kilometres) away in the suburbs of North Hollywood. Toddie was very close to her siblings when growing up in and around Los Angeles, and that bond continued and extended to their families and children; a twelve-hour drive was no disincentive.

•

Toddie's favourite nephew – her brother's adult son, also named Vern (Jr) – was by then living and working in Australia, and the family home still showcased his many achievements, including those as an ocean-going yachtsman, actor, sometime-model, businessman and now successful entrepreneur. Photos, press-clippings, marketing brochures and theatre programs from his Australian exploits featured prominently around Toddie's brother's house.

'Vern Jr's talents know no bounds,' remarked Beezie, looking at the latest in his parents' display of their son's accomplishments. He had first journeyed away from mainland USA in 1965 as a crew member aboard the 66-foot cutter *Nam Sang*, participating in the annual Transpacific Yacht Race from San Pedro to Honolulu. He told his family he wasn't sure when he'd be back. At twenty-two years of age, life had been good for the young man.

'God love him, he was always a blessed child that one,' Toddie commented, as Vern Sr fixed them a drink.

Barely half an hour later, the doorbell rang and Vern Sr went to open the door. A somewhat familiar voice echoed down the hallway: 'Who the hell has taken my parking spot?'

'Vern! I don't believe it. What are you doing here? When did you get back?' Toddie said as she gushed with excitement at this encounter – the first in a decade – with her nephew. She turned to her brother, wide-eyed and open-mouthed, demanding, 'Did you know about this?'

He smiled at her and gave a knowing wink.

'Sorry about your parking space, honey,' said Beezie.

'We weren't to know, and your father didn't say anything. What a wonderful surprise!' Toddie added, embracing her nephew tightly.

'That's a fine rig you're driving,' Vern Jr said. 'I could do with one of those Down Under. All of Australia would be crazy over it.'

'Why?' Toddie asked. 'Don't they have motorhomes over there?'

Vern Jr confirmed they did but explained, 'They're not nearly as self-contained and luxurious as yours. You've got big beds, a kitchen with a fridge, a stove, a sink, a bathroom with a wash basin, a toilet ... even a dinette.' He told her it was just the sort of vehicle he needed for a travelogue he was planning to film in the Australian outback. 'If I had one like this, I could take the family along and still have all the comforts of home,' he said.

The discussion turned to Vern Jr's family, life in Australia, then on to the upcoming presidential election and the Olympic Games underway in Montreal.

Less than an hour later, Vern Jr took his leave, he said, to head to a business meeting, but not before dispensing big hugs to Toddie and Beezie. He departed with a wave and one of his customary megawatt smiles.

It seemed to Toddie that just as suddenly as he'd arrived, he was gone.

•

When Vern Leonard Todd (Vern Jr) was born on 8 December 1943, Toddie was enlisted in the Women's Army Corps (WAC), serving in Army Air Corps Ferrying Command at what was originally the Wright Field near Dayton, Ohio. (She was one of about 50,000 enlisted civilian workers assigned to the sprawling base.) Toddie was excited for her brother Vernon Sr and his wife upon hearing the news they were now proud parents of a healthy baby boy, and she was eager for her first home leave so she could meet her newborn nephew.

Fast-forward to 1966 and approaching the age of twenty-two, Vern had completed an intense five-week stage production in Los Angeles. As members of the Todd family gathered in North Hollywood to farewell him on his next yacht race, little did Toddie and Beezie know what role international travel would play in their future, and how it would shape both their and Vern's lives.

The yacht race provided an escape for Vern in more ways than one. Though he didn't declare it, perhaps one of the reasons for his decision to sail again was his opposition to the Vietnam War. He faced the possibility, once his deferment period expired upon completion of his college studies, that his name could be picked to join the more than two million young Americans drafted to the combat zone from 1964 to 1973.

He had also become genuinely passionate about sailing. He crewed on the *Nam Sang* again in his second Transpacific Yacht Race to Hawaii and then committed to a further 3500 nautical mile race over five days from Hawaii to Bora Bora in Tahiti. His South Pacific odyssey continued to New Zealand where he spent three months, partly due to a growing love interest, before he continued to Australia. He arrived in Sydney in December 1966, just in time to rejoin the crew of the *Nam Sang* for its entry in the Sydney–Hobart yacht race.

Toddie knew from her frequent contact with her brother that in Australia Vern had dabbled in the Sydney arts scene, began appearing in TV commercials and chanced his hand in a small business enterprise. He landed a role in the Harry M Miller production of *Boys in the Band* in 1968, which opened at the Playbox Theatre. He appeared alongside young Australian acting talent such as Henri Szeps and Gerard Maguire. And when Vern wasn't on stage he was often found behind the scenes, bumping bands into and out of their live performance venues, setting up their sound systems, erecting their lights and rigging.

Vern lived in Sydney's eastern suburbs. His good looks, natural charm, Californian accent and self-assuredness helped his name remain on booking agency lists. He also began to build a company – Tubby Products – around an inflatable baby bath invention a friend had designed. Vern was capable of turning business ideas into money-makers, starting with a teenage passion collecting pine cones he preserved and transformed into cupboard handles for a small Californian furniture maker.

Quick to seize upon a money-making opportunity early in his Australian experience, he also discovered ceiling fans had become a popular accessory, especially in homes exposed to high heat and tropical humidity. Before long, he was securing old and broken fans, to be repaired and resold in antique stores.

His Australian business interests regularly took him abroad, and in 1976, he was back in California to visit his parents. Though his family was unaware, US authorities had come to suspect him of adopting different identities to travel – especially into and out of the United States – in an effort to avoid raising any red flags. He was beginning to move in questionable circles negotiating business deals in several countries.

•

Toddie and Beezie both had the company of many brothers and sisters in their childhood, and growing up during the Depression, making ends meet, they developed strength of character and resilience.

Vera Todd (her father's surname) Hays was born on 18 March 1918 in Hollywood, California. She was the third eldest in the family, with two older brothers and two younger sisters. She was the tallest of the girls, nudging six feet (1.8 metres) by the time she'd hit her mid-teens.

Her father was a hard worker and devoted to his wife and children. The family grew up at a time when Hollywood was a safe community in which to raise a family. Toddie was a tomboy at heart, often fighting her brothers' battles and protecting them from playground bullies. She graduated from high school and completed one year of junior college before leaving, aged nineteen. As a young woman, she worked in a variety of odd jobs, but more importantly, her size and strength as an athlete attracted the attention of both a professional softball team and US Olympic selectors in 1936.

The softball league in which she played was one of the highlights of both Toddie's and her family's days in Hollywood. A team sponsored by Bing Crosby – the 'Croonerettes' – competed in a newly established semi-professional softball circuit in Southern California, including appearances at Loyola Stadium. Her prowess on the diamond also attracted US Olympic decathlon coaches for the Berlin Olympic Games. She withdrew from the US team, however, because of injury. For almost four years, the name 'Vera Todd' was synonymous with home runs and pitching strikeouts as she travelled initially in Southern California and then, as the circuit expanded, across the USA. A statuesque and physically imposing woman, she acquired the nickname 'Toddie' during her softball career, a moniker which was to stay with her for the rest of her life.

As with many professional athletes, the aches and pains resulting from her injuries began to take their toll, slowing her down on and off the field. She suffered from spinal disc degeneration – a congenital disease – and her shoulders began to tighten up when she wasn't on the mound or at the batting plate. By 1940, she tired of the physical demands required of a pro softball player and, while not completely alienating herself from the sport she loved, hung up her cleats and mitt, and took employment as a bowling alley manager, a job which lasted about a year.

In 1941, when she was California's single ladies bowling champion, she found work at North American Aviation (NAA) where she worked on the assembly line in the manufacture of aircraft components. In December 1942, she left NAA to enlist in the WAC as a private, first class. The call to war evoked patriotic sentiments and conscientious passion in Toddie, for she is recorded in the US Defence archives as one of few enlisted personnel to have risen from a private to a first-class sergeant in only nine months. Following the war, Toddie received a citation from President Truman for her efforts. The framed document was proudly hung in her home. From 1945 to mid-1947, she was employed by Marine Products, and later by the National Cash Register Company, on their assembly lines.

In 1948, the Los Angeles Police Department's female recruiting drive captured Toddie's attention, and she joined but stayed only long enough to complete basic training. She had tired of the regimentation the military had imposed on her, and was quick to acknowledge she was not a good fit for the police and its strong hierarchical structure.

She managed a shop until 1952, and during that time married, taking on her husband's surname, Hays. The marriage was short-lived and the couple divorced in 1953. There were no children.

Toddie had joined Douglas Aircraft Company's final assembly section in mid-1952, for which she required clearance from the FBI to work on a highly sensitive project the company was developing. It was at Douglas that she met Florice Bessire and began a friendship that was to last the rest of her life.

By 1966, Toddie was made a supervisor. In those days, such a promotion for a woman was rare: she had risen to become Douglas's first female final assembly line boss. However, following an industrial accident in 1969, Toddie received a payout and retired prematurely from the work she so enjoyed. Never one to be idle, she pursued outdoor pastimes such as fishing and hiking, and found her general love of these hobbies was a fulfilling substitute for work at the factory.

Her companion Florice Marie Bessire – better known as Beezie – had a similar love of the outdoors. She was born on 24 May 1916 in Beloit, Wisconsin, where she grew up with her parents, a brother and a sister. Her mother suffered ill health and required regular medical attention. The family moved to Oklahoma at one point but returned to Wisconsin before her parents divorced in the late 1920s, when Beezie was in her teens.

Growing up, Beezie's time after school and on the weekends was spent delivering newspapers, and collecting empty soda pop bottles then cashing them in for a few extra nickels to help the family budget. She was a strong young girl who at 5 feet 4 inches (1.6 metres) had no trouble carrying a full newspaper delivery bag over one shoulder, and a shopping bag of empty bottles she had collected on her paper route on the other. By nineteen, Beezie graduated from high school and began work on the assembly line with the Parker Pen Company in Jamesville, Wisconsin. Paid work was scarce so she considered herself lucky to even have a job. In 1938, she enrolled at the Kellberg College of Swedish Massage in Chicago where she studied massage therapy and early forms of sports medicine, before graduating in 1939.

Until 1942, Beezie worked as a massage therapist in Illinois before joining the giant multinational DuPont, in Washington state, where she was employed on the Manhattan atomic bomb project. Her role required strict secrecy, so all employees were housed and fed on the project base, with occasional company-supervised trips off-site. She remained with DuPont until 1943, when she joined Boeing Aircraft Corporation as an aircraft assembler. In 1944, Beezie started work at the Douglas Aircraft factory. She and Toddie first met working on the assembly line in 1952, eventually sharing a rented house, with a view to saving together for a mortgage.

Theirs was an old-fashioned, respectful companionship built as much out of common interests, trust and economic pragmatism as out of any sort of 'love'. Nonetheless it was a close relationship which was destined to last. It was what some social scientists in the mid-twentieth century described as a 'romantic friendship': an arrangement that was absent of any negative context and which attracted little outside enquiry.

It didn't take long before the pair purchased their first home in Newbury Park in California's Ventura County in 1953. The backyard swimming pool was popular with Toddie's siblings and their families. She even taught her younger sister Hazel, as an adult, how to swim.

Beezie was proud of her awards from Douglas Aircraft, including a medallion melted down from the first *Apollo* space flight which took pride of place in their new home.

As with most companies, especially in the aircraft manufacturing industry, there were periods when work was slow and the assembly line halted production. On several of these occasions, Beezie found other work to keep up with the house payments and, as was her way, also to keep herself occupied. Her friends remember her as someone who loved to 'tinker with tools' and who was able to put her aircraft assembly skills to good effect with most repair and patch-up jobs. She was employed on two occasions during these lulls by the American movie actress Donna Reed as a household manager and personal masseuse.

On another occasion when she was laid off from Douglas, Beezie worked as a dietician in a Wisconsin hospital. Indeed, Florice Bessire was known among family and friends for her good cooking and dietary common sense.

In 1974 Beezie and Toddie decided to move north to Oregon, where they would be away from the rat race of a big city, deep in Mother Nature's domain and closer to Beezie's sister, who was now managing a motel with her husband in nearby Port Angeles, Washington. Toddie and Beezie sold their Newbury Park home, and by now owned an eighteen-foot El Dorado motorhome and a Glasspar Citation motorboat. Through careful budgeting, they didn't owe a dime to anyone.

With the move north, Beezie officially retired and began receiving a monthly cheque from Douglas of about $300 as well as Social Security. She looked forward to a rest from assembly lines and aircraft components. For Toddie, who retired five years earlier – with a regular disability insurance payment, monthly retirement income of $450 and Social Security – the relocation was a more difficult decision. It was a bit of a jolt to finally leave Newbury Park and its proximity to her siblings and their families with whom she had kept in regular contact since retiring from her WAC duty in World War II. Extended family was important to the childless Toddie.

Toddie and Beezie purchased a block of land in La Pine, a small town of fewer than one thousand residents who were mainly retirees and lumberjacks. The township was nestled in the Deschutes National Forest, just off the mile-high Central Oregon Highway leading to Klamath Falls. It was about 776 miles (1250 kilometres) from Los Angeles. Onto their acre block of pine trees, for which they'd paid $18,000 cash, they placed a comfortable white Melody Lane two-bedroom mobile home they had purchased for $10,000, and prepared to settle into retirement. The two women had prepared thoroughly for the move and had done their homework. They were confident the fixed incomes from their modest pensions would enable them to continue to pursue a comfortable retiree lifestyle. La Pine, with its pleasant climate, healthy environment and proximity to numerous outdoor activities, seemed an excellent place to spend the rest of their lives.

Inside their new home, photos of family, work and sport adorned the walls, and Toddie's last pair of softball cleats hung from a nail next to a shelf of her trophies. A twelve-pound trout Beezie bagged on one of her early morning fishing expeditions on the Century Drive lakes was mounted on a wall not long after they settled in.

Oregon was one of the nation's most progressive states, leading the way in pollution legislation, road safety and marijuana reform.

The small-town atmosphere appealed to the women greatly, and they found a sense of community in La Pine, where they knew almost everybody and felt secure and safe. The previous few years at Newbury Park had sometimes been trying for them, with the murder rate in Los Angeles escalating and violent crime on the rise.

After dropping off Toddie's radar for years, Don and Thelma Mitchell, friends from her teenage years in the 1930s, suddenly appeared one day in La Pine. The couple had settled on the purchase of an A-frame home nearby and were enjoying a beer at one of their favourite haunts when they bumped into each other. The friendship was renewed quickly while they caught up on their respective pasts, pushing one beer into another, and another.

In fact, so close was the community of La Pine, volunteers stepped up to help locals Ken and Sharon Boyer in 1976 to renovate the run-down tavern they'd bought and renamed the La Pine Inn. It was to be turned into a restaurant-lounge, and Beezie and Toddie set to work.

'There was no charge for their skills, or tools or labour,' said Ken, 'and no talk of free drinks or anything.' The women became steady customers and good friends of the innkeepers. Boyer found them to be 'good for public relations'.

'They could sit in the cocktail lounge and talk to anybody,' he said, 'especially Beezie. She could handle a drunk better than anybody I saw. She could take somebody who might be pretty hostile and within three minutes she'd have him laughing.'

Part of Beezie's skill might have been acquired when she and Toddie briefly owned and operated a dinner house and cocktail lounge in Sacramento before their move north to Oregon. The pair was generous with advice and suggestions for the Boyers, and gave them a memento they'd kept from their own innkeeper days: a rifle in a glass case, which now took pride of place on the La Pine Inn's dining-room wall. The retirees even helped as servers on busy nights.

La Pine, its altitude-dwarfed pines nestled in view of the Three Sisters mountains, was God's country, the women thought. Not only was there expansive forest, but each season would reveal an entirely different beauty and wildlife was abundant. There was a network of nearby waterways into which they could launch their half-cabin cruiser and set out for a full day's fishing. When the women weren't outdoors traipsing through the wilderness, they were travelling the world in their armchairs, via the pages of *National Geographic* magazines – they had subscribed for many years.

But by 1976, Toddie's back and shoulders were again giving her regular if not constant pain, so reluctantly the pair decided to sell the boat and instead fish from the shorelines. At about the same time, Beezie became a little restless in retirement and looked for part-time work to keep her mind and hands occupied. True Value Hardware, one of the few businesses occupying La Pine's central thoroughfare, offered her a part-time role paid at the minimum rate. To Beezie, the money was secondary; she embraced the opportunity to keep busy. Her modest duties included stocktaking, inventory checks, maintaining the shelves and storeroom, and occasionally helping customers with their orders. Her employers, Nancy and Denis Carter, admired Beezie's dependability and adaptability.

'She was real handy with tools, real mechanical,' Nancy said, 'and one time when we wanted an old pick-up truck bed patched to use for storage, we tried for six months to get someone to do it, until Beezie spoke up. She patched it up just like we wanted.

'They both wore their hair cut short and dressed pretty mannish, but most people do in this part of the country. I'm sure that raised some eyebrows but once you got to know them, they were good people.'

In between work and fishing, Beezie and Toddie enjoyed a few rounds of golf, often conducting post-mortems at the nineteenth hole – not unlike many golfers. Vera and Florice – or, as many were by now calling them, Toddie and Beezie – fit right in with their outgoing natures, senses of humour, warmth and down-to-earth style.

Route 97 – the Central Oregon highway – which doubled as La Pine's main street, made for easy connections to the state's road network and for friends and family to visit. Their home in Birch Road was always open to visitors, and their neighbours and good friends Don and Thelma would regularly drop by to play cards, share a coffee or a beer, and an occasional meal.

Elaine Hempel, the US Postal Service's postmistress, got to know the pair at social occasions such as the Lions Club's community bingo. She got along well with the pair, as did Pat Lester at Patty-Dee Variety Store, and Artie Simpson, who owned the flower shop Floral Fantasies. There were very few, if any, La Pine locals who didn't warm to the women's company.

From time to time, the pair would set off from La Pine to travel north to Port Angeles to visit Beezie's sister, or they'd head south to Los Angeles and Orange Country, where Toddie's extended family remained.

La Pine was the ideal community to meet the women's needs, notwithstanding Toddie's initial misgivings about being so far away from her family. Toddie and Beezie settled comfortably into their new life in Oregon and the community of La Pine, and retired like they meant it.

CHAPTER TWO

HOME BY CHRISTMAS

Within the Cascade Ranges in north-west Oregon and the Deschutes National Forest, the ancient caldera of the Newberry Volcano surrounds the twin Paulina and East lakes.

It was April 1977, and the tall conifer forests hugging the deep Paulina Lake shore gave off a heady pine fragrance. In spring, dusk was always a reliable time to wait on the banks, patiently trolling lures for brown trout. This was America the beautiful; the home of the brave and the land of the free.

As dusk fell and with a couple of good-sized fish bagged, Toddie and Beezie packed their rods and their ageing poodle, Suzette, and set off in their orange Volkswagen Fastback for the drive home, about twelve miles (twenty kilometres) to the south-west.

Shortly after returning home and preparing the catch for dinner, the telephone interrupted Toddie's concentration. She reached for the black wall phone.

'Hello,' said Toddie.

'Aunty Vera, it's Nephew Vern calling. How's my favourite aunt?'

Toddie instinctively pulled a cigarette from the packet on the card table and reached for her lighter. She hadn't heard from her nephew since he'd arrived, unannounced, during the summer visit to her brother's in Southern California the previous year.

'Well, I'm fine, honey,' said Toddie. 'Heck, it's wonderful to hear from you.' She tucked her hand over the mouthpiece as her neighbour Thelma came through the front door to catch up on their latest fishing exploits.

'I'll be a few minutes; it's my nephew calling long distance,' Toddie explained, and turned her attention back to the phone call.

'Listen, Aunty Vera, I have a wonderful proposition for you. Are you sitting down?' asked Vern.

'Sure I am. What have you got on your mind, honey?' replied Toddie. She wasn't sure where he was calling from, such was the sometimes patchy connection.

Vern and Toddie's conversation lasted less than ten minutes. By now Beezie, who had come inside, and Thelma were curious as they'd caught a reference to an 'all expenses paid vacation'. Toddie's facial expressions weren't hiding her excitement either.

Toddie had started on a second cigarette, while the first sat idly burning to the filter tip in the ashtray. She finally got off the call, and both Beezie and Thelma anxiously awaited the details.

'I don't believe it!' Toddie declared. 'Nephew Vern has offered Beezie and me an all-expenses-paid trip through Europe,' she said.

'Well, did you accept?' asked Thelma.

'No, not yet. He's giving us a couple of weeks to think about it. Heck, what did we do to deserve this?' she said breathlessly.

The evening was filled with talk about Vern's generous offer. Neither Toddie nor Beezie had travelled overseas before – their only 'international' travel had been a quick border hop into Mexico shortly after they'd moved in together, to purchase pottery and some leather shoes. This trip was in a whole new league to travel they'd ever done before.

Beezie was initially hesitant and not quite as enthusiastic as Toddie, and wanted to go over the details, as scant as they were.

'So you say Nephew Vern has offered us an all-expenses-paid trip across Europe ... doing what?' queried Beezie.

'Driving a motorhome,' replied Toddie. 'He is filming for some sort of project in Australia and figured we could handle a big vehicle. He said we would enjoy the trip more than anyone else he knew. I told him I'd speak to you about it all, and he'll phone us back in a few weeks to get our response,' added Toddie.

Beezie thought for a moment about their poodle, Suzette. She was going on fourteen and was not enjoying the best of health. She was now completely deaf and blind but had grown accustomed to her limitations and was otherwise healthy and happy.

'How long would we be gone for?' asked Beezie.

'Well, Vern reckons we'll be home by Christmas,' answered Toddie.

Caught up in the excitement, Thelma chipped in, 'You'd both be crazy not to go', and in the same breath offered to look after Suzette and arrange for Don to tend to their home and garden while they were away.

CHAPTER THREE

BATHED IN OPPORTUNITY

After much discussion between the two women, Beezie increasingly warmed to the proposal and the travel bug began to bite. They started to make lists, albeit with no firm idea about the finer details. Having made up their minds, however, they set to the task of preparing for the trip. Certainly driving long distances wasn't an issue for them.

A trip had been in the offing for Toddie and Beezie, at least in their imaginations. They had considered the idea of flying to Hawaii for that Christmas, but the opportunity to travel to Europe seemed incredible.

As promised, Vern phoned several weeks later to gauge the women's response, and as he expected, they were both keen to take him up on his offer. Toddie plied him with questions from the list she and Beezie had made. Vern said he'd be travelling to the United States soon and he'd visit them to provide further details and help organise their documentation for the trip.

In the meantime, Beezie continued working at the hardware store, Toddie and Thelma fished and played cards, and summer prepared to replace spring in the northern hemisphere.

Around mid-June 1977 there was a knock on the front door one morning. Toddie glanced at the wall clock. They weren't expecting a visitor, but then, in a small town like La

Pine, friends and neighbours were just as likely to drop by unannounced. That's the way it was.

In a quick glimpse through the curtained windows Toddie could make out a well-dressed man, carrying what appeared to be an aluminium briefcase standing with his back to her. Toddie approached the door and opened it. Her face immediately creased into a smile.

'Vern!' she said, enveloping her nephew in her arms. 'You didn't even call us to let us know you were coming, damn it! We wanted to have everything all fixed up, but no matter, come on in, honey,' she said.

It had been almost a year since they had seen him and at thirty-four, he was a fine looking man. He was tall with an athletic build, not unlike his father and aunt. His thick brown hair was collar length, but neat and styled. A gold ring on his wedding finger and a gold chain hung about his neck added to his chic but casual look, completed by an open-necked shirt.

Vern Todd now co-owned and operated an import/export business in Sydney, which would become known as Tubby Infant Products and gain global shelf space for, among other products, its inflatable Tubby Bath. Vern's company, in its early days, supplemented his acting and modelling income, which was neither regular nor necessarily always enough to sustain his lifestyle. He explained the company's success meant they were now expanding to markets in Europe and Asia. Toddie and Beezie marvelled at his achievements and were impressed to see how the once independent, adventurous youth had matured into a successful, jet-setting entrepreneur.

In fact, Vernon Leonard Todd, the Los Angeles–born university review actor, who, according to theatre programs in Australia, had once scored a role in the TV series *Mr Novak*, was, in addition to his business operations, also getting work in TV commercials and on modelling shoots.

During the national tour of *Boys in the Band*, an American play about homosexuality – a topic considered risqué in

Australia at the time – at the behest of government censors and prudish politicians, police attended performances in Sydney, Canberra, Melbourne, Perth and Hobart. Some senior police and politicians believed the play offended people's morality, but their narrow-mindedness failed to halt the show's successful run over almost two years. When the Tubby Bath was launched on the Australian market in December 1972, the *Sun-Herald* newspaper prominently covered the event with a profile on Vern. He was described as an actor who 'likes sailing and making beach buggies'. It told the story of Vern's arrival in Australia in 1966 to compete in the famous Sydney to Hobart yacht race in which the *Nam Sang* finished a creditable seventh. It was after the race, the newspaper said, that Vern decided to stay in Australia.

Vern was one of the first people to introduce modified dune buggies to Australian beaches. On 8 February 1970, hardly an eyebrow was raised when Vern and his bride, 21-year-old New Zealander Maggie, drove away from their wedding in one of the black and gold vehicles he and an actor mate had rebuilt in Melbourne, and which the mate drove to Sydney for the wedding celebrations.

The origins of Vern's relationship with Maggie followed the *Nam Sang*'s 1966 voyage through the South Pacific, including a New Zealand stopover. He became a landlubber for several months and with a fellow crewmate hitchhiked around the North and South islands, meeting his wife-to-be along the way. Together they travelled to Australia in time for Vern's crew briefings at the Cruising Yacht Club on Rushcutters Bay. He rejoined the Santa Monica Yacht Club–berthed *Nam Sang* under the command of owner and skipper John Thompson. The converted ketch was tipped as a favourite to win the Sydney to Hobart line honours.

Vern Todd made his first formal foray into business in the early 1970s along with a business partner. The two registered their company with the NSW Corporate Affairs Commission on 26 September 1972 and listed among their objectives the 'manufacturing of and dealing in plastics, textile, timber and metal goods and vehicles, plant and machinery'. The 'dealing in ... vehicles' aspect was clearly an opportunity to tap the growing market for imported foreign cars, motorcycles and perhaps one day campervans. Vern's business partner never anticipated what Vern would do with the vehicles, or any of the activities undertaken beyond the scope of the Tubby Bath products.

The limited liability of the company had a share capital of 10,000 one dollar units, and both Vern Todd and his business partner held a management share. At the same time, they had settled with a designer for a new inflatable baby bath prototype, which they hoped to produce in Taiwan cheaply and export to Australia for retail sale. The designer – 23-year-old Ken Beatty, a fellow student from the University of New South Wales – said he learned his first business lesson about trust and mistrust thanks to Vern.

As Beatty remembers it, Vern Todd commissioned him to design a baby bath which was both safe for babies and cheap to produce. Beatty was already designing inflatable rubber toys called Snibbos that were made from thick plastic and then heat treated, so the bath – lightweight and portable – was an easy concept to adapt to Todd's requirements.

Beatty set to work and in 1970 came up with a prototype, which Todd and his business partner approved. The design specifications were dispatched to Taiwan, where manufacturers went to work on samples with a variety of chemicals and plastics, before the business partners settled on a mainland Chinese company to produce a commercially viable product – the Tubby Bath. Beatty graduated to become a successful furniture designer, sculptor and installation artist, later creating inflatable sculptures for Sydney's Pact experimental art theatre, Ubu Films and the Mildura Sculpture Triennial.

The bath was an overnight success once the manufacturers sorted out the early problems with broken seals and poor-quality materials. Demand outstripped supply with the first shipment of 1000 units selling overnight through a handful of Sydney retail outlets. But for designer Beatty, the new product amounted to only a few hundred dollars' income. His Tubby Bath was a commercial opportunity on which he believed he had been sold decidedly short. There was no commission and there were no ongoing royalties.

On the other hand, to Vern's immediate family, aunts and uncles, their understanding was that his business dealings were further proof of his capacity to do well at just about anything he attempted – acting, modelling, importing and now manufacturing and distributing. As a gesture of their faith in him, his mother and father purchased 100 shares in the company in 1973; an uncle and aunt also purchased shares.

•

As Vern relaxed with the women in La Pine, he chatted about family with Toddie while Beezie prepared lunch. Soon conversation turned to the matter at hand – the trip to Europe – as Vern had proposed in his earlier telephone conversations. He explained to the women there were two reasons for the trip.

First, he said, they would drive the camper van with Tubby Baths on board and help to stage product demonstrations with him and other business partners in shopping hubs along the way. The two women would have an opportunity to travel through the Continent at a leisurely pace, stopping when and where they chose, merely acting as 'transport agents' for the bath promotions while Vern and his associates attended to the business side of things.

Second, as he explained it, his company needed a new van for a film they were shooting in the Australian outback – the 'bush' he called it – and this would be a cost-effective way of purchasing and delivering a mobile home otherwise unavailable in Australia.

'But you made no mention of travelling to Australia before,' interjected Toddie.

'No, you don't have to go to Australia – just drive it from Stuttgart to Bombay where we'll have it shipped by sea to Australia,' explained Vern, reassuringly. 'I'll take care of all that.'

They discussed the proposition further, but Beezie was still troubled by its simplicity. Okay, she thought, he has done well as a businessman, but nobody gets a free lunch.

Vern also raised the idea of payment. In addition to their travel expenses, he would pay them a sum of US$25,000 upon reaching Bombay.

Beezie felt there had to be a catch. She leaned back in her chair, rested one elbow on the armrest and the other along the back of the chair, as she tilted her head to one side and queried: 'Okay Vern, what's the deal? Is it pedal-powered?'

Vern laughed off her concern, ignoring any suspicion creeping into Beezie's disposition. With a smile he said to both women, 'No, there's nothing primitive about this trip, except perhaps the towns and cities you may visit along the way. Anyway, Aunt Vera, you are my favourite aunt; I could ask anyone to make this trip, but I would rather have you both make the money instead,' he explained.

Toddie and Beezie relaxed and Vern continued: 'I will tell you something though: I've driven that route before. I know those countries, and I know their roads. You'll have earned every cent of what I'm offering you, and that's without any exaggeration at all. It will help me get the campervan to Australia and enable me to do Tubby Bath business along the way.'

It still seemed a lot of money to Beezie, but neither of the women had any reason to distrust Nephew Vern.

Toddie leaned forward and looked into Vern's eyes: 'There's nothing fishy, is there?'

Vern waved off the suggestion with a hand gesture.

'No!' said Vern. 'Nothing like that ... although I do smoke a little marijuana and I may take some to smoke along the way.'

Vern smoking 'grass' was nothing new to Toddie or Beezie; they'd known about this from Vern's college days when they heard he once dared smoke some in front of his parents. And after all, it was nearly legal or actually legal in some American states now, while minor possession was lawful in their own state of Oregon.

'Well, the hell then,' said Toddie. 'I smoke cigarettes. I don't give a damn what you smoke, as long as what you do doesn't affect either Beezie or me!'

By now, Toddie's and Beezie's thoughts were focused on visions of travel and the adventure ahead. All they could think of were international airports, passports and the other side of the world, hitherto only experienced through the glossy pages of magazines and TV documentaries. They agreed and gave the proposed venture the nod.

Vern departed, telling them he would arrange to wire them $3000 for their tickets to Frankfurt, their passports, and visas and vaccinations. He gave them a list of things they needed to get organised and suggested they be ready for a departure sometime in August.

Toddie and Beezie were abuzz. They popped over to their neighbours' to confirm they could leave their beloved Suzette and the house keys with them for a few months. Don and Thelma, who also had a poodle, were more than happy to oblige, and were equally enthusiastic about the women taking up the offer of such a thrilling adventure. 'Be sure to send us lots of postcards,' said Don.

Toddie and Beezie went methodically about the essential tasks of compiling the personal records required for their first-ever US passports as well as ensuring their needles for chickenpox, diphtheria, tetanus, measles and polio were all up to date. Their doctor recommended additional coverage, such as for smallpox, cholera and rabies because of their travel through high-risk areas such as India and South Asia.

Vern phoned Toddie and Beezie from overseas in mid-July. His call was to flag a later start date for the overland journey once they'd landed in Europe. The campervan's fit-out had been delayed, he said. He told them it might not be until September that they would need to fly to Germany. The women made the necessary ticketing adjustments and found it easy to fill the summer days. In fact, they were glad of the reprieve. Beezie continued working at the hardware store while Toddie prepared their home in anticipation of their four-month absence. It was rare for a day to go by without Beezie telling her boss Nancy Carter something new about the planned trip.

Unexpectedly, Toddie suddenly fell ill with what doctors believed at the time was an internal infection. She was admitted to hospital in nearby Bend overnight and placed on medication before being sent home the next day. An appointment was made to see a specialist. Neither Toddie nor Beezie could believe their misfortune.

Toddie found that the antibiotics she was prescribed caused headaches and interfered with her nightly drink over cards. She became uncertain whether she and Beezie would be able to complete the overseas trip, so in fairness to Vern she sent a telegram to him in Australia to say they were no longer available on account of her ill health.

Vern immediately telephoned them. He inquired about Toddie's health and wanted to know if she was still under her doctor's care.

'Absolutely,' Toddie replied. 'I'm a bit of a wreck at the moment, what with my back, my leg and now this damn infection. I'm sorry, honey, but I think we'd best just forget about this trip,' she said. Toddie was inclined to be dramatic at times but Vern couldn't tell in a trans-Pacific phone call just how sick she was. He told her the van fit-out was still a work in progress, and assured her that if she continued on her course of medication he was confident she would fully recover, and the trip offer would still stand. 'Let me know when your health picks up,' he signed off optimistically.

CHAPTER FOUR

THE HIPPIE TRAIL AWAITS

Beezie and Toddie could not quite shake the anticipation of the trip that Vern had proposed, and as Toddie's health began to improve, the pair allowed themselves to become excited once again. Toddie especially didn't want to let Vern down.

Fortunately, by early August, doctors gave Toddie the all-clear to travel. When Vern next called, he was delighted to learn of the improvement in his aunt's condition and the women's readiness to embark on the adventure.

Toddie and Beezie took their poodle to Don and Thelma's and made arrangements for their pensions to be paid into their local bank account in Bend, while Beezie's sister managed their bills and rates notices. Don, a former earthworks contractor, was looking forward to trying out Toddie's metal detector while they were away, although he baulked at their penchant for collecting and polishing rocks. The Mitchells, Ken and Sharon Boyer, and next-door neighbour and retired plumber Bill Tokstad threw them a bon voyage party. 'You're two sixty-year-old hippies,' joked Ken Boyer as they farewelled Beezie and Toddie late in the evening and headed home.

On 22 August 1977 the women set off for Port Angeles to spend a few days with Beezie's sister and brother-in-law, before being driven to nearby Seattle airport to catch their flight to JFK Airport in New York City, and then travel on to Germany. Their adventure of a lifetime was underway.

•

'Good afternoon, passengers,' said the flight's purser. 'We are now approaching Frankfurt International Airport, where the weather is warm and sunny and the temperature is a pleasant 22 degrees Celsius, 72 degrees Fahrenheit. We would ask that you extinguish your cigarettes, fasten your seatbelts, secure your tray tops and return your seats to the upright position.'

Toddie and Beezie peered through the small cabin window to catch a glimpse of the city of Frankfurt.

On 27 August 1977, the two weary travellers, after clearing German customs, transferred their bags from the international terminal and headed for the forty-minute domestic flight to Stuttgart, where they were looking forward to meeting Nephew Vern. He had explained in his last phone call that if there were flight delays or if for some reason he wasn't able to be at the airport for their arrival, they were to catch a taxi and go to the Stuttgart Klein Hotel, where he would meet up with them as soon as possible.

As it turned out Toddie's nephew wasn't there to meet them, so they hailed a taxi. The beauty of Stuttgart approaching fall – some leaves beginning to change colour on deciduous trees, pearl grey skies and the deep green of the conifer trees – made up for Vern's absence. Nonetheless, the signs in a foreign language, passport queues, and airport transfers were all very new experiences for the women, who were exhausted but chuffed they had successfully negotiated the first step on their journey to the other side of the world.

After settling into their hotel room, they soon discovered what jet lag was all about. The huge eiderdown blankets and European square pillows weren't what they were used to, but nonetheless they slept for fourteen hours uninterrupted and awoke late in the afternoon. They headed out to stretch their legs before returning to the hotel. A dinner reservation made, they proceeded to play a couple of rounds of pool to keep themselves awake and help adjust their body clocks.

It was two days into their German adventure and Vern had still not materialised, so the women decided not to waste time and rented a car. They made short forays through the old city, spotting buildings and monuments they recognised from the tourist brochures they picked up in the hotel lobby, and tracing the cobblestone roads high up into the mountains. It was a good opportunity to familiarise themselves with new road signs, foreign-language directions and the detailed European maps upon which Beezie, as designated navigator, would rely.

Vern finally contacted the women on day three and dropped by the hotel just after lunch, with three associates whom he introduced as Australian film producer Bob Lange, Mr X and his wife; the couple had their baby daughter with them. Vern said the couple and their child would accompany the women on the trip, although details were sketchy about sleeping arrangements. They chatted briefly about the flight, their sightseeing and Toddie's health. Vern and his associates didn't stay long. They wanted to head off to check on the van's preparations. Vern told them he would try to speed up the workers who were installing beds, a sink, cupboards and other accessories.

The women hadn't expected to remain for long in Stuttgart, but now, given the delay, were a little disappointed their nephew wasn't going to be there to show them the sights. They put it down to Vern being a busy man – they couldn't expect him to be at their beck and call, even if he was family.

Toddie and Beezie explored the area and neighbouring towns, sampling German wines, tasting new dishes, coming to grips with the unfamiliar language and enjoying the local hospitality.

Vern returned several days later to take them to the workshop where the vehicle was being worked on. He hoped they would be impressed by the fit-out of this European campervan. Vern knew of their experience with American motorhomes and recreational vehicles, and said he wanted to ensure the comforts were to a standard they were expecting.

They arrived at the workshop, surrounded by a large yard packed with motorhomes and campervans in various stages of fit-out, which Vern said were all being altered to their owners' specifications. The company specialised in body work and appeared to be very busy. Their vehicle was 7.9 metres (about twenty-six feet) in length and manufactured by Mercedes-Benz in Germany, so had the steering wheel on the left-hand side. It was only a four-cylinder motor, but this didn't bother the women too much as they weren't out to break any land-speed records crossing the Continent. They were impressed with the cupboards, windows and kitchen area being cut in, and asked for a chemical 'porta-potty' to be installed in the bathroom. A cassette player and speakers they had bought duty free en route were still awaiting installation in the driver's cabin. Toddie was well accustomed to the rigours of long-distance driving and had brought along her favourite easy-listening music on cassettes to play during the trip. Vern instructed the workers to proceed with the latest alterations and the trio departed. He gave Toddie money to shop for personal items to furnish the van so, not wasting any time, the women went shopping for bedding, pillows, cutlery, crockery, pots and pans, sheepskin seat covers, tinned foods and, as Vern recommended, plenty of bottled water.

When he arrived at the hotel the next day, Vern told them that Toddie needed to accompany him to London to arrange a Customs carnet for the vehicle. The suddenness of the arrangement took Toddie by surprise. She hadn't counted on a side trip to England. 'What the hell is a carnet?' both women asked.

'It's just a necessary registration formality,' replied Vern.

As far as Beezie was concerned, she was just a passenger and didn't need to know any more about what she termed this 'mumbo jumbo'. She remained in Stuttgart while Vern and Toddie made the quick trip to London.

Vehicles travelling from country to country are required to be accompanied by a carnet in the owner's name, effectively preventing the vehicle from being sold along the way unless the appropriate taxes are paid. The carnet reference is also stamped inside the vehicle owner's passport and must be sighted each time the vehicle crosses an international border.

Vern insisted, without explanation, that the carnet could not be issued in Germany and that they needed to travel to London for the procedure. About twenty-four hours later, after a rushed day attending several offices in the British capital, the *Carnet de Passages en Douane* (International Passage through Customs – Tourist Treaty) was issued, and the campervan was also insured. The carnet listed Vera Todd Hays as the owner, and further obliged her not to 'dismantle, sell, or lease' the vehicle while it was outside the country of registration, which was listed as England. It all seemed so foreign and complex to Toddie, but she trusted Vern's worldly experience and let him handle everything. She didn't bother asking him to explain it further and with the paperwork completed, Vern and Toddie returned to Germany.

Back in Stuttgart, during the final check at the workshop, Toddie discovered the high-powered driving lights still needed to be affixed and a bull bar mounted on the front. Bob Lange took care of those arrangements and sent Toddie and Beezie out to stock up with even more essentials, including two extra five-gallon tanks for water and a spare jerry can for petrol. About four hours and more than US$500 later, Toddie and Beezie returned to their hotel to wait. Mr and Mrs X and their baby, Bob Lange and Vern were going to meet with them in their room to map out the best route to take. When the couple and their baby arrived, they brought with them baby food and nappies, which they asked the women to load into the campervan for them.

What the women didn't know at the time was that the proposed route was essentially the Hippie Trail on which thousands of Western adventure seekers embarked annually as a pilgrimage through Europe and into North and South Asia. The trail was popular because of its cheap hotels, local foods and exposure to local culture. For some, the availability of high-quality cannabis and hashish was an added bonus.

Mr and Mrs X handed over traveller's cheques to the women issued on the First National Bank of Berlin. Each woman was given US$2500 in $20 and $100 denominations for petrol, food and general expenses along the way. Mr X also handed them two tickets from Bombay to Seattle for Toddie and Beezie's flight home at the end of their road trip. The group, which by now no longer included Vern – who had left 'on urgent business' – discussed the various countries through which they would be travelling, the likely road conditions, points of interest and possible locations for the Tubby Bath promotions where it was expected Vern would meet up with them. Toddie and Beezie toasted the upcoming adventure with a couple of local beers before turning in to get a good night's sleep.

The following day, 6 September 1977, they departed from Stuttgart but, much to their surprise, without Mr and Mrs X or their baby. The last-minute change of plans arose from a domestic dispute which Vern said had flared up between the couple. The baby clothes, toiletries and accessories loaded into the van now seemed unnecessary, but Vern insisted they should all remain on board.

Toddie cruised south down the autobahn as Beezie navigated the first leg of their road trip to Munich. They then headed south-east for the Austrian border. Upon arrival at the crossing, Austrian officials took exception to the heavy-duty bull bar affixed to the front of the van. It was specifically designed to clear cattle and stock and wasn't suited to city roads. They demanded it be removed before proceeding as it was considered dangerous and not consistent with the campervan's original manufacture.

Toddie did her best to placate the officials, explaining that the bull bar may be necessary when they encountered wandering cattle in India later in their journey.

An hour later, they were clear of the Austrian border – bull bar intact – travelling south towards Yugoslavia. They were finally doing what they loved: driving on the open road in a campervan as they took their time enjoying the sights and regularly stopping to visit towns, stretch their legs and fuel up.

'We're seeing this big, beautiful world,' wrote Toddie in her diary. But the excitement gradually turned to frustration at times as the women encountered again and again foreign languages they didn't know or understand. It was quite a challenge as their expectation was that everyone would speak at least some of *their* language – American English. Toddie wrote:

> The border crossings are unreal. No-one could understand English. Sign language and a big smile however seemed to work wonders, sometimes. The passport and vehicle checks could take anywhere from three hours to all day. Customs officers were in and out, over and under, but since we had nothing to hide, we had nothing to worry about.

They struck trouble crossing into Yugoslavia, where border officials were perplexed about the excessive quantity of Vern's Tubby Bath merchandise they were carrying. Again, Toddie used her best American diplomacy to explain the purpose of the baths and their promotion planned for different parts of the Continent. Concerns were set aside and soon they were off again, with no taxes levied. Toddie opined in her travel diary that night: 'The country is Red but we minded our manners and checked into a beautiful Americanised motor inn.'

The campervan's five forward gears made for pleasant driving, but gradually the roads deteriorated. In Yugoslavia, the shoulders of the roads were littered with wrecks of assorted vehicles purchased for resale in countries as far afield as Turkey,

Syria and Lebanon whose drivers, unaccustomed to the high-powered European engines, sometimes crashed their recent acquisitions and abandoned them by the roadside.

The women noticed ever-present Yugoslavian police and army officers standing by the highways flagging down cars and lorries at whim, checking identity papers and, in the case of truck drivers, closely inspecting their documentation and log books. The women learned from fellow travellers to be careful as there were often 'fines' to be paid for the flimsiest of transgressions.

Days passed without further incidents and the women pressed on to Bulgaria where Toddie and Beezie found the scenery beautiful but the drivers' road skills lacking and their behaviour death defying. Their overnight stops were a good opportunity to stretch back in their campervan, recharge their batteries and prepare for each new day's surprises.

'The country is breathtaking and it is hard to describe the quaint little towns. But they speed like idiots and drive with their horns,' Toddie wrote.

The first promotion of the Tubby Bath was scheduled to be staged in an Istanbul shopping centre but Vern had listed the exact date as 'to be determined', so the women were under no time pressures. Toddie was careful and kept to the speed limits, if not under them, especially as she was driving in foreign countries with often puzzling road rules. The scenery continued to please them, but the food was sometimes a mystery. In one of Toddie's phone calls to her nephew to keep him across their progress, she said the tinned foods with which they'd loaded up in Stuttgart were beginning to pay off as they found the national dishes on offer not at all to their liking.

By the time they were approaching Turkish territory, the roads had become thin passages, the bitumen patchy and often worn through to the dirt beneath. Stones thrown up by passing vehicles proved a constant danger. Still, the different languages seemed less confronting and more of a novelty the further they went, and they continued to admire the ever-changing scenery.

The campervan so far had served them well, and the inclusions worked perfectly. It wasn't 'home', but they didn't travel halfway around the world to sit in the comfort of their own living room. Their daily plan was to drive for about eight hours then pull into a trailer park where they felt safe, usually situated close to a petrol station or supermarket. Toddie had so far been able to maintain good health and she took care not to strain herself driving without regular breaks. Beezie navigated, made the coffees and checked the oil and water at each rest stop and gas station. She prepared and cooked all of their meals. Theirs was a relationship founded on each woman's independence but reliant on co-operation and mutual tolerance.

By now they were successfully through the Edirne border into Turkey and were skirting the Greek border at its northernmost tip on the way to Turkey's largest city, Istanbul. It was already after midday. They had 150 miles (240 kilometres) to cover, and the roads weren't in great condition, so it was late afternoon by the time they approached the city outskirts. It had been a particularly long day for Toddie. She was losing concentration fast. The bridge crossing the Bosphorus gave them a magnificent view of Istanbul. But the Turkish drivers were no delight. Their haphazard and dangerous driving had the women on the edge of their seats. The constant cacophony of horns was deafening. Road rules seemed non-existent, while road etiquette was completely absent, and the campervan felt far too wide and long for the narrow lanes and streets of the city.

Toddie and Beezie understood that on this occasion they were to leave several demonstration Tubby Baths at a department store, with explanatory information and a special package Vern had prepared to introduce and promote the product. After map-reading help from a friendly English-speaking local, they completed the errand and with grateful thanks to their guide and directions on how to exit the city, they departed by late afternoon. They were relieved to finally leave the horns and hubbub of Istanbul and make their way south-east in search of somewhere they would not be bothered by inquisitive locals, or noisy children constantly begging for money and cigarettes.

The next destination was Ankara, a good two hundred and eighty miles (450 kilometres) south-east. Toddie did a quick mental calculation and figured if the roads weren't too bad, she'd be able to last the distance despite her weariness. The sun began to dip in the sky and the traffic began to ease as they moved away from Istanbul. They followed the road along the Sea of Marmara and decided to pull into a rest area near Izmit, half an hour or so out of Istanbul. Both women were mentally exhausted and decided not to push on through the night.

Beezie prepared a quick meal on the stove, and Toddie stretched out on her bed, badly in need of sleep after a very tiring day. They ate a late dinner without much conversation, and then Toddie retired for the night. While Beezie cleaned up the dishes, it dawned on her that she had seen warnings in one of the tourist brochures about bandits on the outer roads. Travellers were advised not to stop unnecessarily at night on the wayside.

She pushed the warning to the back of her mind and prepared for bed, pulling the drapes across the living section of the van before turning out her light.

Not long after, Toddie sat bolt upright, reached across to Beezie's bed, and grabbed her arm, shaking it and urging her to wake up. Flashes of light were penetrating the campervan windows and raised voices from all directions could be heard outside. The voices became louder and broke into shouting. The women worked out it was flashlights casting eerie shadows, criss-crossing the walls and ceiling of the campervan. Beezie leaped from the bed and grabbed for a knife from the kitchen drawer. The male voices they could hear, they figured, must be speaking in Turkish. The shouting was then accompanied by loud banging against the outside of the van.

Toddie, the more physically imposing of the two women, dressed quickly. She moved to the front of the van towards the driver's seat. Grabbing the edges of the drapes Beezie had drawn earlier, Toddie flung them aside and put her hands on her hips to create an impression of fearlessness. The flashlights shone on her, and she could see rifles raised and pointed directly at the campervan's windscreen.

The 'bandits' turned out to be Turkish police who, upon sighting a woman, lowered their weapons. The commander motioned his men to move aside and walked around to the driver's side of the van. Toddie's and Beezie's hearts were racing. Toddie wound down the passenger window and looked directly at the commander.

'American tourist, American tourist,' she said, pleading for understanding. '*Tourista, tourista.*'

None of the soldiers spoke English. The commander approached the window, gesturing with his hands, pointing into the distance and drawing his forefinger across his neck from side to side. There was no mistaking it was a clear warning that the rest area in which they were parked for the night was dangerous and vulnerable to attack by bandits. Another policeman uttered in his best cowboy vernacular 'bang', pressing his forefinger to his temple. Toddie and Beezie needed no further convincing to move along. With adrenaline pumping, and thankful nods of understanding, the women handed out American cigarettes gratefully received by the now smiling policemen. Toddie looked at her watch. It was 10 pm. Meanwhile Beezie pored over their maps, trying to decide their next move.

Soon after, Toddie started up the van and they were on the road again. They agreed the safest bet would be to keep driving but didn't relish the thought of heading back to Istanbul, so they struck out for Ankara.

They carefully drove through the night towards their destination, arriving on the city's outskirts at around 3 am.

'We stopped a cab and tried to make him understand to lead us to a hotel in Ankara,' Toddie wrote in her diary. 'I told him we would pay him like we were a fare. Explaining this transaction took almost half an hour, but he finally understood.'

Finding a hotel, they parked, checked in and collapsed into their beds, sleeping soundly for the next twelve hours.

•

They were making good time on their journey across the Continent and estimated they would reach Kabul in Afghanistan by 27 September; there they were scheduled to meet Vern, Bob Lange, Mr X and, if the couple had made up, Mrs X and the baby. However, the Turkish roads were the worst they had driven anywhere. The trucks were so overloaded with people that when their drivers failed to negotiate a bend – often due to a combination of speed, bad handling, and overbalancing – they merely tipped and disgorged their cargo onto the roadway, the surrounding vehicles shuddering to a stop. Adults and children, bags, goats and live chickens would be flung through the air, almost as if in slow motion, but little damage or harm seemed to come their way. The passengers inevitably scrambled for safety and, unperturbed, would produce a cooking pot, some tea and water, and then proceed to light a small fire amid the bedlam.

'If only they could see this at home,' Beezie thought, 'they wouldn't believe us.'

The women remained in Ankara for three days before continuing across the rest of Turkey, headed for Iran. At times there was no apparent road, or if there was, it boasted potholes the size of which neither woman had ever seen before. Then there were the drivers, many of whom the women thought drove with a death wish – aiming straight for their van like a projectile, only to swerve at the last possible moment. In some places young children, from the age of five or six, stood armed with rocks by the roadsides, their free hands gesturing for cigarettes. It took Toddie no time to realise that if they stopped and passed out cigarettes, the rocks remained clasped in those little hands. It wasn't for Toddie to criticise the parenting when she remembered that she too, as young as twelve years old, had snuck out at night to try a cigarette and a nip of brandy on more than one occasion growing up in North Hollywood.

As they approached the city of Agri, they found road crews digging up what was left of the highway. They were stopped from proceeding any further. They had no choice but to turn back, deciding to call it a day shortly afterwards at a campsite where they fortuitously enjoyed the company of two American couples, also travelling by car but in the direction of Nepal. The four adults – two of whom were doctors – and their children were on their way to a small village outside Kathmandu to teach English and operate a health clinic. Both groups of American travellers enjoyed each other's company so much, they arranged to meet the next evening at the BP campsite outside Erzurum.

Upon arrival around 3 pm in the province's largest city, the now three-van convoy of Americans headed off to secure their visas for Iran, only to discover it was Holy Week and they would have to wait seven days for the embassy to reopen. With no choice but to bide their time, the group spent the week at Erzurum, relaxing and swapping stories of their families, their homeland, recent travels and experiences on the road. For Toddie, it was like being in a family fold again. At the week's end, with the necessary visas in hand, the group prepared to head off, convoy-style, for the Iranian border.

Both doctors were unwell – one with a dislocated knee, the other with diarrhoea – so Toddie and Beezie offered to transport them in their campervan, with its toilet facilities, while the wives drove their own vehicles. The alternate route took the convoy along the Russian border where at one stage a Soviet border patrol ordered the convoy to a halt, and with guns pointed at their heads, demanded the Americans hand over cigarettes. The women were becoming experts at sign language. By 2 am, still driving in the hope of avoiding further Russian patrols, Toddie reached the Iranian border, with the two other vehicles close behind. All they had to do now was wait until Customs opened at 6 am, so they could cross into Iran. The doctors left Toddie and Beezie to head in a different direction, thankful to the two women for the comforts of their campervan, and rejoined their wives, who had pulled in behind the campervan for a short break. As Toddie and Beezie bade farewell, little did they know they were about to enter a country on the cusp of a revolution.

At first light the Customs inspectors arrived for duty, and once cleared through it took Toddie and Beezie another eight hours to reach the capital, Tehran. The city was wall-to-wall people. After almost four hours following roads which seemingly led nowhere, they pulled in behind a truck whose driver was able to point them in the direction of Herat on the Afghanistan border. The trip into Iran was heart-in-mouth mind-boggling and the conditions were taxing. The locals were intimidating, and the going was very tough and slow. Toddie recorded in her travel diary:

> The trucks we followed lead us through the sewers of Tehran. The pot holes were so big that I had to drop down to first gear. The campervan had five forward gears so you can see we were barely moving. I had to carefully inch each wheel down into the pothole, and then up again. We finally hit one main road leading to Afghanistan although it was not the one we wanted. Again, we didn't have any choice. After about five miles, we found a place to pull off. I was dead tired. Safe place or not, at this stage we didn't care, and just fell asleep in our clothes, where we were. The next morning we drove on, even though it was not a road we should have travelled. We found out later the route was for very experienced drivers only and was very dangerous. The Lord does watch out for fools.

The women finally made it to Kabul. They parked the campervan in the outdoor parking lot next to the Intercontinental Hotel and booked themselves two nights' accommodation. They had previously organised to rendezvous with Vern there. The next morning, bright and early, Toddie's nephew and his associates Bob, and only Mrs X joined the women for breakfast. It was never quite clear to Toddie or Beezie why Vern would be accompanied – or be unaccompanied – by his business associates from time to time. There was no rhyme nor reason to the arrangement, but at this point it was of little consequence to the women.

The trio spent the morning with Toddie and Beezie discussing the trip so far. It had been hard work, Toddie assured her nephew, and the roads weren't anything like what she had been anticipating. While they weren't expecting autobahns and freeways all the way, they had found the conditions more than tough going. Toddie said she understood what Vern had meant about 'earning every cent' when he'd offered them $25,000 all those months ago in La Pine as their fee for driving the van to Bombay.

Before leaving Kabul, Vern made arrangements with Toddie to drive to the Pakistan border, where they were to pick him up after completing border crossing formalities. Neither of the women understood why Vern couldn't just accompany them on this leg.

'You could travel with us from Kabul, couldn't you?' asked Toddie.

'No,' said Vern, 'the carnet for the vehicle says you are the owner and there is only one passenger,' he confidently explained, 'and in these countries, that means you cannot have any other passengers in the vehicle when you cross borders.' It seemed strange but plausible, they thought, and as Vern had travelled these parts before, they figured he must know all of the regulations.

Toddie, however, gave this more thought overnight and recorded her misgivings in her diary:

We felt like we were back in civilization, staying at the Intercontinental Hotel. I asked Vern about the Tubby Baths we were carrying for his promotions, and when did he need them next. He told us we'd had a rough trip and just to relax. He didn't have to tell us twice on that! Last night Vern came to our room and said 'I want you to drive to the border, clear Customs and [Mrs X], Bob and myself will be there and we will ask you for a ride'. I asked him how they were going to get to the border. He said by cab. I said that's ridiculous; why not ride with us? I was told by Vern that the registration of the vehicle included the driver and companion only. I said this still doesn't make sense. I'm allowed to pick up and give a ride to whomever I want. I got the usual response: 'Do it my way and then there's no trouble.' All the time I'm thinking: what's he up to? I don't want to worry Beezie. After all, she is my travelling companion and you might say co-pilot with all the maps and seemingly having the time of her life with not a worry in the world.

In a note Toddie added some time later to this entry, she elaborated on the doubts beginning to slowly creep into the trip:

It's too bad we didn't talk more about our thoughts and ideas for I found out later Beezie had the same doubts and feelings about Vern as I did, but she didn't want to worry me. We both felt that Vern would never let any harm come to his aunt and her friend.

After three days in Kabul, the women set off for the Afghanistan–Pakistan border where they were to meet Vern and his associates on the Pakistan side. The closer they got to the crossing, the more treacherous the roads became.

When they arrived at the border, there was a long line of trucks ahead of them already waiting, and it appeared no border officers were on duty. Often the guards spontaneously downed their pens and headed off for a break. It had already happened on several occasions while the women waited in the queue.

Finally they made it through and about a mile inside Pakistan they followed the signs taking them towards the Khyber Pass. Beezie spotted Vern ahead, standing alone by the side of the road, his shiny aluminium briefcase in hand. Toddie pulled the van over and he climbed in.

'Hi honey, going my way?' asked Toddie, and as Vern settled into his seat, he explained that Mr and Mrs X had been arguing in Kabul, and yet again wouldn't be travelling with them for this part of the journey. Bob, he said, had returned to Stuttgart on business. Toddie drove on, but the going, especially at altitude, became even more perilous. The side of the road slipped away into nothing but sheer drops on either side. The Khyber Pass was living up to its treacherous reputation and Toddie was fearful of driving any further.

Vern, who was sitting in the front passenger's seat, then suggested he could take over. It was the best idea Toddie had heard for a long time. She was relieved to hand over the responsibility to him. There was a problem though on taking up the offer: there was absolutely nowhere to pull off to switch drivers. But Toddie wasn't going to waste any time and told Vern they'd switch as she drove slowly. At a crawl and precariously balancing the van on the thin strip of road, Toddie slid sideways from the driver's seat and out of the way. For a moment, there was no power as Toddie withdrew pressure from the accelerator so she quickly pulled on the parking brake.

Almost simultaneously Vern's foot hit the gas pedal, the engine responded and the van slowly inched forward. It had been dangerous to attempt, but Toddie was relieved she was no longer driving.

About an hour into Pakistan territory during what was a slow and perilous nail-biting drive, Vern pulled off the road outside Peshawar, where there was a conveniently located government bungalow.

Peshawar was not far from the Pashtun Tribal Area. It sat on what used to be the Old Silk Road that linked China to the

West via the Khyber Pass through Afghanistan. It was highly novel for Westerners visiting the ancient city to see goats, cattle and oxen being herded through the streets, or hear the imams' calls to the mosque five times a day. For many tourists on the Hippie Trail, the main reason to visit Peshawar was because it was the 'nerve centre' of the region's marijuana plantations and hashish shops. It was not uncommon for Pashtun youngsters to learn the family business growing cannabis, making hashish, working in hashish shops or smuggling, all from a young age.

By now it was dusk, so the women were happy to wash, change into fresh clothes and settle in. They were to spend the next few days in Peshawar in a bungalow, or *dacha*, a type of low-cost accommodation common throughout Pakistan and India that provided the basics for travellers passing through.

CHAPTER FIVE

NEGOTIATING AN INDIAN PASSAGE

The following morning Vern told the women that he would need the keys to the campervan as he wanted to take it out to do some filming and test out new camera equipment he had brought along. He said he'd be a day or two and suggested they should use the time to catch up on some sleep and relax. Toddie gave Vern the keys and he was gone.

The women spent their time taking walks into Peshawar, photographing the local inhabitants and testing the food. It was curry, curry, curry ... and more curry. They surprised even themselves that they were finally beginning to develop a taste for the famous South Asian staple, although even mild versions they sometimes found too hot for their finely honed American palates. Three or four days passed before Vern eventually returned with the van, surprisingly in the company of Mrs X and Bob Lange. Vern told Toddie and Beezie they had completed their filming and should now prepare for the drive to Lahore, where he would again meet up with them. Lahore was at least a day's drive away, and if they took their time would be two or even three days' travel.

Vern explained Mrs X was returning to Germany while Bob was needed at a business meeting elsewhere. Vern said he was hoping to do one or two more Tubby Bath promotions, including in Lahore, before they arrived in Bombay.

Even with several days' rest in Peshawar, Toddie's blood pressure was beginning to give her cause for concern. The endless driving was taking its toll, and the conditions the women were enduring would have made even the hardiest world adventurer think twice about continuing. Toddie took her time on the drive to Lahore. Beezie questioned her several times about whether it was worth risking her health to complete the trip to Bombay – a further 3700 miles (6000 kilometres) and likely an arduous ten-day road trip at best. Toddie assured her she was managing and could complete the journey as planned.

Toll gates every thirty miles (fifty kilometres) or so interrupted their journey to Lahore, and the collectors were a sight to behold by the roadside. Some had visible running sores covering their faces, arms and legs. They demanded cigarettes and threatened to touch the Americans if they didn't get them. At times Toddie had to get out of the van, walk up a hillside and pay the fee.

The narrow shoulders of the roads were lined with people, sheep, water buffalo, camels and even the occasional elephant.

Toddie wrote in her travel diary:

In Pakistan we changed over to the other side of the road. Here I am driving a left-hand drive vehicle on the wrong side of the road. Thank God for my good co-pilot. At night people slept on the road. I tried never to drive at night, but so far most of the driving was done at that time because we could never find a place to stay, and it wasn't safe to pull off the road.

Eventually in Lahore, they headed straight for the Intercontinental Hotel. Vern appeared within a few hours and said they would need to depart early the following day because the Indian border traffic was going to be heavy and there could be a long wait at the crossing if they didn't get into line before midday.

Without telling Vern of her deteriorating condition, Toddie rose early the next morning and, with Beezie, prepared for the short drive to the crossing which would lead them to Amritsar, in India. When they arrived at the crossing at about 8 am, as Vern had predicted, there was already a long line of trucks, as well as cars and hundreds of people on foot. The women waited almost two hours before they were attended by a Customs official. He informed them that they no longer issued tourist visas at the border and instructed them to drive back to Islamabad to have their documentation processed.

Toddie was furious, as well as tired. She didn't need this bureaucratic mix-up. Vern was supposed to have managed all of these arrangements beforehand, and he'd let them down at a time when they needed picking up. She parked the van out of the line of traffic and sat on the grass verge awaiting Vern's arrival by rental car. This was the procedure he had arranged with them in Lahore, and for all they knew, he too would now need to return to Islamabad for his visa.

Vern arrived half an hour later and pulled his rental car over behind the women's campervan. Before he could ask what the problem was, Toddie told him in no uncertain terms he had screwed up. 'Anyway, I've had it, Vern,' Toddie announced matter-of-factly. She was levelling her frustrations and anger directly at her 'favourite nephew'. She had been holding back for too long and now was venting the stress she had felt building up.

'There's no damn way I'm gonna drive these roads again. I've been sideswiped twice already. They've got a death wish if ever I've seen it. I just plain refuse to drive back to Islamabad,' she informed Vern.

Toddie had made her point. Vern evaluated the situation and, not wanting to upset his aunt any further, offered to drive the campervan to the Pakistan capital himself. 'I'm not driving all the way to Islamabad with you,' she snapped.

'No, I understand,' said Vern. 'We'll catch a flight from Lahore to Islamabad and have our visas processed the same day.'

Toddie, Beezie and Vern climbed into the van – leaving the rental car by the roadside – and Vern drove the campervan back to Lahore. The women thought his driving was bad at the best of times, and although it was only a short journey back to the hotel, he managed to scare the living daylights out of his aunt and Beezie several times over.

They checked into the hotel and went to their new rooms: Toddie and Beezie in theirs, and Vern in an adjoining suite. Vern was unpacking his bag when there was a knock on the door. He opened it to find both Beezie and Toddie standing in the doorway. There was a look of deadly seriousness on their faces. Toddie didn't waste any time speaking her mind.

'Vern, I refuse to go any further, no matter what,' she blurted at her nephew, who was clearly caught off guard by the message, and its blunt delivery. He ushered them inside his room and shut the door. 'Beezie and I have been discussing it and we want to go home now. We're taking our tickets and we're going home. You can take the van and here are the keys,' Toddie said, holding them out to him. 'Do with it what you want. Personally, I don't give a damn what you do. I will not drive this van anymore, come hell or high water. And what's more, we don't think you are being honest with us,' she said, wiping away tears.

'Oh Aunty Vera, please don't cry like that ... come on now,' pleaded Vern, ignoring the keys held in his aunt's outstretched hand. 'I know it's been tough driving in some parts, but look, I'll drive for a while. I'll drive to Bombay. But you know my driving; you'd probably wish you'd never driven with me.'

Beezie had been concerned over the past week that Toddie's nerves were shot and her demeanour and mood were signalling some sort of emotional breakdown. Their predicament was becoming untenable, and the incident at the Indian border hadn't helped.

Vern tried a different tack. 'Look, I'll drive to New Delhi and show you how good the roads get and you'll see that conditions aren't that bad from here on.'

Toddie shook her head and took some deep breaths to bring her emotions under control. Beezie sat mutely by her side. This was a matter to be resolved, she thought, between aunt and nephew. Toddie finally stood up and said she would think about Vern's proposition, then left the room with Beezie. As always, Beezie feared Vern had his aunt in the palm of his hand, able to manipulate her at will. He was working overtime on it at the moment.

Back in their own room, Beezie gently probed Toddie for her thoughts, mindful of the close family bond that existed between Vern and his aunt. 'Toddie, I'm beginning to get a little suspicious about this trip, you know,' said Beezie finally. 'Vern wouldn't be in some sort of trouble, would he, or be involved in something and leading us astray?'

Toddie ignored Beezie, still wrestling with the recent outburst she'd had with her nephew. She was lost in her own thoughts and didn't answer.

They were distinctly aware they were a long, long way from home … in fact, they were feeling quite homesick. No more was said on the subject that evening, and the pair turned in early to sleep.

By the next day Toddie had calmed and capitulated, and with the campervan parked safely at the hotel, Vern and the two women boarded a Pakistan Air flight to Islamabad. Vern organised their Indian visas without any complications. Toddie had resolved that they would complete the journey to Bombay, but Beezie still harboured a nagging doubt about Vern's intentions. She knew it was best to stifle her doubts because when Toddie had to make a difficult decision involving family, logic and sense didn't always factor into the equation. The trio returned to the hotel in Lahore that evening.

Following breakfast the next morning, the trio headed off for their second attempt at crossing the Indian border. Just before the frontier, Vern alighted, reminding the women that he couldn't travel in the van lest there could be trouble at the crossing. He would meet them on the other side of the border after he had crossed independently. The women cleared Pakistan Customs, but the Indian authorities identified important entries missing from the carnet.

The document they carried listed neither the vehicle's engine nor chassis serial numbers. For over an hour Toddie pleaded with the officials, explaining they had travelled through seven countries so far without any hitches regarding the omissions on the carnet.

Toddie and Beezie spotted someone resembling a 'boss' whom they dubbed the 'sultan'. They approached him and with utmost respect and tact explained their position. He eventually cleared them into India, and so it was on towards New Delhi.

About a mile beyond the border crossing and inside India, Vern once again appeared; the familiar yet mysterious solitary figure carrying a shiny aluminium briefcase at the side of the road, waiting for his ride. He boarded the van and, as promised, took over the driving duties. Sure enough, the highway through to New Delhi was, by comparison, a superb freeway. Toddie's outburst the previous day remained the elephant in the room or, rather, the campervan.

Along the way to Bombay, which lay 1500 miles (2400 kilometres) to the south-west, she boldly raised the issue of the trip's purpose with her nephew. 'Vern, I think there's something going on. Both Beezie and I feel it, you know.'

Vern's reply took them both by surprise. He was curt and to the point. 'Well, frankly, Vera, it's none of your god-damned business.'

The women were stunned into silence. Vern continued driving, concentrating on the road ahead. This wasn't what they had imagined. It certainly wasn't feeling like a 'holiday' anymore. What had happened to the enduring charm for which Toddie almost worshipped her 'favourite nephew'? Perhaps he was subject to 'off' days too?

Nothing further was said about the women's concerns and they drove on to New Delhi to find a hotel to stay in for the night. If Vern was concerned about the women's doubts, and his aunt's uncertainty about completing the trip, he didn't let on. Sitting down over dinner in the hotel, in an effort to shore up the relationship, he offered to drive all the way through to Bombay.

'Aunty Vera, I can see the strain is taking its toll on you, and I don't want you to push yourself any further than you have already,' Vern said in a sympathetic tone. Beezie felt he always seemed to know how to inject just enough compassion in his voice to manipulate his aunt. 'The problem is, though, the carnet is in your name and you are going to have to be with the van when we get to Bombay. But I'm concerned and I don't want you overextending yourself, so if you want me to drive I will,' he offered. Toddie's view of Vern's driving ability hadn't changed. The women did not feel particularly safe with him at the wheel and had no desire to ride as passengers with him ever again.

'No, Vern, I am not overly fond of your driving, and if we have to get to Bombay, then I'll make sure we do,' Toddie announced. Vern professed further concern for his aunt's health. He could charm the pants off a policeman, thought Beezie.

●

Before he flew out of the Indian capital, Vern had dinner at the hotel one last time with Toddie and Beezie. The conversation kept turning to the weather, and specifically to the rain that had begun to fall in the early evening, which was now steadily increasing. They had been based in the city for almost a week by this stage and began to wish they'd set out a day or two earlier.

The deluge continued through the night and in the morning it was still raining. The dirt road on which the hotel was situated began to flood. It did not look promising, the two women thought. October was monsoon season in Delhi and if they weren't careful, they'd be caught in the middle of it. They decided to set off midmorning. Vern had already left for the airport, ostensibly to fly to Bombay to make arrangements for the van's shipment to Australia. The women weren't to know that Vern was in fact returning to Stuttgart for a week, and in November flying from London to Sydney to oversee his company's operations in readiness for the impending arrival of the campervan. It would be discovered much later that Vern was organising the shipment of other vehicles to Australia at the same time. It was quite the 'film production transport fleet' he was assembling.

The women hadn't travelled thirty miles beyond New Delhi before they struck trouble. The road was flooded with water that was lapping under the first step up into the van. There were craters in the road they estimated to be two and almost three feet deep, and Toddie sensed they would have to proceed with extreme caution so as not to snap an axle.

Grabbing Toddie's walking stick, Beezie got out and, like a shepherd leading its flock, stepped gingerly into and around the potholes, guiding the campervan through the pouring rain. Toddie was at the steering wheel, peering through the windscreen with the wipers working furiously to provide some visibility. For at least a mile they crawled along, the water bubbling at the exhaust pipe as they made cautious and slow progress, sounding like an old motorboat.

Toddie monitored the gauges on the dashboard and did her best to keep the engine revolutions over 3000 to avoid any chance of the floodwater finding its way up the exhaust pipe. The appalling road conditions and stress on the van's engine by now had begun to dislodge the radiator from its mounting. The constant vibration from the revving engine made matters even worse and just as they cleared the last section of floodwater and hit dry roadway beyond a tributary of the Sahibi River, the fan blades broke loose and pierced the radiator lining. Although Toddie didn't hear the loud crunch of metal on metal, Beezie certainly did and waved Toddie to a standstill. Beezie feared something dire had just happened under the engine's hood, but they kept the engine idling while they unscrewed the grill from the front of the van.

It was no easy feat manoeuvring around the bull bar and driving lights that had been specially installed in Stuttgart. As Toddie was grabbing a tool from inside the van, she noticed the needle on the dashboard temperature gauge had shot up into the dangerous red zone. She had no choice but to immediately switch off the engine, and soon discovered the cause of the overheating.

The radiator had been gouged by the fan blades and had emptied itself completely of coolant. There was no way anything could be done without a mechanic, or at least someone, fitting a new radiator to the campervan. It was just after noon by now, and if they could flag anyone down, they could get back to New Delhi or into the next major city. According to their maps, they were not far from Alwar.

But there was no traffic in either direction. The locals obviously knew better than to travel in this weather, thought Toddie. They started the engine up again and moved the van as close to the side of the road as they dared. Toddie's heart lifted a little when she saw tracks leading down from the surrounding hills to a nearby well. All they had to do now was wait for one of the locals to come down the hill.

They waited. And they waited.

As the day waned, they had not seen a single soul – either trekking down from the hills or along the road. Then suddenly out of nowhere, five women dressed in saris with children in tow appeared from out of the hills with water jugs and containers in their hands. They spoke animatedly among themselves as they drew closer and, while appearing shy, gestured to convey to Toddie and Beezie that they should move their van along. It seemed they were warning the Americans not to remain there any longer.

As if to make herself better understood, one of the women stepped forward and made a motion of her hand cutting across her throat. This warning was all too familiar to Toddie and Beezie – it was universally understood. Bandits roamed the region and the women would be sitting ducks if they stayed put. Toddie desperately tried to explain their van had broken down, and until someone came along they could do nothing but wait. And pray.

The village women simply smiled and filled their water jugs before returning to the hills with their offspring and disappearing from view. Toddie and Beezie climbed back into the van and continued to watch the road for vehicles or any sign of help, but to no avail. As the shadows began to lengthen, they closed up the van and kept watch in the direction of the hills for bandits.

Beezie began asking herself why they hadn't upped and left Vern with his campervan when they'd told him they'd had enough. But this was not the time to be discussing that with Toddie. Suddenly, in the distance, in the fading light, human shapes began to appear, wending their way down the hillside towards them; perhaps, the women hoped, simply for more water from the well. The women locked the van up from inside, pulled the curtains and waited, closely watching through a small gap the twenty or so figures approaching their stranded campervan. Toddie hoped offering cigarettes might help, so she handed out enough cigarettes through a half-opened window to appease them, smiling all the while. The women were relieved to see the men take their cigarettes, turn and head back up into the hills. Or so they thought.

Beezie wasn't convinced they'd seen the last of the group, but after thirty minutes had passed without incident, she told Toddie to take a sleeping pill and try to get some rest. Toddie would have to be fit and alert to steer the campervan over what was left of the road the next day if they were fortunate enough to secure a tow, Beezie figured. When her sleeping pill didn't take effect quickly enough, Toddie downed several shots of scotch and finally fell asleep.

Beezie had a sense of foreboding and remained awake and on guard. She prepared a small arsenal of weaponry from the kitchen drawer by her side, as well as the wheel brace, and with the internal overhead light on, opened the pages of her book and began to read. A couple of hours later, Beezie was beginning to get drowsy when her focus was suddenly interrupted by noises coming from outside the campervan. She listened carefully trying to determine what – or who – was making the sound, but was having difficulty pinpointing its origins.

At first it seemed to be coming from down around the rear wheels of the vehicle, then sudden scuffling came from the right-hand side and from the front, followed by the murmur of low voices. As the noises became louder, she peered through a crack in the curtain to see the distinct outline of a large group of men who were now appearing to surround the van.

Beezie remained hidden and motionless. The men were back but this time in larger numbers, and she doubted it was just for cigarettes. The male voices were getting louder and sounded distinctly menacing but she couldn't establish how many there were because they were constantly moving and there was no moon. The reading light inside the campervan remained defiantly on; however, it made it difficult for Beezie to see clearly outside into the dark without being visible inside. The best strategy she felt was to keep the men outside guessing. If the mob was uncertain about the vehicle's occupants and whether they were armed, they might not rush the van.

Toddie remained blissfully unaware of the drama unfolding outside in the dark until she was abruptly woken by sudden shouting and yelling from the mob outside. The commotion made Beezie jump but she had taken hold of a long kitchen knife and was ready to defend them both. As Toddie began to sit up, Beezie put a steadying arm on her until she fully regained her senses.

The men were now pounding on the campervan with fists, sticks and rocks. Toddie was still somewhat groggy, but stood beside Beezie, who by now was holding a knife and screwdriver, determined not to give up without a fight. The van began to rock as the men climbed onto the bull bar and jumped up and down, continually pounding on the van's exterior. Toddie and Beezie stood back to back in the centre of the van with feet braced and arms pressed against the interior cupboards for balance, all the while clutching their weapons. For what seemed an eternity as the bandits kept up their attack, the women remained silent and focused on any access point that might give way.

The men could not penetrate the van's exterior, or possibly they just chose not to smash its windscreen. Suddenly the noises ceased and the van stopped rocking. The only movement was the trembling of Toddie and Beezie's hands as they held their breath and stood stock still. As abruptly and mysteriously as the attack began, it ended. The women sat quietly, waiting for the next onslaught, but it never came. Sleep, however, overtook Toddie, who could no longer fight the sleeping-pill-and-scotch cocktail, and she lay where she fell back onto the bed. Beezie remained seated in silence with the interior light on for the rest of the night, not daring to close her eyes until the safety of daybreak.

Beezie dozed off shortly after the sky began to lighten, and about an hour later she awoke. Both women ate a small breakfast before checking that the exterior of the van was intact – scratches and some slight dents but nothing major – and set up watch for signs of traffic ... of any sort.

At last in the distance, a young man wearing a brightly coloured turban appeared, cycling along the road towards them. He was making slow progress around the flooded potholes but seemed to know what he was doing. Toddie and Beezie emerged from the van and stood by the campervan to catch his attention as he approached. He stopped, and in slow English Toddie explained they needed help. He was able to understand a little of what she was trying to say. She asked him to get a message to the nearest police station. In fractured English, the young man offered to take one of the women on his bicycle to the next village. Beezie, being the smaller and lighter of the two, agreed and hopped onto the handlebars of the young man's bike. The slender Indian manoeuvred the now overloaded pushbike, pumping his legs furiously as he pedalled away in search of help. Toddie and Beezie had convinced him of their desperate need and he had proudly taken on the role as their 'agent'.

It didn't occur to Toddie until they disappeared off into the distance that this could be the last time she saw her companion, a sentiment she shared in her diary: 'I will never forget in a million years the rear view of her riding away to only God knows where, wondering to myself would I ever see her again. If she was scared, she never showed it. What strength.'

It seemed to Beezie that they cycled an awfully long way before they eventually encountered a tiny settlement consisting of about two dozen inhabitants. Their shelters were made from clay and buffalo dung. As she rode ceremoniously into the camp under the people's curious gazes, Beezie also noticed a few scrawny-looking hens, a weedy goat and two lumbering water buffalo, but no well or obvious source of water. She moved stiffly from the bike when they reached the centre of the compound, and a camp elder motioned to her to sit on a small stool he proffered. It was time to share a cup of tea. He placed an obviously much-loved cup and pot ensemble on another stool, and poured the liquid for Beezie to enjoy. Like a proper lady, her small finger extended, Beezie sat among the onlookers, making as if to sip the hot beverage. She wasn't game to drink it.

The young man designated as Toddie and Beezie's agent was a resident of the camp. He began bartering for the services of a vintage World War II jeep kept under cover of rags, rugs and an original army tarpaulin. From all appearances the vehicle had not seen action since the war. The jeep was heavily rusted, with grass growing through its floorboards and springs protruding from the seats. As the villagers tried to get the old jeep's engine started, Beezie imagined she would still be there sipping tea at sundown. However, as she had offered to pay them a generous 200 rupees for their help, they were determined to succeed. When the engine failed to start, the entire community was called upon to assist.

It was a comic scene and Beezie had to stifle her amusement. The men, women, and children were employed to help push the jeep uphill – in reverse. Beezie feared it was an accident waiting to happen. She was troubled by visions of the jeep wiping out the entire camp when it eventually gathered momentum and careered downhill. However, there were functioning brakes fortunately, and while the driver held the jeep in position the entire group swung behind the vehicle and pushed for their lives forward and downhill. This routine was repeated four times before finally the relic sputtered to life. Beezie couldn't believe it was actually operational. A dirty, dusty rug was produced, and after three shakes it was placed on a seat and she was invited to take her place in the vehicle. With the triumphant agent in the rear, the three set off, but heading in the opposite direction of the campervan. Beezie gestured frantically, telling them they were headed the wrong way, but they were determined to maintain their course. Finally, she understood where they were going: they needed more petrol before they could go anywhere. After a bone-jarring journey bumping and rattling along, they parked atop a rise while the agent headed off to a nearby village he knew had a petrol bowser, to fill his two jerry cans.

When they finally made it back to the incapacitated campervan, Toddie was negotiating with some men from a truck she had flagged down. This was going to be a ticklish situation, Beezie realised. As she had already commissioned the young agent, a driver and his jeep, they were morally bound to rely on them first. The men from the truck whom Toddie had hailed felt slighted, and an argument ensued between Beezie's and Toddie's helpers. Beezie's young agent won out, and a wire cable about seven feet long was fastened beneath the campervan and onto the old jeep. Fortunately, Toddie was high enough up in her driver's seat to be able to see over its roof, so could steer safely. But less than a mile along, the jeep engine died.

The truckload of men whom Toddie had engaged, but who had lost their commission, was trailing close behind. There were cheers as the men realised the first agent's rescue attempt had failed. Beezie flagged the truck down, thanking and dispatching her agent with his promised 200 rupees and her thanks. The men from the truck were delighted to be able to now come to the women's rescue. Regardless of what the women said, their helpers would simply nod emphatically, smile and utter the words, 'No problem'. It seemed they were the only English words they knew. They leaped into action, connecting their truck to the campervan with ropes and towing it towards the nearest town.

As the truck towed the van, Toddie had to carefully use her handbrake, as the campervan's engine needed to be running and the electronics turned on to activate the power brakes. One man stood on the side of the truck's running boards while another took up a position opposite to help their driver. They all wore cheerful bright yellow and blue turbans.

The men acted as lookouts, signalling upcoming turns and dangerous road conditions. It was about thirty miles (fifty kilometres) to Alwar, and along the journey the truck and its load was regularly forced to pull out to pass ambling cows, or tractors towing open trailers crammed with passengers.

As they finally pulled into Alwar, there initially appeared to be no facilities where the van could be repaired. Residents emerged from their dwellings when the American women and their campervan appeared, and while their hearts reached out to the locals, inwardly they cringed. Toddie's travel diary didn't mince words: 'The dirty, betel nut–chewing people ... swarmed us.' The odour was also overwhelming. Children began pulling, tugging and touching Toddie when she alighted to pay the truck driver. The word *baksheesh* was repeated over and over, until Toddie had had enough and shouted at those crowding her. Though they didn't understand her language, there was no mistaking her tone, and they backed off.

The head man of the neighbourhood appeared, resplendent in a purple turban. The truck and van were pushed down a side street by the children and soon two young boys were dismantling the radiator. It was no easy task working around the bull bar.

Once the damaged radiator was removed from the engine, the purple-turbaned man loaded it onto an oversized tricycle, complete with a passenger seat between the rear wheels aft of the driver. He took his place in the passenger seat, nursing the damaged radiator. A second man peddled the tricycle off to the repair shop.

Meanwhile, the women were safely 'booked' into the town's one and only hotel. Before he had headed off, the head man implored the women to have a pot of tea on the hotel veranda, with his compliments. So as not to be rude, they accepted. Again, Toddie and Beezie made out to be drinking but, so as not to risk any germs or ill-health, discreetly emptied their beverages onto the damp floor.

Later the women wandered down to the campervan, now minus its radiator, to await completion of the repairs. They sat inside the van playing cribbage to pass the time. Three hours later, the makeshift job was complete. The bill: a mere US$5.50. The boss wouldn't hear of a tip.

The women set off for Jaipur but weren't far down the road when the radiator coolant was again boiling, and the engine overheating and in danger of seizing. The women were able to get a message to the purple-turbaned man once more, and he arranged for the campervan to be towed back into town. Again, his boys set to work on the repairs.

When finished, the man insisted on riding with the women to prove his handiwork was guaranteed. Further down the road when he was sure the vehicle was travelling smoothly, he bade them farewell and headed back to Alwar. In a short while, the temperature gauge again warned the women the engine was overheating and after another five miles, they were ready to walk away and abandon the van by the roadside.

They allowed the engine to cool down and in time saw a small sedan travelling along the road, which they flagged down. Out jumped five middle-aged, immaculately attired Indian men with bright red bandoliers, all armed with holstered pistols strapped to their waists. One of them identified himself in English as the Jaipur chief of police, and politely inquired as to the nature of the women's problem. Toddie explained their quandary, and instantly all of the policemen became expert mechanics. They rolled up their sleeves and, with tools Toddie produced from the van, began to tinker around the engine in an attempt to stem the radiator leak. Before long they had used all the spare water the women were carrying, as they tested their repairs, pouring the water into the radiator, only to watch it flow from the supposedly welded leak. The Chief of Police decided then the safest and most comfortable place for the women to be was in a government bungalow, while in the meantime he and his men would continue on to Jaipur to summon further assistance.

As it turned out, this was Bengal tiger country and it was necessary for the women's safety to be secure inside a bungalow, especially at night. The women proceeded to tell the police chief of their experiences with bandits and not tigers that led them to fear for their lives. He laughed aloud as they described the bandits' shouting and their pummelling and rocking of the van. 'That interior light is what saved your lives, you know,' said the chief. 'The bandits know little about electricity and lights, they know only of bonfires, flame torches and the moon for light in darkness. Artificial light is still a mystery to them.'

His explanation for their lucky escape was that the bandits would have been sufficiently intrigued by the light inside the campervan. They would have been trying to force it out of the van, the Police Chief said. When their shouting failed, they would have become wary of the continual glow, and also the people inside who somehow had the 'power' to keep the light burning. The women were able to laugh at the episode, but Bombay and their return flight home could not come soon enough.

Toddie's diary account captured the details of the day:

> The radiator overheated yet again and then the van just plain stopped. We had just stepped out when we spotted this car approaching. It slowed down when passing us but we caught a glimpse of five men inside, all in white uniforms. We yelled and waved frantically. Slowly their car stopped, turned around then came back. How smart they looked in their white uniforms, compared to the dirty-looking people we had come to see in India. We found out the head man was the Chief of Police in Jaipur. His name was Surendra Sharma, and along with him were his four subordinates. They refilled the radiator and since they were on their way to Jaipur they would follow us. We managed to drive a couple of miles and it happened again. Finally Mr Sharma said he would drive our vehicle. I could feel the workings of his mind. 'Women don't know how to drive cars; she must be doing something wrong.' So with my best charm, I let him behind the wheel. The van gave out again. We only had enough water for one more fill-up. He advised us to turn around and follow them and they would take us to one of the government bungalows.

The women made the bungalow their home for five days while they waited for a mechanic to be brought out from Jaipur, about forty miles (sixty-four kilometres) south-west of the compound. Their room was spacious – about thirty feet square and was filled with large, hand-carved furniture which included two large beds, two chairs, an extra-large divan, a coffee table, two bedside tables, several lamps, hand-woven rugs, tapestry cushions and heavy drapes. Their meals at the bungalow were served family-style at a long communal table. There were about ten other tourists staying almost every day. Whether it was curried goat or chicken with rice, or vegetables, everyone ate the same thing. After two nights, Toddie decided she wanted a change of menu, and they instead decided to cook their meals in the campervan. A number of young European travellers from Germany, France and Sweden staying at the compound enjoyed a beer or two from the women's stash, a valued commodity, in the campervan. It wasn't cold but it was beer.

The first morning at the compound Toddie shot up from her bed, calling out to Beezie, 'What the hell was that noise?' Beezie remembered from childhood hearing the same noise at her grandparents' farm. 'They're peacocks,' she said. Peacocks, she recalled, were man's 'beautiful watchdog'. The women looked out the window and there were dozens of them, and what a raucous noise they were making.

The nights were still, and as they were close to the jungle, they could hear the roar of the Bengal tigers. One night they took an escorted tour into the tigers' backyard where local guides tied live bait to the roof of a vehicle that the tourist bus followed. On most nights, the tigers caught the scent of the panic-stricken goat, attacked and tore into their catch to the accompaniment of flashes and cameras.

The Chief of Police was as good as his word. Upon arrival in Jaipur, he went straight to the Mercedes-Benz dealer, United Motors, and secured the exclusive services of their best mechanic who was then dispatched to the compound to repair the van. Within a day of his arrival the campervan was once again operational, though it had to be driven slowly and carefully over extremely rough terrain as it limped into Jaipur.

The women left the van at United Motors and had the mechanics remove the unserviceable radiator to install a new one. In the meantime, the Police Chief continued to entertain the two women and looked after their welfare like a true gentleman. He even loaned them rupees so they could purchase some essentials when their traveller's cheques weren't accepted. They promised to reimburse him as soon as they reached Bombay.

Their accommodation at the Rambagh Palace was comfortable, but the menu offered nothing but more curry.

They collected their repaired vehicle after their three days in Jaipur, and farewelled their hosts, taking almost an hour expressing their deepest thanks to the local residents living near the auto shop who had befriended them. They were now on the final leg of their journey and were headed south to complete the last 600 mile (950 kilometre) leg to Bombay.

With the finish line in sight and the United States beckoning, Beezie and Toddie pressed on and drove to Bombay without further incident.

CHAPTER SIX

CARNET OR BUST

Vern had promised to meet them at the Oberoi Sheraton hotel in Bombay on 17 October. As was now becoming a pattern, he was not there for their arrival. The women nevertheless parked the van on the main road outside the hotel, facing the Arabian Sea.

The next day there was a knock on their hotel room's door, and Beezie went to open it. In the doorway stood Bob Lange. Toddie was surprised and disappointed. She invited him in, asking where Vern was. 'He said he'd meet us, take the damn van off our hands and pay us for all the work we've had to do getting it here,' she told him. Lange didn't have a lot to say; he never did. He seemed just as mysterious and unreliable a character as Vern had become.

However, Lange was able to report that Vern had flown to Hong Kong at the last minute to check on a boat he was having built.

'We've driven all those miserable roads through half a dozen countries, across multiple borders,' Toddie said, 'and we've broken down and our lives have been threatened. I bet none of you would have cared. You wouldn't have even given a damn whether we'd have died out in the middle of nowhere or not, would you?'

Toddie was seething, trying to keep a lid on the frustration that had built up over the past three months. She was not comfortable with the powerlessness she felt in their current situation and it was exacerbated by the abandonment she perceived at the hands of her own nephew. Lange decided to break the tension and restore more cordial relations, so suggested they all head down to the hotel bar where he'd buy them a drink. It was likely that in a public setting, he must have figured, Toddie was less likely to cause a scene.

Downstairs, Lange reclined in the armchair and looked out the window of the hotel bar, staring off into the distance. He appeared inwardly unmoved by the women's distress but let them vent their frustrations before speaking again. Beezie eyed him carefully and decided she trusted him no more than any of the bandits they'd encountered in their travels.

'Vern has asked me to apologise for his absence,' Lange finally said, 'and I'm to complete all the arrangements from here to get the van shipped to Australia.' That suited the women just fine. They didn't care who took over now. They had completed their journey, fulfilled their obligation and they were ready to fly home.

Lange then took them completely by surprise, saying, 'The thing is, though, you're going to have to see that the van gets to Australia safely because that carnet has your name on it, Vera.'

Toddie didn't react immediately as she tried to grasp what it was he was demanding. She simply glared at Lange. Without even raising an eyebrow, she replied coldly: 'You're out of your ever-lovin' mind, boy. We're not going any further. We have our tickets and we are going home to the United States from here, just as we agreed.'

If only it had been so easy. Toddie now knew why her nephew had not come to Bombay. He didn't have the guts to front his aunt with this latest change of plans.

'I'm sorry, ladies,' interrupted Lange, sitting up straight. He coolly and matter-of-factly delivered the ultimatum: 'The carnet is in your name and you won't be able to leave India without being arrested because the passport is stamped with the carnet and it shows you came in with the vehicle.'

That damned carnet again. Why were they being held like prisoners with this ridiculous document? Why was it so important? The carnet wasn't *their* business, although now it appeared it was very much so.

Lange continued, 'I've made arrangements with shipping agents Forbes and Frenkel to have the van sent to Melbourne on the *Straat Luanda* and it sails from Bombay on 5 November, so you'll have to get the things you need from the campervan for your flight before it is loaded on board.'

Australia had never been a part of their travel plans; their journey was to end in Bombay. They were road weary and fed up. After all they had experienced, thought Beezie, it was crazy to even consider going any further. There was silence again. Lange stood up and looked at Toddie. 'Vera, might I have a word with you?' He moved with Toddie down to the far end of the bar in a quiet corner. Beezie remained seated in an armchair, casually looking about at the other patrons and inspecting the decor, but straining to hear the nature of the conversation, and surreptitiously observing the body language between the two. There was a lengthy and, at times it seemed, heated conversation. Above the noise from people coming and going and socialising in the bar, Beezie could make out raised voices. It did not augur well for their imminent return home to La Pine.

Whatever it was that Lange said to Toddie during their discussion, her attitude changed. Her defiance was replaced with resignation – they were now obliged to continue to Australia, and then they could fly home. Later, back in their room, Beezie raised the subject. Toddie explained that due to the carnet, she'd be thrown in jail if she didn't fly to Australia to take delivery of the vehicle at its final destination. Lange told her that Vern would be there to meet them and take possession of the van once it had been offloaded and cleared through Customs.

'And then we can go home? Is there anything else that I should be told?' asked Beezie.

'No,' snapped Toddie. 'Nothing.'

Beezie could pick Toddie's moods. After almost two decades together, she knew if Toddie was angry, she was also healthy. But if she brooded and kept her emotions within, Beezie became concerned that Toddie's health was at risk. The latter part of the trip had, at times, tested their relationship.

Resigned to the next stage of their journey, they drove the van to the shipping agent several days later. They had removed their suitcases, packed with their personal effects, before handing over the keys and necessary documents. They found a post office and wired the money that had generously been advanced to them by Surendra Sharma, the chief of police in Jaipur.

Indignant at the change of travel plans Vern had sprung on them, Toddie began to wonder whether he would still honour their $25,000 fee for driving the van from Stuttgart to Bombay. Toddie pressed Lange for their promised payment. He said he didn't have the funds, but Vern would pay them once they landed in Australia.

Toddie didn't mince words when she wrote of her encounter with Lange to finalise arrangements before the ship set sail from Bombay as scheduled on 5 November, headed for Brisbane, Sydney and then on to Melbourne: 'Bob Lange and I never did get along and now here we were sparring again. I told Bob he was an S.O.B. He got up to leave with the parting remark "I'll keep in touch".'

On 6 November the two women booked their flights to Sydney, via Hong Kong, where they could obtain their tourist visas to enter Australia. The island colony stopover was an opportunity to put behind them their unhappiness at how the holiday had become such misery.

The women were relieved to be unencumbered and relished the comforts of their luxurious hotel after almost two months on the road. The hotel's all-day buffets were a welcome change from the curry they'd endured for the past few weeks. After four days in Hong Kong, they boarded a Qantas flight for Australia, arriving in Sydney on 10 November. Once through Customs and Immigration, Vern's instructions, as provided by Bob Lange in Bombay, were to hail a taxi and proceed to the Wentworth Hotel, where a booking had already been made for them. There they would meet up with Vern, clear the van through Customs once the ship arrived and fly home to the United States. They would still be back in La Pine with their little dog, Suzette, in time for Christmas and able to resume their uncomplicated lifestyle in retirement.

The Wentworth Hotel was one of Sydney's prestigious hotels in the downtown core of the central business district. It was a short walk to Circular Quay, a ferry to Manly, and a stroll to the beautiful Royal Botanic Gardens. Toddie and Beezie had already mailed postcards from Hong Kong to friends and relatives, telling them of their unexpected 'detour' to Australia, but assuring them that they would be home soon.

For two days after arriving in Sydney, there was still no word from Vern. Late in the afternoon on the third day, he arrived at their room while the pair was having an afternoon rest.

They were relieved to finally see the elusive nephew. Vern was resplendent in a white safari suit, beaming a disarming, warm smile with both arms open to greet the women.

'Well, shit!' cursed Toddie, not one inclined to cuss unless she was under stress or very angry ... or both. 'If it ain't a ghost from the past, come to haunt two poor old ladies,' she added wryly. Vern walked into the room and made himself at home.

'God damn, where the hell did you get to, honey?' Toddie asked. 'You had us so worried not showing up in Bombay, and then sending that Bob Lange to tell us we had to come here. Didn't you have the guts to come and tell us yourself?' she demanded.

Vern raised his hands as if to defend himself and to brush off the questions, sidestepping the interrogation with questions of his own. He wanted to know whether they were happy where they were, because, he advised them – for the first time – they might be in Sydney for several weeks waiting for the ship. Not only was the Wentworth Hotel expensive, but he suggested it would probably be more to their liking to be in a small serviced apartment where they could do their own cooking.

'Vern, you don't seem to realise how lucky we are even to be alive,' said Beezie, not satisfied that Toddie had been frank enough with her nephew. 'We broke down twice, were attacked by bandits ... but I guess you couldn't have cared less whether we'd dropped dead.'

Vern scoffed at Beezie's words. 'No, no, not at all. We'd have found you even if we had to put a helicopter up to search. We had it all worked out how long it would take you to get to Bombay, and if you hadn't been there, well, sure, we'd have gone out looking for you,' Vern added reassuringly.

Beezie was far from convinced Vern had any idea of the terrors and trauma they had endured.

'That would have been a bit hard considering you weren't even there,' she retorted.

'I was there until I was recalled to Germany on urgent business,' Vern replied. His story was always changing.

'Well, you're here now, and that's all that matters,' said Toddie, trying to break the tension building between Vern and Beezie.

Vern arranged for them to move to the Sunset Motor Lodge in Kings Cross, the heart of the city's sometimes seedy night life. Still, the women found the self-contained apartment well-appointed and comfortable. It had two bedrooms, a living room and a small kitchen – just like a home away from home.

While they waited for the ship to eventually wend its way to Sydney, the women passed their time taking tours around the city, travelling on ferries on its famous harbour, visiting Taronga Zoo, riding commuter trains across the Sydney Harbour Bridge, walking around the harbour foreshore and touring the Opera House on Bennelong Point. They also spent several leisurely afternoons which slid seamlessly into the balmy late spring evenings enjoying beers in the historical precinct, The Rocks. Toddie purchased tickets to the Colgate International Women's Tennis Championships in late November at White City, where they cheered for 1971 Wimbledon champion Evonne Goolagong Cawley in her comeback, which included a win over compatriot Kerry Reid.

Vern invited Toddie and Beezie to a party at his John Street, Woollahra home where the pair would meet, so they were told, Vern's friends and associates – some of Australia's leading actors, designers and lawyers. When they arrived at the house, the party was in full swing, and among the milling strangers they spotted the familiar profile of Bob Lange. During the party, they thought they heard several people refer to him by the name of 'Phillip', although he made no attempt to speak to Toddie or Beezie. Toddie made a mental note to follow this up the next time they saw Bob ... or was it Phillip? Vern's wife and their young children also joined the party, for which Vern had arranged caterers and serving staff.

It was quite the show, and it was what Toddie expected of Vern, who on the one hand was living up to her expectations as a flashy and successful businessman, but who on the other hand was giving her cause for concern about his character, reliability and trustworthiness.

But the bottom line as always was that he was family, and that after all was what Toddie valued over everything else.

The morning after the party Vern dropped by to see Toddie and Beezie, and advised them to begin scanning the newspapers for the daily shipping list in order to monitor the *Straat Luanda*'s expected arrival in Melbourne. They would have to fly to Melbourne, he said, where he'd rendezvous with them at the Hilton Hotel. This was yet another surprise – that they would now have to clear the van in Melbourne – but Vern explained it away as having something to do with the bad weather offshore affecting the ship's progress. The women were enjoying the

Australian weather and lifestyle, so they didn't complain about the minor delay or a quick trip to Melbourne before their final flight home to La Pine.

Toddie and Beezie spent a total of three weeks in Sydney until the shipping movements finally listed the impending arrival of the ship carrying their campervan. It was due to dock in Melbourne on 6 December. Yet again Vern's arrangements seemed peculiar to the women. If the ship would be pulling into the harbour city on 5 December to unload its Sydney-bound cargo, why not clear the campervan in the city in which they were already situated? Instead he wanted the women to fly to Melbourne, while the ship spent twenty-four hours sailing down the east coast to the Victorian capital, and clear the vehicle there. The only positive they took out of the arrangement was that they would get to see a bit more of Australia. Vern gave them the assurance everything was under control.

The women packed their luggage and flew to Melbourne and, as Vern had arranged, checked into the Hilton Hotel.

At least, the women thought, they were in a civilised country with comfortable hotels, reliable services and good food which, while it wasn't quite the fare to which they were accustomed, was certainly closer to American cuisine than what they had experienced over the past few months.

PART TWO

OPERATION GENIUS

CHAPTER SEVEN
YOU KNOW THE DRILL

As the *Straat Luanda* sailed down the Australian coastline, separate checks were being made on the ship's cargo in two cities by two different Australian government officials.

One of the officials was Foreign Liaison Officer in the Federal Bureau of Narcotics intelligence section Alex Taylor. Since 1974, it had been Taylor's responsibility to manually scrutinise shipping manifests, flagging suspicious cargo of interest. He was especially keen to identify the movements of an international drug syndicate shipping cannabis and cannabis resin – hashish – into Australia, using cars and vans into which the drug loads were secreted.

The Narcotics Bureau, established in 1969, had been subjected to varying degrees of harassment at the hands of state police forces, jealous of the role the 'new kids on the block' at the bureau were playing. It could best be described as a turf war. Some senior state police were also critical of the recruitment of their drug squad officers to the new Commonwealth force whose pay, conditions and political support were vast improvements on some of the state forces' own arrangements.

The campervan in which the women had driven almost seven thousand miles (over 11,000 kilometres) and listed on the *Straat Luanda*'s manifest immediately caught Taylor's eye. He recalled similar vehicle shipments appearing on ship manifests from Bombay over the past twelve to twenty-four months – but that was before the bureau had begun targeting this style of drug importation. The appearance of a campervan on board a cargo ship piqued his curiosity.

A quick check of the vessel in Lloyd's – the 'bible' of the maritime shipping industry – confirmed for Taylor the *Straat Luanda* was a regular visitor to key Australian ports such as Brisbane, Sydney, Melbourne and Adelaide, and had a dead weight tonnage of 8600 tons. When originally launched by Dutch shipbuilders Gusto in 1958, she carried the name *Van Linschoten* before being renamed *Straat Luanda* in 1967. He had enough background information to take his hunch a step further.

Taylor telephoned a Narcotics Bureau agent in Brisbane, asking him to run a drill inspection on the campervan. This would entail discreet holes being drilled into various sections of the campervan and a visual inspection of what the drill bits drew out from the cavity. The ship was due to pull into Brisbane, Sydney and Melbourne on this voyage, which enabled proactive intelligence gathering for which Taylor's instincts were well regarded.

At the same time, an alert Customs preventative officer, also in Brisbane, was studying his copy of the *Straat Luanda*'s manifest, acting upon a memo Taylor had previously circulated, and had also been ready to run a drill inspection of the suspect campervan. But it was not to be.

Because of delays in Bombay, and poor weather on the voyage, the *Straat Luanda* was bypassing Brisbane and sailing directly to Sydney to make up some lost time.

Customs' Sydney-based Special Search Group was now briefed on the operation. Preventative officers Cummins and Scott boarded the ship in port at about 7.30 am on 5 December and, as had been the recent practice when inspecting suspect vehicles, began now boring into the underfloor of the vehicle using a portable electric drill.

The team drilled six small holes beneath the floor of the van, and each time they extracted the drill bit, they deposited their findings into a plastic evidence bag, recorded the time and date onto it with a permanent marker, and sealed the bag tight. A dark, sticky substance had coated the threads of each of the six drill bits. It was almost like drilling for oil. The Special Search Group was earning its money that day.

The bureau assigned the name 'Operation Genius' to the investigation. For Alex Taylor, it was almost like a dream come true: his charts, meticulously maintained spreadsheets, endless reports and hard work over recent months tracking suspicious vehicles being shipped by 'tourists', 'film makers' and returning Australians seemed to be finally paying off.

Operation Genius's running sheet reveals from its genesis the Narcotics Bureau's keen sense it was on to a substantial importation that was part of an even more substantial global syndicate.

0915 – 5 December, 1977
Telephone call from Inspector T. Alton, Narcotics Bureau, Sydney, to Inspector Robinson, Melbourne, to the effect that a Mercedes campervan, German registration number 853Z6217, consigned to a female, Mrs. Vera T. Hays, Melbourne, was deck cargo on the *M.V. Straat Luanda* which arrived in Sydney this morning. A search by officers revealed narcotics concealed in steel bearers which appeared as support to the floor at the rear of the vehicle. Estimated weight of cannabis resin contained in the hide is 60 kilos.

0925 hours
Checked with narcotics coordinators Melbourne, and established the motor vehicle concerned in this instance appears as item 29 on the manifest *MV Straat Luanda*. Particulars as follows:
  SHIPPER: Vera T. Hays
  CONSIGNEE: O/N Automobile Association of Melbourne
  MARKS AND NUMBERS: 853-Z-6217.

DECLARED CONTENTS: Unpacked 1977 model Daimler-Mercedes Benz car fitted with radio cassette tape deck.
WEIGHT: 3290 kilos.
Narcotics coordinators to ascertain the following:

1. Anything known re: the shipper and/or consignee.
2. Approximate weight of similar type of vehicle.
3. Name of customs agents to clear vehicle in Melbourne.

1420 hours

Inspector Alton, Sydney, advises that information from the officers of the *Straat Luanda* has established that the vessel will now depart Sydney at 2200 hours and will possibly arrive Melbourne 24 hours from that time, i.e. 2200 hours on 6.12.77. The hide has been drilled and representative sample was extracted and handed to the Customs Chemist, Sydney. The sample has been identified as cannabis resin. As far as Alton is concerned, there is no connection between this motor vehicle and a similar type vehicle – Mercedes campervan – which had similar type concealment that was detected and seized in Sydney some time ago.

1517 hours

Commander Mitchell advises that two preventative officers from Sydney will remain on the vessel *Straat Luanda* and surveil the vehicle during the voyage to Melbourne.

1523 hours

Alton advises that a search of the interior of the vehicle resulted in the discovery of a number of photographs – mainly of old persons. However one photo shows a grey-haired woman with a male person in uniform. (Possibly the male is an Indian customs officer.) The concealment of the narcotics in this instance is situated in the sub-frame. If it is anything like the first hide detected in the other Mercedes, a small piece of steel will be glued over the end of the sub frame. This piece of metal is easily removed by cutting the glue.

0929 hours on 6.12.1977
The priority is now to ascertain the identity of the shipper of the target vehicle.

1215 hours
Mr. B. Lugar, Appraisal Officer, Customs, called Narcotics Bureau office and advised Narcotics Agent Giblan that the target female Hays was at his office, Appraisal section, first floor, Customs House, Melbourne, seeking information in connection with the clearance and delivery of the target vehicle.

1238 hours on 6.12.77
Surveillance units begin. Members of the Narcotics Bureau units consists of agents Kalbarczyk and Robinson. N7 consists of Owens and Lovell who commenced surveillance of the female Hays when she left Customs House, Melbourne. She was seen to enter a Silver Top Taxi Cab T1592 and occupied the rear seat of the vehicle with another female.

1340 hours
Gary Cox, Security Manager, Hilton Hotel, Melbourne was contacted and a request was placed for a check of the hotel register.

1351 hours
Cox returns telephone call and advises Hays is booked into the hotel.

1450 hours
Narcotics Agent Giblin and Roberts say target appears in hotel register under her correct name and she occupies room 510 in the company of another female named Florice Bessire.

1517 hours
Telephoned Donald Chippendale, Overseas Liaison Intelligence Analysis, Canberra and advised him we required checks with the Drug Enforcement Agency and C.R.R.B. re: the females Hays and Bessire.

1540 hours
Chief Narcotics Agent Robinson briefs all staff in connection with Operation Genius.

1600 hours
Commander Southern Region Mitchell advises that Senior Narcotics Officer Wackett will travel to Melbourne on the morning of 7.12.77 with crocodile equipment for eventual attachment to the target vehicle.

Meanwhile in Melbourne, Toddie and Beezie stayed close to the Hilton, going for walks, and in the evening, dining at nearby eateries while they awaited confirmation the van could be collected. They were counting the hours before they would finally be free of the albatross around their necks – the carnet and the campervan. Vern had reiterated that the carnet required them to clear the vehicle once landed, and he told them to drive it from the Customs sheds.

Vern arrived at the Hilton Hotel on 7 December and booked a room two floors above them, but not before first renting a car. Narcotics agents later discovered the car had in fact been leased under an alias.

Vern told the women he had driven around the wharf area but the ship had not yet berthed. He was keen to know whether they'd finalised the import paperwork with the shipping agent.

'Where do you want to meet us once we have signed the van off the ship?' asked Toddie.

'Well, Aunty Vera,' said Vern, casting his eyes to the floor and then raising them to meet squarely with his aunt's, 'due to the change of port for its arrival, I need you and Beezie to drive it to Sydney,' he said.

'No way,' said Toddie, shaking her head. 'No way. That van is yours now and there ain't nothing going to make us drive it any further than off the wharf.' She continued defiantly: 'You told us in Stuttgart that we had only to get it to Bombay, and you'd meet us there – you didn't. I told Bob Lange in Bombay we wanted to go home then and there, but he said the carnet wouldn't allow that, so we listened to him. He said we would only have to come as far as Australia and you would take it off our hands and get your damn film done or whatever it is you wanted. I told you before what you could do with this van, Vern, and if it won't fit, then I'll make it fit.'

Toddie was shaking and Beezie thought she was going to have a meltdown as she had with Vern in Lahore at the border.

'Alright,' said Vern quickly, 'I promised you $25,000 for driving all the way, and if you'll do me this favour driving to Sydney, I'll give you an additional $200,000.'

Toddie laughed dismissively at the proposition.

'C'mon Vern, what in the hell would we do with $200,000 even if we did believe you?' she said. 'We wouldn't know what to do with that sort of money.'

Vern paused for a moment and replied, 'You can invest it if you want to in Sydney with a lawyer and he'll make sure it gets good interest.'

Then it was Beezie's turn to speak. 'Vern, as far as I'm concerned, you're nuts, and the sooner you take responsibility for it, the better.' Turning to Toddie and looking directly at her companion, she said, 'Toddie, I think we should just give Vern the van now and let him take care of the rest of the things and let's just go home.'

'Beezie, you'll be hounded for the rest of your lives if you try that on me.' Vern didn't mince words. 'No matter where you go or what you do, you'll regret it for the rest of your lives if you dump that van now.'

Conveying more menace than the carnet obligation with which he had up until then held the pair hostage, he was clearly making a threat.

'You'll regret it for the rest of your lives...' Beezie repeated in her head, unnerved by the intimidation buried in the warning. Vern was sounding like a criminal, as if he had something to hide.

Vern was offering a ridiculous amount of money for them to drive the van to Sydney. What was he up to? She was concerned about Toddie's health – her high blood pressure, her back pain, swollen knee and daily headaches – she didn't need the added stress. Vern said they would enjoy the drive to Sydney, and would be able to take their time and enjoy the scenery on the way.

Toddie sat on the bed with her head buried in her hands, a handful of tissues scrunched beside her. Slowly she regained her composure and was ready to address Vern's threats. Turning to her nephew, she said, 'Alright Vern, we'll drive to Sydney, but when we get there, that's it. No more.' It was as much a plea as a statement.

Vern got up, crossed the floor and hugged his aunt, although she made no attempt to return his embrace. She sat up straight, her arms by her side and eyes closed. She couldn't bear to look at him. Beezie by now was dumbfounded – that once loveable and adoring nephew had smiled, beckoned and conned Toddie once again into doing his bidding. There was nothing Beezie could do about it.

Vern didn't waste any time – it seemed the going was good, so he left them in their room, but not before telling them he would expect a phone call once they had cleared the van through Customs. He was returning to Sydney briefly, but would keep in touch with them, he said as he slipped out the door.

CHAPTER EIGHT

THIS WAS NO HOLIDAY

For Australians, the approach of December evokes images of sunshine, beaches and holidays. In the southern hemisphere, it's the time of year when most workers take their annual leave, and when school closes for the six-week end-of-year summer break. Holiday-makers flock to the beaches and campgrounds around the nation. Time is spent in front of the television watching Test cricket or tennis. Not unlike most working folk, many of the Narcotics Bureau agents had also booked their annual holidays well in advance. Inspector Bob Drane was no different. He was attached to the Melbourne office and was enjoying his first few days of leave when he was telephoned by his regional commander and summoned to its Melbourne headquarters. He was instructed to cancel the remainder of his holidays in light of a major operation afoot for which he would be immediately required to coordinate surveillance teams to track a suspect vehicle imported from India and at least two persons of interest.

Drane attended his first briefing on 7 December – the bureau's running sheets record the operation's next steps.

0900 – 7 December, 1977
Narcotics Co-ordinator Wake advises that confirmation has been received that *Straat Luanda* will arrive Melbourne at 2000.

0905 hours
Commander Mitchell advises Senior Narcotics Agent Wackett with crocodile equipment will arrive Melbourne on Trans Australia Airlines Flight 411 at ETA 1455.

1000 hours
Narcotics Agent Giblin and Senior Narcotics Agent Peers go to Hilton and see the security manager re: parking facilities at the hotel. Decision made to use the Nagra (tape recorder) when Mrs. Hays calls at 26 South Wharf to collect the target vehicle. Narcotics Agent Walshaw will carry the Nagra and will work with Mr. D. Stelling, Chief Area Inspector for 26 South Wharf, as one of the uniformed Customs Officers. It is anticipated Narcotics Agent Walshaw will be in a position to question Hays re ownership of the target vehicle etc.

1105 hours
Narcotics Agent Giblin and Senior Narcotics Agent Peers return from Hilton. It is highly unlikely target vehicle will be parked at hotel.

1117 hours
Senior Narcotics Agent Wackett arrives at Bureau office with crocodile equipment. (Arrangements made for it to be tested this afternoon.)

2130 hours
Narcotics agents Giblin, O'Brien, Walshaw and Preventative Officers Roberts and Dewhurst enter shed at 15 South Wharf and inspected target vehicle. Two random samples of cannabis resin extracted. Narcotics agents vacated shed about 2343 hours.

1015 hours on 9.12.1977
Narcotics Agent Walshaw proceeds to 9 South Wharf fitted

with Nagra to record all conversations between target Hays during the course of clearing the vehicle. Seizure notice prepared re target vehicle. G Group under the control of Senior Preventative Officer Roberts will be available to remove the narcotics from the target vehicle. This will take place immediately the vehicle is seized.

1245 hours
Telephone call from Senior Narcotics Agent Peers from 29 South Wharf that Hays has just left Quarantine Section and all paperwork has been completed. All surveillance teams alerted via channel 3.

1410 hours
Target females Hays and Bessire arrive at 29 South Wharf to approach Storage Clerk and Narcotics Agent Walshaw. Conversation recorded.

By 3 pm, the van was ready for collection by the women, but not before a final check by Quarantine officers whose responsibility essentially covered undeclared importation of fresh fruit, salami and exotic pests.

Toddie and Beezie were now at the wharf. The Customs shed was in view, and parked outside it, their campervan. The end of their journey was finally in sight, they thought.

However, bureaucracy is bureaucracy, and the Australian Quarantine and Inspection Service, which was responsible for upholding the nation's animal, plant and human quarantine regulations at border entry points, including both cargo and passengers, had staff stationed at the wharf more interested in the timepieces on their wrists than on clearing the campervan.

It was Friday mid-afternoon by the time the officers saw the size of the van to be checked, and then steam cleaned. Realising it was already after 3 pm and approaching the traditional Friday beer-o'clock at 4 pm, they advised their Customs colleagues they'd have to return Monday to complete the quarantine process. They claimed not to have time to thoroughly vet the campervan.

Quarantine officer Harvey Caple was a plant specialist working for the Victorian Department of Agriculture. As officer-in-charge of the Plant Quarantine Station at Port Melbourne, it was his job to explain the next steps to Toddie.

'Your vehicle won't be steam cleaned today owing to the vehicles in front of yours having to be cleaned first,' Caple said. 'It will be ready for you about 9 am on Monday.'

Toddie asked, 'Okay, but do you want me to leave the van here?'

'Yes, just leave the van where it's parked and I will put it in the shed over the weekend for security,' Caple told her.

Toddie used the office phone to call a taxi to return to their hotel.

The vehicle was held by Quarantine, and over the weekend Narcotics Bureau agents maintained around-the-clock observation of the campervan in the event anyone attempted to interfere with the hidden load.

On 11 December at about 10 pm, Vern arrived on an Ansett Airlines flight at Melbourne's Tullamarine Airport and approached the Avis Rental Car desk where Mary Soutis was on duty. Todd told her he had a booking in the name of a 'Mr Anthony'. He told the booking clerk Mr Anthony had not appeared and that he was taking his place. He then offered the clerk an Avis credit card in the name of Vern's company and Mr VL Todd.

He also showed the clerk his licence in the same name – Vern Leonard Todd. It was a NSW licence, number 4858NW with an expiry date of 17 February 1978. Miss Soutis recorded the details on the hiring contract. Todd indicated he would be staying overnight, so she asked him for a contact address. He said he was staying with friends in Toorak or South Yarra, but he didn't know the address. Vern hired a green Holden Statesman De Ville, registration AAB-642.

When interviewed later by the Narcotics Bureau, Miss Soutis remembered Vern Todd because he had also hired a vehicle about a week earlier. On that occasion, his booking was in the name of 'Mr Millar', and he gave his contact address as the Hilton Hotel. On the night of 11 December though, Miss Soutis distinctly remembered he was using a different name. She made a mental note of his features in case the car was later abandoned or reported stolen. She observed he was wearing blue jeans, a green shirt, and a pale-coloured jacket. He wore several rings on both hands and was well spoken, she recalled.

At about the same time that Vern Todd was renting his car, at the other end of town, Narcotics Agent Giblin was trying to determine how much cannabis resin was actually secreted in the campervan currently in Quarantine. After careful examination, and ensuring not to upset the women's arrangements inside the van, agents concluded the *entire* floor of the van was carrying drugs. The original estimate from the drill-bit extractions was around sixty kilograms of hashish. Little did they know that an under-floor mounted water tank, which had been disconnected from the internal sink, was also used to conceal many more kilograms of smuggled hashish.

Operation Genius's running sheet continued:

0925 hours on 12/12/1977
Narcotics agents Robertson and Thorn see Hays and Bessire at the Quarantine station at Port Melbourne. They entered the campervan and Hays drove the vehicle. Robertson saw a male person in an Avis hire car, metallic green Statesman De Ville with a white vinyl roof registration AAB-642. Upon checking, the car was hired to a Vern Leonard Todd, (D.O.B. 8.12/1943) of NSW (known to the Narcotics Bureau).

0955 hours
Both vehicles drove in a westerly direction along Lorrimar [Lorimer] Street. Thorn and Robertson followed the hire

car with Todd which continued to follow the campervan for some distance. The hire car then turned sharply left and suddenly pulled over and stopped. A short time later, the hire car moved off. Thorn and Robertson continued to follow the hire car. At the intersection of Salmon and Woolboard Road, Robertson saw the campervan stopped with Hays and Bessire standing beside the vehicle. The hire car continued past the van and Robertson continued to surveil the hire car.

At the same time as this surveillance was being carried out, Senior Narcotics Agent Peers and Narcotics Agent Lovell saw the Mercedes campervan with the two females proceed along Salmon Street and turn right into Plummer Street into the Mercedes Service Centre. Both females alighted from the vehicle and appeared to have a conversation with the employees of the establishment. A short time later, mechanics began working on the front section of the van.

1140 hours
Senior Narcotics Agent Yurisich and Narcotics Agent Nixon who were on duty at the Ansett terminal at Tullamarine airport see Holden Statesman De Ville, driven by suspect Vern Leonard Todd, 1.83 metres, dark brown bushy hair, shoulder length, thin build, clean shaven, cocky bush jacket, faded blue jeans, carrying a large brown leather shoulder bag and a silver metallic equipment suitcase. Vehicle parked in Avis carpark, silver case removed from trunk of the car.

1145 hours
Todd entered Ansett departure lounge where Ansett flight 20 for Sydney was preparing to depart.

1158 hours
Todd entered the lounge and approached the seat allocation office but turned and walked back to the concourse. He

looked about and returned to the lounge and then took a seat behind the office out of sight of the concourse.

1210 hours
Todd boarded the flight having allowed the majority of the other passengers aboard first.

1415 hours
Approximately 1415 Robertson and Thorn followed a Yellow Cab number T296. Surveillance was continued in front of taxi and Narcotic Agent Hansell was on a motor cycle following it.

1425 hours
Taxi stopped outside Matilda's Tavern in Queen Street. Hays alighted from taxi and entered RACV office. Robertson took up position on foot opposite RACV office.

1430 hours
Hays returned to taxi and returned to Hilton Hotel arriving 10 minutes later.

1500 hours
Hays re-entered the foyer from the lift area and walked to the public telephone area.

1522 hours
Hays re-entered the foyer from the lift area and walked to the public telephone. Narcotics Agent Thorn, who had by now joined Narcotics Agent Robertson, followed Hays to the telephone area. Thorn heard Hays ask the operator for a reverse charge call to Sydney 328-1780 (A.V. Todd, 47 John Street, Woollahra, NSW). This was confirmed by a piece of paper Hays had on which the number was written and sighted by Narcotics Agent Thorn. He heard Hays say to the person

on the phone 'I have been trying to reach you. I'll see you at lunchtime tomorrow.'

Meanwhile at the Narcotics Bureau headquarters in Melbourne, Commander Douglas Mitchell, the southern region boss, was preparing to send a telex to the bureau's director, Harvey Bates, at Central Office in Canberra. It was just before 6 pm when the telex machine kicked into action, dispatching a top priority, restricted message which began: 'I Douglas John Mitchell, Regional Commander, Southern Region, Narcotics Bureau, hereby state ...' followed by a dense text recounting the week's events, beginning on the first day of Operation Genius on 5 December. Bates was still at his desk when his assistant brought the print-out to his office. He was pleased with the progress his agents were making, but he knew from his career in Customs, these sorts of investigations could not only take a long time to successfully conclude but, worse still, could easily fall off the rails.

Bates was known as a dedicated Customs man who had risen through the ranks as a preventive officer on the Melbourne wharves, then was promoted into undercover operations where he excelled, before heading up the prevention and detection section in NSW, where he set out to challenge the corrupt practices of the old-style Customs men on the knockabout Sydney waterfront. Bates was an outsider, disturbing Sydney's tranquillity, and his physical appearance – small in stature, bespectacled and almost cherubic – hardly endeared him to his staff. He overcame these obstacles, ridding the team of corrupt officers and earning the respect of like-minded colleagues keen to promote Customs' law-enforcement credentials. Bates was recognised for his achievements by The Queen, who made him a Member of the British Empire in 1968. The following year he was appointed the Narcotics Bureau's first-ever director.

•

In their hotel room, Toddie set to work recording the day's activities in her travel dairy. She wrote:

> For the first time we are sure now our feelings about Vern all along were right, but what is it, what's he done and how involved are we? I'm mad now and the tears are not from being hurt, or being scared; it's just downright madness. I really want Beezie to go home as we have a house to maintain, property taxes to pay etc. But she said she would not leave me alone because of my poor health.

•

As Operation Genius entered its second week, the running sheet activities moved from Melbourne and into rural Victoria. The women were once again on the road, taking their time as they dealt with the challenges of travelling in a left-hand drive vehicle on the left-hand side of the road.

1255 hours on 13/12/1977
Target vehicles leave Mercedes centre and Mazda leads campervan with occupants Hays and Bessire. Vehicles take route which leads them to Mobil service station road house, Broadmeadows, where they arrive at 1350 hours. Narcotics Agent Robertson is already seated inside roadhouse.

1355 hours
Hays, Bessire and male enter roadhouse and have refreshments. (Narcotics Agent Robertson is seated two tables away and listens to conversation.)

1415 hours
Campervan with two females continues out the Hume Highway towards Sydney.

Toddie and Beezie were completely unaware that they were now front and centre of what was fast becoming Australia's largest surveillance operation outside of wartime, which would ultimately involve not only the Federal Bureau of Narcotics, but also state police, the Australian Army, and a host of characters who ranged from the viciously criminal to the powerfully political.

The web of Operation Genius being spun around the two women would, in time, encompass an international drug smuggling organisation worth more than $US40 million and responsible for organising a number of sizeable drug importations into Australia.

CHAPTER NINE

YOUR CAKE AND YOU'RE STUCK WITH IT

As Commander Mitchell in Melbourne had expected, the return telex from Canberra instructed him to deploy all available resources to Operation Genius. It would be, if it all worked out as they hoped, the bureau's greatest bust to date. Since its establishment within the Department of Business and Consumer Affairs, complementing the Bureau of Customs' investigations but with a focus exclusively on the importation into Australia of prohibited drugs, it had so far been credited with making mostly minor drug busts. No operation had ever generated as much interest within the Australian drug enforcement community as this campervan.

Inspector Bob Drane was assigned officer-in-charge of Operation Genius as it surveilled the two women on the open road. In addition, Drane had eight other agents, affording him the luxury of 24-hour surveillance. He knew it was going to be a difficult operation, not only because of the extent of the task ahead, but also because of the personalities within the team he had been assigned. Three of the agents had been pulled from their holidays to go on the road, while two others had their impending Christmas holidays cancelled. They all now found themselves, Drane included, behind the wheels of unmarked bureau surveillance cars and a motorcycle tracking two American senior citizens.

Narcotics Agent Michele Khoury was Drane's number two, and the only woman agent on the road in his team. She was to play a vital role in Operation Genius. Drane's prime concern was the team's ability to monitor every movement the women made. He would have preferred even more agents, an extra vehicle or two, and some newer electronic monitoring devices, but in reality he had the best available resources at his disposal. The crocodile (tracking device) and transmitter that agents had covertly strapped to the underside of the campervan when it first arrived in Melbourne continued to emit a constant signal to Drane and Khoury in their vehicle. It was good for a radius of up to seventy-five miles (120 kilometres), so anywhere the van went, the device kept the agents informed of its location.

Meanwhile in the campervan ahead of Drane, Beezie was busy sifting through the masses of brochures and caravan guidebooks Toddie had picked up at the Royal Automobile Club of Victoria office. The first leg of their road trip ended at the Victoria Lake Caravan Park in Shepparton, about 150 miles (240 kilometres) north-west of Melbourne, where the Goulburn Valley Highway meets the Midland Highway. That evening, before retiring, Toddie and Beezie headed to the site's laundromat to do some much-needed washing. If they were lucky, it might begin drying overnight and just need a few hours' sunlight the next morning before it was ready to wear. They bundled their clothes into the machine and sat down to wait, each with a book, while the load ran through.

Shortly after, they were joined by a young woman also doing her washing.

The young woman struck up conversation. Her name was Miche, and she was an Australian holidaymaker enjoying her annual leave. She was travelling with her de facto husband, Bob, and they were public servants. It was always wise for agents working undercover to use their own first names or nicknames lest they drop their guard when using aliases and arouse suspicion. Beezie and Toddie welcomed the conversation. They truly enjoyed meeting new people. Miche asked where they were headed, how they were travelling and where they'd been. She said the women seemed to have been very brave to have survived their experiences so far and to want to continue travelling. When her load of washing had finished and spun dry, Miche headed off to her trailer with her bundle – which was filled out with all her fellow agents' underwear, socks, singlets and t-shirts, since it was her first night on the road – while Beezie and Toddie waited for theirs to finish.

It was Narcotics Agent Michele Khoury's practice in her undercover role to positively identify her targets and learn about their movements over the coming days. Khoury had joined the bureau in 1975 shortly after one of her closest friends died of a heroin overdose. She had always wanted to be in law enforcement, especially undertaking undercover roles, and the bureau gave her that opportunity.

On the day Operation Genius was conceived, she turned up for work like Drane and her fellow agents, and with little warning was suddenly sent out on the road in pursuit of the campervan as it headed towards Shepparton. Fortunately, she always kept a small travel bag in her work locker with the personal essentials for just these sorts of assignments.

The American women were up bright and early the next morning and headed north-east along the Goulburn Valley Highway, eventually reaching Deniliquin and finally Narrandera, where they stayed the night at a caravan park a short distance outside the town of five thousand inhabitants. Each night they were on the road, the narcotics agents did their best to squeeze as many officers they could into one room to save on their allotted travelling allowance. This enabled them to build up a kitty for Christmas celebrations they had already begun planning back in Melbourne.

From Narrandera, Toddie and Beezie headed in a north-easterly direction and booked into a Dubbo motel. Bob Drane covertly arranged with the hotel manager to have the women's calls also switched into his room, so he'd be able to monitor any calls to Vern. Toddie tried but failed to make contact with him, and instead Drane heard Toddie speaking to an unidentified voice on the other end of the line that instructed the women to drive to Dunedoo, an even smaller town, where they would be met in two days' time at 10 am in the main street. The women spent two days and two nights in Dubbo before moving off north-east to Dunedoo.

Drane had strong suspicions that if the syndicate ringleaders were planning to meet the Americans in Dunedoo, then there might be an attempt to unload the drugs at the same time. Dunedoo seemed an odd choice for the rendezvous, he thought, until he arrived to scope it out early the next morning. There were nine different approaches converging on the town's centre – some were highways, some were main roads, and others were akin to goat tracks. Drane radioed Canberra and sought approval for air support to monitor the multitude of intersections. An Australian Army helicopter was soon hovering high in the air, maintaining a discreet distance from the targets, trying not to attract attention. It would be a challenge in a small town of only a few hundred inhabitants for a chopper to go unnoticed.

In total, with extra vehicles and staff from Sydney dispatched to the scene, Drane had seven cars as well as two undercover officers on foot. By 8 am it was hot, heading towards 100 degrees Fahrenheit (38 degrees Celsius). At 9.30 am, the campervan could be seen approaching the main street. Following instructions she'd been given in her phone call to Vern, Toddie parked it on the left-hand side of the road, parallel to the kerb and across from the post office. Both she and Beezie got out and walked across the road to the small restaurant, where they ordered breakfast. Half an hour later, and still with no sign of Vern, they returned to the campervan and played some of their music cassettes to pass the time. The van's door and windows were propped open as the temperature began to rise. The cold beers in the fridge became more and more inviting. They had a few drinks and played cards, but when Vern failed to turn up, they packed up and headed out of town.

'Target vehicle is pulling out, heading due west. Maintain your positions,' Drane instructed his team by radio as he and Khoury seamlessly pulled into traffic, three car lengths back from the campervan. He had a sneaking suspicion there was counter-surveillance being maintained, but he was unable to pin any one car or person to confirm his suspicions. He remembered the report that Vern Todd had conducted counter-surveillance when the women took delivery of the campervan in Melbourne, and he knew the drug kingpin's organisation had the nous to mount such an operation itself.

Or maybe the presence of the chopper above them had given the game away.

The women had no plan at this point so they set off for Gunnedah, but were unable to secure a room on arrival, and continued on to Tamworth. They booked into the Tamworth Lodge.

The Narcotics Bureau duo of Drane and Khoury arranged for a team member to secure them a room so they could maintain a watch without being seen checking in. Again, Drane made arrangements with the hotel management to patch the women's calls into his room so he could monitor any conversations with Vern and his associates.

Over the next three days Toddie tried several times, unsuccessfully, to make contact by telephone with her nephew, each time connecting with an unidentified voice on the other end of the line. On the third day she decided she had had enough of the inland heat, the flies and the sunburnt countryside. She informed the voice at the other end of the telephone they would be heading to the coast and then south where they expected to spend Christmas as a family with Vern in Sydney.

The pair headed due east until they reached the coastal resort town of Port Macquarie, about 250 miles (390 kilometres) north of Sydney. They pulled into the Aquatic Gardens Caravan Park, next to the Hastings River, and hooked up their campervan to the mains power supply. Toddie again called Vern's number several times from the park. On one occasion, the voice at the other end told her he had had a fight with his wife and couldn't be located. The unidentified man gave her the instruction to be at the first hotel (Sunset Motor Lodge) they'd stayed in after the Wentworth Hotel by Christmas Eve. Vern would collect them to celebrate Christmas Day with 'part of the family', as he put it.

Toddie and Beezie left Port Macquarie on 22 December and arrived in Sydney the same day. It was not the first time Toddie had to negotiate the left-hand drive vehicle in busy city traffic, but still she took extra care while Beezie acted as her lookout and navigator. They booked into the Sundowner Caravan Park on Mona Vale Road, in the outer suburb of North Ryde. The next morning, 23 December, Beezie and Toddie caught a taxi into the Sunset Motor Lodge and booked themselves a room for the evening. They'd no sooner settled down when the room's telephone rang. A woman's voice on the other end said she wanted to speak with 'Mrs Hays'.

'This is Mrs Hays speaking,' answered Toddie.

'Well, I think it must be the wrong Mrs Hays,' said the caller, and immediately hung up. Toddie had no idea who the caller was, or what her purpose might have been in making the call. She thought possibly it was a call from Vern via an associate to confirm she and Beezie had checked in. She waited for the phone to ring again, but it didn't. Vern never called, never visited; he never even wished them a Merry Christmas.

Toddie was shattered by Vern's snub and offhand treatment. She wrote only a few sentences on Christmas Day in her travel diary:

Christmas arrived, and as usual there was no word from Vern. This was our first Christmas away from home and our loved ones, and we were so blue and homesick. I tried calling Vern on several occasions but I would always wind up talking to a stranger. I was told Vern and his wife had another big fight just before Christmas and that is why we didn't hear from him. He apparently went out of state, and she went to friends in the bush.

Beezie too had never spent a more unhappy Christmas in all her life. On 26 December, the women checked out of the motel and caught a taxi back to their van at the trailer park. They spent the night there and decided to move on the next morning, to be near the water. Before leaving the caravan park, they checked their guidebook and decided on heading to Brooklyn, a small community of about three hundred residents on the Hawkesbury River north of Sydney. But before they set off, they travelled back into the city and visited The Rocks again. Their absence gave Inspector Drane and Agent Khoury an opportunity to secretly enter the women's campervan, photograph the interior and search through their belongings. They also inspected a small hole behind the driver's seat that had been drilled while the vehicle had been in quarantine on the docks in Melbourne. It enabled them to check the haul was still intact and hadn't been tampered with.

When the women arrived in Brooklyn, they parked in a reserve next to the river not far from the highway connecting Sydney to the northern steel and coal city of Newcastle. Toddie located a public phone and made a call to Vern's home in Woollahra. She was instructed to travel back into Sydney. Vern had apparently returned.

On 30 December at about 3 pm, Toddie took a Sydney-bound train from Brooklyn. After catching a taxi from Central Station to a Paddington art gallery as directed, she got out and walked along the main street of the trendy eastern suburb, whereupon a stranger unexpectedly beckoned her to follow him. She trailed him through several different lanes, all interconnecting, turning right, then left, doubling back until they finally stopped in a back alley and a gate opened into a small courtyard. She followed the young man in, and there waiting for her was Nephew Vern.

Without giving her a chance to speak, Vern ushered her inside and asked Toddie how they were enjoying Australia. She told him the scenery was beautiful and the people very warm. Then she got straight to the point: something was causing her great distress.

When she had phoned a few days earlier, it had coincided with a discovery the women had made ... totally by accident. Beezie, she said, was dislodging pebbles caught between the treads of the rear dual wheels when she chanced upon a small foreign object attached to the van's rear springs. Toddie had been inside cleaning up with a pot of coffee brewing when Beezie called to her to come and look. Both women examined the black object, removed it and took it inside the van to study it more closely. That was the point at which Toddie went to telephone Vern.

This black object was the tracking device narcotics agents had placed on the van when it was at the wharf in Melbourne. The agents were also monitoring telephone conversations to the Todd household as well as calls to his company's business number. They distinctly heard Vern advise his aunt in that phone call to reattach the transmitter to the van springs and to come to Sydney immediately.

Vern's major task was now to placate his aunt as she demanded answers to her questions.

'Why is there a device on the van?' queried Toddie. 'And why did you want us to put it back on?'

Vern leaned back in his chair and said with very little emotion, 'I want them to know where you are.'

'What do you mean, you want *who* to know where we are?' demanded Toddie.

'It doesn't make any difference now. I wanted you to put it back on because it was the only option to take,' replied Vern.

Toddie's record of the day's events reveal a growing realisation of how seriously complicit she and Beezie were becoming as their situation became more and more unbelievable:

> Beezie and I got into an argument today over this whole situation and mess. I flew into a rage and said I'm going to get some answers once and for all. I took the train and arrived in Sydney. I had a funny feeling I was being followed but this can't be true I said to myself; it only happens in the movies but I still couldn't shake the feeling. I decided to go to the Rocks for dinner and while there, a fellow came in that was in the phone booth next to me at the train station. I was trying to call Vern, without luck, so then I called a cab. Was this coincidental or was I being followed? Again, the shivers. My God, what's happening? Now I was feeling remorse for storming out on Beezie. I told myself I would make it up to her by doing some shopping. We both needed swimsuits and fortunately the night I was in town was late shopping. I found the swimwear and while there went to the restroom. I saw a pay phone and thought I'll try once more to call Vern. I finally reached him and asked him where in the hell he had been and just how long did he expect us to stay in Australia? He asked me if I was being followed. I told him that I had the feeling that I was, but why? He said I'll be seeing you soon and I'll tell you then.

Back in Woollahra, Vern by now had been joined by Bob Lange and another one of his business associates. They talked about how they could get inside the campervan without the narcotics agents detecting their presence. They pored over a map of western New South Wales, looking for a town with a suitable rest area where they could hide behind trees and bushes then jump into the van through the passenger door when the women stopped to 'stretch their legs'.

Toddie was beginning to think she was in some cloak-and-dagger movie scene. She listened to the men huddled around the map, discussing options. It was quite apparent now it was no longer a matter of 'taking a little marijuana along to smoke on the way', as Vern had claimed at the outset. The men were discussing large quantities of drugs. What were they proposing to put into the van and when?

When Vern began mentioning 'throwing packages from the van every hundred yards', and later collecting them from the roadside in the dead of night, red flags were well and truly raised for Toddie. It was clear that for her nephew it was just a game. She told Vern she wanted no part of whatever he was caught up in. She wanted out and to go home as promised. The conversation became heated. Vern leaned forward to level his gaze at Toddie and barked at her that it was an international syndicate calling the shots and she – and, for that matter, he – had no choice but to follow orders, or else. She didn't want to know what the 'or else' would be.

Toddie was speechless, but more than that, she had become very frightened.

'Aunty Vera, you can't go home with the carnet in your name. If you want to leave, you are going to have to ship that van back to Germany. You make the choice,' he said. 'It's your piece of cake, and you're stuck with it.' A short time later, Vern departed.

With that, one of Vern's business partners told Toddie he would be taking her to Palm Beach later that evening, where they would meet Vern again and have further discussions.

Of course, the American women weren't to know that Sydney's eastern suburbs of Paddington, Woollahra, Vaucluse and Double Bay were not only home for much of the city's society families but also for many of Sydney's acting fraternity, musicians, fashion designers, politicians and even drug kingpin. Nor were they – or any of the extended family in the United States – aware that large parties in mansions, including Vern's, were common; and in her nephew's case, auctions were staged in which the participants bid for truckloads of cannabis stashed in a van parked nearby. The highest bidder would be given the keys and instructions as to where to locate the vehicle. It was a relatively safe way of disposing of the drugs, and it was always a good party.

Vern Todd's group was well known for this modus operandi. At one such party, a leading Sydney criminal lawyer specialising in drug cases was in attendance when the Narcotics Bureau raided the mansion. They were looking not so much for the party-goers smoking cannabis but for the location of the van loaded with drugs about to be auctioned.

The agents identified themselves and announced the raid, to which the lawyer jumped onto a table and declared authoritatively: 'I am a lawyer and you are advised to give only your name, your address and your date of birth, but say nothing more until you have legal representation.'

The Palm Beach connection had direct links with not only the eastern suburbs set, but also with the traditional 'flock' of the Sydney underworld. The Northern Beaches were the stomping ground of one of Vern's associates, James 'Jimmy' Sweetnam, a convicted drug thief sentenced in 1970 to twelve months' jail for his part in the theft of half a million dollars of amphetamines from a Sydney pharmaceutical warehouse. Sweetnam and another associate – Neville Stevens – and Vern Todd were all called in 1977 to appear before the NSW Royal Commission into Drug Trafficking, headed by Justice Philip Morgan Woodward. Todd was named before the commission as one of Sydney's leading marijuana dealers specialising in moving huge quantities of cannabis from Griffith in south-western New South Wales into metropolitan Sydney. There are some who believe Australian cannabis was in fact so good, growing conditions so productive, and corruption of NSW politicians and police so effective at this time that much of the east coast's cannabis crops were exported to overseas markets in

North America and Europe. Australian domestic consumption was only one element of overall demand.

When Toddie and one of Vern's associates did arrive at Palm Beach in the dark, as usual Vern was nowhere to be found. She waited for Vern to appear, but in vain. Vern's associate was convinced by now he wasn't going to show, so drove Toddie back to the campervan at Brooklyn in the early hours of the morning.

At the same time – 3.10 am on 31 December – a narcotics agent observed and noted in his running sheet that one of Todd's associates approached the reserve at Brooklyn, driving a white 1964 Valiant station wagon. He saw Toddie exit the vehicle, walk several hundred yards to the van, enter it and turn on a light. The light remained on for a short time and was then extinguished.

Agents followed the Valiant back to Sydney and then to John Street, where the driver parked the car in a lane, walked to the backyard gate and entered the Todd home via the rear of the premises. The next morning after Toddie had slept in until about 11 am, Beezie learnt from Toddie that Vern and his wife, now reunited, had invited the two women to spend New Year's Eve with them in Sydney. Beezie was hoping, more for Toddie's sake, that this might be Vern's opportunity to make up for the upset he caused when he didn't show up to celebrate Christmas. But little did she know how seriously deep into the web both women were now ensnared. Toddie had not shared details of the conversations to which she had been privy the day she stormed out on Beezie and went to Vern's home to 'get some answers once and for all'.

With each passing day, and every conversation Toddie had with Vern, another red flag was raised with Beezie, prompting her to ask more questions of her companion but getting fewer answers in return. As both women sat and discussed their predicament, they reached agreement on one important aspect: whatever Vern's inducements, risking their lives and their health – especially that of Toddie's – simply weren't worth it.

They resolved they would be tough with Vern and demand he *get* them, rather than *let* them, out of this horrible situation.

Shortly after 2.30 pm on New Year's Eve, after a long walk from their van, Toddie and Beezie boarded a Sydney-bound train at Brooklyn Station. Upon arrival at Sydney's Central Station, they caught a taxi to Woollahra. They followed the same routine as Toddie had previously undertaken – standing outside the art gallery in Paddington. The regular watch, however, didn't appear to be on duty. Toddie found a pay phone and called her nephew. The voice on the other end of the line said he was expecting them, but at the Sunset Motor Lodge. They hailed a taxi and headed into Kings Cross to the serviced apartments and waited in the foyer for Vern.

He finally made contact by phone through the motel's reception at about 6 pm and instructed them to walk down to Rushcutters Bay Park, where he would pick them up in a white van. The women waited at the park by the water for Vern to appear. Shortly before 7 pm, his familiar face appeared but driving an unfamiliar vehicle. He stopped and the passenger door opened for them. Vern didn't say much except that he was taking them to a quiet spot to have a talk. He drove around the bay and found an alley into which he reversed and parked. The discussion was about their attitude to what lay ahead and a proposal for them to transfer ownership of the campervan to Bob Lange, who by this stage they had discovered was in fact Phillip Shine. (Shine, they were told, used the alias 'Bob Lange' to keep an ex-wife off his trail, and ultimately away from his money.) Toddie was close to blowing a fuse again.

'We trusted you from the start,' she said, 'but you've lied to us on so many occasions, didn't turn up when you were supposed to, and played such peculiar games that we don't believe you anymore. I can't trust you, we can't trust you and I told you before we don't want any part of whatever you're involved in. We're not interested in financial gain or anything … we just want to go home.' With that, she began to sob.

'Vern, stop playing games with us,' Beezie said. 'There is something terribly wrong and you won't tell us and now we are caught up in it … something you know about and have known about all along. I think it is time you levelled with us.'

Vern continued to sidestep the issue, but Beezie pushed on. 'Vern, there is something in that van, and we want to know exactly what it is. Have we been carrying drugs? You said you smoked mari—' but Vern interrupted, reassuring them as he had initially that they need not worry about more than a little grass being in the van for his own personal use.

But Beezie wouldn't let it rest this time. 'If that's the case and we get caught with whatever it is, what is likely to happen to us?' she asked.

Vern glossed over any consequences, saying that even if they did get caught, they would get off lightly because it would be a first offence.

'But if they find it, won't they find your fingerprints or something like that?' asked Beezie.

'No,' said Vern. 'Fingerprints disappear after a while.'

Beezie spoke up again. 'We're in this situation that you've put us in, where we stand to lose every goddamned thing that we have worked hard for all our lives. We don't want no more of this.'

Vern remained silent. A minute passed, then Toddie sighed deeply and said, 'Well, it's getting late and we have to have a place to stay for the night, Vern.'

They were intending to celebrate the New Year as a family, but again Vern changed plans. Vern had never invited them to overnight at his John Street home since they'd arrived in Australia. Tonight would be no different.

Instead he drove from the alley heading for Sydney's inner suburbs, through areas the women didn't recognise and which they found particularly unattractive. Vern pulled up outside a rundown motel, but Toddie flatly refused to stay there.

'I'll sleep on the streets before I would bed down here,' she told her nephew.

So Vern drove back towards Kings Cross and eventually arrived at the Southern Cross Travelodge at Rushcutters Bay, close to the park where they had begun their little tour of Sydney and its inner city. The women secured a room, checked in and Vern drove off into the night, and into the new year of 1978.

It was the last time Toddie and Beezie ever saw Vern Leonard Todd.

•

The following morning the women returned by train to Brooklyn and began cleaning up the campervan. They had decided to head north to Gosford. Following Vern's suggestion, they went to the local post office to send a telegram to Bob Lange, who was now back in Bombay, which read: 'We are waiting for you to collect van. Please advise arrival date urgently. Signed, Vera Hays.' The women truly believed they were on the homeward trek and would soon be able to hand the van over, ridding themselves of it once and for all.

Narcotics agents took a copy of the telegram once the women left the post office and resumed surveillance of the campervan. Toddie and Beezie drove on to Terrigal, one hundred miles (150 kilometres) north of Sydney, and booked into the Hillshaven Van Park.

A white station wagon with tinted windows was posted alongside other holiday makers' panel vans to keep a check on the women and their campervan. The bureau intended to make the most of this convenient arrangement to expand its technical surveillance capabilities by planting a bug inside the campervan's dashboard.

Agents John 'Shobby' Shobbrook and Bruce Wackett had a small window of time, once the women left to catch public transport to the local club for drinks and dinner, to get in, plant the device and get out without detection. Shobbrook's objective was to connect a small radio transmitter and microphone to a live terminal underneath the dashboard. It was the early hours of the evening in a crowded caravan park; campers, kids and bicycles were still about as the sun slowly set on a long summer day. The agent found a glass window slightly ajar and after sliding it open, quickly climbed through with the help of his partner. Shobbrook then crept forward to the driver's cabin and searched for the live wire that powered the car radio. After connecting the bureau's transmitter to the live wire, he found another connection for an earth, and a dim red light glowed on the transmitter. Bingo! He covered the light with electrical tape and then taped the transmitter out of sight up under the dash. Shortly after, Shobbrook exited the van undetected and returned with Wackett to the bureau's unmarked station wagon.

Job done. Or so they thought.

The next morning, the women drove off to do some shopping, with the agents following closely. Their conversation was picked up clearly by the newly installed bug. The content of their idle chatter had little significance to the investigation. Agents Shobbrook and Wackett shadowed them through Gosford and then into a small industrial area where the women turned into the driveway of a car radio repair shop.

'Oh no,' Shobbrook said, as they quickly realised what was happening. 'I've buggered up the van's radio when I connected the transmitter.' They knew the repairman couldn't miss the suspicious-looking black plastic box with an antenna once he peered under the dashboard. As the women entered the shop, Shobbrook darted around to a side door, taking a step into the workshop where he could see the owner of the business in conversation with Toddie.

'What do you want?' the shopkeeper turned and called out to the stranger now just inside his workshop, but out of sight of the two customers. The agent discreetly showed him his Federal Bureau of Narcotics identification and motioned for him to step into the workshop. The shopkeeper left the women at the front counter and Shobbrook quietly explained that the women and their van were involved in a drugs investigation. He asked what they had said. 'They told me their radio isn't working and want me to have a look at it,' he replied.

Agent Shobbrook told the shopkeeper, 'I connected a radio transmitter up to it last night that must have killed the radio. When you have a look, can you leave the transmitter hidden up under the dash and in a working state?' The startled shopkeeper replied, 'Yeah sure, mate, but they said the radio hasn't been working since they first started driving the van in Melbourne.'

After repairing the radio, the helpful shopkeeper left the transmitter operational and the two women continued on their way. They remained in Terrigal and visited the Central Coast Leagues Club in nearby Gosford, where they enjoyed the restaurant and had a flutter on the poker machines. It was here one evening, and then again a few evenings later, that Miche and her de facto, Bob, 'serendipitously' ran into the American women.

This encounter in early January 1978 was remembered well by both parties. The four of them drank together until closing time before the women were given a lift back to the campervan in Bob and Miche's car. Upon reaching the campervan, Toddie and Beezie invited the two agents in for a nightcap. They discussed politics, sport and the problems they had encountered with their jobs into the early hours of the morning. All the while, the conversation was being monitored.

Drane still wasn't sure about the women. They were very cool customers it seemed, but he doubted they were aware of the extent of their valuable consignment. They were relaxed, and open about their travels and their lives; they were not your average criminals, he thought.

At around 3.15 am, the 'touring couple' finally decided to call it a night and head back to their motel. Toddie and Beezie were glad to have met up with the pair again; a wonderful coincidence that the couple they should meet nearing the end of their travels were the same people they'd met at the beginning of their Australian trip in Shepparton.

Minutes later, as Toddie and Beezie cleaned up the glasses, cups and plates and were about to retire, they heard a car approaching, a door open and then footsteps outside the campervan. A knock at the door revealed a breathless Miche. She had forgotten her purse, which she suspected was somewhere in the van. Sure enough, the undercover agent's purse, containing her Federal Bureau of Narcotics identification, some money and make-up, had slipped down behind the bench on which she had sat, but appeared to have remained there undiscovered. Miche thanked them, bade them goodnight again and headed back to the car where her partner was waiting.

When the agents arrived back at the motel where the rest of the team was staying, there were chuckles and relief all round. The team monitoring and recording the conversation from the campervan had heard Drane's remarks about their 'boring public service jobs'.

None the wiser, Toddie was almost gushing as she described their catch-up in her diary:

One evening while at the club in Gosford we ran into Bob and Miche. We had met them earlier, especially Miche, at one of the caravan parks. You would have thought it was old home week. After much embracing we asked them how their holidays were going. Miche said 'great; we are having a wonderful time and really living it up'. On a previous meeting they had told us of their vacation and the wonderful trips they had planned. We were on a first name basis and friends. We met them at different times at the club eating, drinking, and gambling. To them, we were Beezie and Toddie.'

The two women now focused on arranging their flights home while squeezing in a few more days' Australian sunshine before the cold and snow they expected would greet them upon their return to La Pine. Part of the arrangements included formally ridding themselves of any responsibility for the campervan. On a visit to Sydney on 5 January, Toddie went to the US Consulate, where she spoke with the consul's assistant, Irene Wallace. She told Mrs Wallace she was an American citizen who was seeking a consular appointment. Mrs Wallace asked about the nature of the matter, and when she ascertained it was a legal issue, provided Toddie with a list of solicitors the mission kept on file to specifically address these types of consular requests.

On 6 January, Toddie sent another telegram to Bob Lange in Bombay: 'Am sick of waiting. Van in storage for you to collect. Signed Vera Hays.'

Again, the narcotics agents took a copy of the telegram. They were convinced Vern had given Toddie instructions to contact Lange by telegram in an attempt to create a cover story.

Toddie's diary entries began to convey a feeling that they might need to take matters into their own hands:

> I asked the manager of the caravan park if he could recommend a good storage place for all of our excess luggage. By now we had too many suitcases and they were forever in our way. We had purchased Christmas presents for our loved ones in the States and here it was … January and we are still here in Australia. We stored the suitcases and headed north. On the way we checked with the owner of a nearby storage warehouse to see if it would be possible to store the campervan. He said 'yes'. I had already sent one telegraph to Bombay so I decided to follow up with another one.

It was likely, authorities now believed, the women knew they were being watched, and if so, it was only a matter of time before the game was up. Surveillance kept the fourteen-person Operation Genius unit in Sydney occupied around the clock, but given the bureau knew the extent of the Todd organisation's operations, it was felt that the overtime costs could be justified. Particularly if, as the bureau's regional commander Tom Mullaly hoped, it would provide them with a big catch: Vern Leonard Todd and maybe even Phillip Shine (aka Bob Lange), whom they had been tracking for several years now.

CHAPTER TEN

DON'T 'AUNTY' ME

In early 1977 the NSW premier, Neville Wran, had been enjoying almost unanimous support from the electorate in most parts of the state. Elected on 1 May 1976, he and his wife, Jill, resided in leafy and exclusive Woollahra, just a stone's throw from the comfortable Todd residence and also the nearby premises of his company now located at 50 John Street.

In July 1977, the Premier had stalled in establishing a royal commission into the disappearance of Griffith anti-drug campaigner and former Liberal Party candidate Donald Mackay, but on 5 August he finally announced the inevitable: that Justice Philip Woodward would be appointed to head a royal commission into drug trafficking in New South Wales and that among other objectives, it would try to identify Mackay's killer or killers, yet to be apprehended or identified.

Now, some six months later, in January 1978, plainclothes narcotics agents had been in place in John Street from the time the suspect campervan departed Melbourne and Vern Todd had returned to Sydney to oversee the drug shipment. The Sydney unit of the bureau under the eastern region commander, Inspector Tom Mullaly – a one-time New South Wales police drug squad senior investigator who left for the bureau's better pay and conditions in 1969 – had been fully briefed on Operation Genius. Round-the-clock surveillance was placed on both Todd's residence and his business premises. His home phone was being monitored and his business partners were also under close surveillance. Wire-tapping for the purpose of obtaining evidence in criminal trials was still unlawful in Australia, although the practice nonetheless flourished. Police hoped planned federal legislation approving the use in court of evidence gained through intercepted communications would be passed in parliament. It had been talked about since 1969.

At any given time, the undercover surveillance of John Street comprised a narcotics agent on a motorcycle (concealed from time to time behind bushes in a laneway, which gave good vantage points of the Todd residence and nearby business premises, as well as the street and laneways often used by Todd and his associates); another pair of agents slunk low in an old unmarked Ford Falcon; and a third team working the area from time to time on foot.

On several occasions in January 1978, one of Sydney's most influential socialites looked out her second-storey study window and noticed a scruffy-looking, leather-jacketed man below, possibly a biker ... it was in fact the undercover bureau agent and his motorcycle. On the third occasion she spotted him in as many days, she called her husband to the window and drew his attention to the suspicious figure. He feared their home was being staked out and had an assistant contact the local sergeant at Paddington police station.

Two uniformed officers were dispatched to the street, where they found the undercover agent and his motorcycle in his hiding spot. Stern words were exchanged between the bureau's agent, who flashed his ID, and the young constables. The New South Wales police reported back to their sergeant with the results.

When the socialite looked out the window a few hours later and could still see the leather-clad figure there, she once again summoned her husband. He in turn contacted a senior New South Wales police officer to complain about the local constabulary's apparent inaction and threatened his next call would be to the Police Commissioner if nothing was done. It was then that Inspector Mullaly took a call from a senior-ranking officer in the New South Wales police and was told in no uncertain terms of the socialite's agitation. She did not appreciate the presence of those loitering just outside her home, although she was never made aware of their true purpose. Mullaly checked with his team and was advised: 'We told the coppers it was none of their fucking business what we were doing.'

The animosity between the bureau and state police dated back to the new agency's creation in 1969 and was still unresolved almost a decade later – at every level of operation. Mullaly phoned a contact in the New South Wales police and told him his team's presence in John Street was of paramount importance to a major operation and that their key person of interest resided in that street. He reassured his contact that the Federal Bureau of Narcotics agents posed no threat to the security of the socialite and her husband, and requested his support to allay their fears. Mullaly took a call minutes later from an even higher ranking police executive who demanded the surveillance team be moved immediately to another, less conspicuous, site.

Mullaly acceded to the request – which was in essence an order – and the surveillance team was relocated to a more discreet position. They had now lost the excellent vantage points of their original stake-out.

It was during this changeover of surveillance that narcotics agents are convinced Vern Todd escaped their dragnet. Narcotics Bureau investigators were not permitted to reveal the socialite's involvement – of her identity – in the operation, but harboured deep-seated anger that one of the contributing factors to the qualified success of Operation Genius was the order, or 'request', to move the surveillance team from John Street, Woollahra.

•

Meanwhile on the New South Wales Central Coast, Toddie and Beezie remained in Terrigal. Inspector Drane and Agent Khoury maintained their vigilance and tracked the women's movements almost twenty-four hours a day in conjunction with the bureau's team of city agents. On 11 January narcotics agents visited the storage warehouse in Erina where Toddie had left their large brown suitcases for storage. Upon interviewing the owner, the agents discovered the women planned to shortly place the van in storage once arrangements to take delivery of the registration documents were confirmed with the 'new' owner arriving from overseas.

On 12 January, Toddie travelled to Sydney and again visited the US Consulate, demanding to see the consular official who had previously been unavailable to speak with her and who had instead instructed staff to provide her with a list of solicitors. Consul General Ralph Jones met with her shortly after 2 pm when he returned from lunch. Toddie explained to him the predicament she faced, relating details of her European and South Asia experiences and the extended journey through Australia. She told him it had become a trip under duress.

Mr Jones's advice was simple: speak to Australian Customs about the disposal of the vehicle and, at the same time, contact one of the lawyers from the list supplied to inform them of its full registration details and carnet documentation. Toddie was fragile, both emotionally and physically, but little was she or the Consul General to know her hypertensive condition would soon require hospitalisation.

That afternoon Toddie entered the chambers of James Linton, a solicitor who worked from a small office in Endeavour House at the corner of Pitt and Bridge streets, Sydney. She produced all the documentation she could find: licence papers, registration, insurance and, most importantly, the carnet. She also had with her a telegram she had collected from Sydney's General

Post Office, from Bob Lange in Bombay, which explained he was delayed because of insufficient funds, but would arrive in Australia within six weeks. Toddie repeated to the lawyer what she had told the Consul General: she was placing the vehicle in storage and would leave it for Mr Lange to collect upon his return to Sydney.

The lawyer queried what it was she actually wanted him to do now. Toddie answered that she was handing everything relating to the van's registration over to him under a power-of-attorney arrangement, but that she was unsure how the carnet regulations operated. She told him she had been led to believe throughout her travels that the idea of the carnet was to prevent the owner leaving the country without the vehicle, especially if it had been sold without the appropriate tax or duty being paid to the state. He phoned the National Roads and Motorists' Association and inquired about the workings of a carnet. A motoring adviser proceeded to explain that Toddie's understanding of carnets was incorrect. Mr Linton told his client it would be quite proper – legal in fact – to hand over all documentation relating to the campervan to him. There was nothing to stop her from now leaving Australia.

Toddie was relieved but also flummoxed; it seemed too easy. So she asked the lawyer to repeat himself. Yes, he confirmed, she could leave Australia at any time. All she had to do was sign the van ownership to whomever she wished – the lawyer as her representative, or to Mr Lange. With a simple signature she could transfer the ownership legally and be free from any further obligation.

For the first time in months there was a light at the end of the tunnel and she and Beezie could go home. Trembling, Toddie handed over the files she had brought with her, signed the disposal notice for the campervan, and was given a receipt and a photocopy of the registration document to enable her to continue to drive the vehicle, and leave it at the warehouse. The solicitor indicated that while he held the documentation, the keys should be turned over to the warehouse manager, who might need to move the campervan in the interim. He also instructed her to dispatch another telegram to Mr Lange informing him of the vehicle's disposal and its storage address. This Toddie did without delay. She had an enthusiasm for the future that had been absent for many weeks.

Toddie stayed overnight in a Sydney motel, and the following morning returned to the consulate to advise the consular staff of what she had done. She took a commuter train to return to the Central Coast and informed Beezie that they were now relieved of the shackles of the carnet; Lange could collect the van in six weeks when he said he would return; they didn't have to answer to Vern; and they were free to go home any time they chose. Beezie was ecstatic.

Convinced they were now clear of any responsibility for the campervan, the women began to list the tasks they'd need to address before their return, including ensuring the water pipes hadn't frozen up, the gutters had been cleared of leaves, and the heating was turned on by neighbours in advance of their arrival home. Toddie felt her blood pressure might be through the roof, so wasn't inclined to immediately begin the long flight back to the United States and La Pine. She thought she should first try to get some genuine rest, especially now that the pressure of the van's ownership was resolved. A doctor's appointment to have her blood pressure checked and stabilised if needed could wait a few more days.

The women decided to drive north to Seal Rocks, where they relaxed for several days staying at the local coastal holiday park, before meandering further north to Hallidays Point, about nine miles (fifteen kilometres) north of the resort town of Forster.

By now it was 17 January, and Toddie and Beezie were beginning to again enjoy themselves with the warm weather and coastal scenery, finally free of the yoke of the carnet and, they believed, any responsibility for the ownership of the campervan. It also signalled the end of dealings with Vern and his associates; and they felt no desire to even contact him.

Toddie's sense of liberation was reflected in an entry written later:

When I went to the US Consulate again, I explained about the campervan, the carnet, my failing health, and our wanting to go home. I often wondered why I didn't tell the Consul General of our fears that something was legally and morally very wrong. I think this was mainly because Vern was blood-kin and for my brother Vern Sr, whom I love dearly, it would break his heart. Like I have said before, we eventually knew something was very wrong, but we didn't know the what, where and how. I was advised by the Consul-General to take the campervan back to the Customs officers. Oh how I wish I had complied with his advice. What a relief now anyway: no more damn campervan to worry about. It is their problem now. Let them take care of it. Good riddance. It's amazing we both still have our sanity.

On 24 January, Toddie and Beezie drove towards Sydney, stopping in at the storage warehouse, where they removed some of the Christmas presents for their families and souvenirs they had bought, deciding to take them to Sydney where they could post them by sea mail before they flew home. It would save paying for excess baggage.

When they finally reached Sydney they booked themselves into the Travelodge in Ashfield, an inner-western suburb. Toddie visited a doctor to check her hypertension. Her leg and her right eye were also beginning to cause her acute pain. She'd had a cataract diagnosed before her departure from La Pine, but her eye had never ached like this. The doctor examined her eye, and said an ophthalmologist would have to be consulted for expert advice on her condition. He recorded her blood pressure as being 225/115, abnormally high, and prescribed medication to bring it down to safer levels. She explained it would not be possible to attend a specialist ophthalmologist's appointment immediately as she had other personal business to attend to first. The doctor asked that she at least return to see him, and she made the appointment for two days hence.

By now, the pair had decided it was time to phone Vern and tell him the news. Surprisingly, the women felt, they reached Vern on the first call – he had obviously been waiting impatiently for word from them. In a matter-of-fact tone, Toddie read the riot act: 'Vern, I have been to see a lawyer and have turned all my registration and carnet papers over to him. He advised that Beezie and I could have surrendered the van at any time, and left Australia without any problem. That carnet meant nothing, and you have lied to us all along. The van's being stored in a warehouse north of Sydney and the responsibility is yours.'

Vern quickly pleaded, 'Aunty Vera, will you please be reasonable and get the van back and bring it to Sydney? I will give you the name of a Mercedes dealer to book it into.'

'I will not, Vern, I will not, and don't "Aunty" me anymore,' Toddie shot back. 'I want no further part of it. I'm not going anywhere near it again. I'm sick, and if you want it, you fetch it.' And with that, Toddie ended the conversation and placed the phone back in its cradle.

It was the last time Toddie ever spoke to her nephew.

•

On 26 January 1978, Toddie and Beezie drove north in the campervan from Sydney towards Gosford and placed it in storage. Toddie had written a letter which she placed on the dashboard. The letter was addressed to Bob Lange and it explained to him where the papers were, and what storage fees had been agreed with the warehouse manager.

The women returned by train to Sydney that afternoon, and Toddie went to her doctor's appointment. The doctor conducted an electro-cardiograph and found her blood pressure remained dangerously high. He warned his patient it was close to the point where her sustained high blood pressure could cause a stroke. He wanted her to rest and discussed possible hospitalisation, but she initially objected because she had run low on funds and didn't know whether her US travel insurance would cover the costs. She was eventually convinced her life was worth more than a hospital bill, and accepted the doctor's recommendation to book into St Luke's Private Hospital in Darlinghurst that weekend, on 29 January.

In the meantime, the women moved their belongings into the Top of the Cross Travelodge at Kings Cross, where Beezie would be closer to Toddie when she was eventually booked in for treatment. After Toddie's admission, they both reluctantly agreed it would be better for Beezie to book her flight home, especially if it seemed possible that Toddie was to be hospitalised for a prolonged period. With their trip now extending into its fifth month, there were matters requiring their attention in La Pine. And there was Suzette. What the women did not know was their dog had died peacefully in early December, and their neighbours were withholding the sad news until their return.

Beezie confirmed her departure with Qantas for 31 January. Toddie wrote a short postcard home to Don and Thelma Mitchell, telling them of her health woes as she had recorded in her diary:

> Around the latter part of January, I was having severe high blood pressure, also sciatic nerve is acting up, and I can hardly walk, and on top of that I lost my vision in my right eye. Was under doctor's care and he admitted me to St Luke's Hospital in Sydney. I was told I could be there from one to two weeks. Being the case, we decided Beezie should fly home as we had so much luggage, Christmas presents for family and friends. We also had a lot of personal business to take care of plus Beezie filing her Social Security.

With Toddie now settled into her hospital room, her bags by her bedside and a paperback novel to keep her occupied, Beezie went back to check out of their hotel. She left her suitcases in the foyer while she returned to the hospital to bid Toddie a final farewell. They spoke little of the past months and all they had endured. This was not the moment to reminisce about the 'trip of a lifetime'.

Beezie took a taxi to the airport in Mascot. Given the considerable amount of time she and Toddie had spent in airports all over the world in recent months, there was no destination she was looking more forward to than the USA: she was heading home.

She hoisted her suitcases onto a luggage cart and wheeled it into the bustling airport terminal. After consulting the flight departure board, Beezie proceeded to the Qantas counter and checked her bags in for the long flight across the Pacific Ocean.

PART THREE

BUSTED AND COURTSIDE

CHAPTER ELEVEN

YOU LOOK FAMILIAR

It was Wednesday morning on the first day of February 1978. Toddie was napping on her hospital bed in St Luke's when a nurse entered the room.

'Hello, Vera?' she called out to the patient, and when Toddie didn't respond immediately, the nurse cleared her throat and repeated, 'Hello Vera? Vera Todd Hays?'

Toddie emerged from her light slumber and began to sit up.

'Yes, yes ... I'm Vera Todd Hays,' she said, blinking as she shifted in the bed to prop herself against the pillows.

The nurse smiled and retrieved the chart at the end of the bed to allow Toddie a moment to settle herself and gather her wits.

'Vera, I'm just going to take your blood pressure,' the nurse said as she scanned the notes, adding, 'I see you've been taking your anti-hypertension tablets without any problems?'

'Yes, ma'am,' said Toddie. 'I'm feeling much better, thank you.'

The nurse placed the cuff on Toddie's arm and proceeded to squeeze the rubber bulb to begin taking her blood pressure. She seemed pleased as she entered the most recent details onto the patient's chart.

'You had a close call there, Vera,' said the nurse, referring to her admission to St Luke's several days earlier. 'Your blood pressure was at a very high level and you were a serious candidate for a stroke. Were you aware of that?'

Vera nodded. 'Yes, the doctor has warned me if I don't get it under control I am even more at risk being up in a plane,' she said. 'Something about less oxygen at high altitude would increase the blood pressure even further. They said I needed to bring it down before flying or I might not make it home alive.'

'Absolutely,' said the nurse.

'So I've been resting and catching up on my sleep and that's made a big difference along with the medication,' Toddie assured the nurse.

'Well, that's reflected in these notes. Your blood pressure readings show a steady decline and you are back to a safe range again,' the nurse said.

'They've given me the drill about the low-salt diet and cutting out smoking. I'm ready to go home and make some changes,' said Toddie.

'You want to be sure to check with your own doctor to keep your hypertension monitored and have the cause further investigated. You're not out of the woods yet,' the nurse replied.

'I have my plane ticket ready and when I get the all-clear I just need to phone through to book my seat and I'll be on my way. When will the doctor be coming today?' she asked.

'The doctor will be on his rounds soon, so put your feet up and relax. You can discuss it with him when he comes by,' the nurse advised.

With that, the nurse left the room and disappeared out into the corridor.

An hour later, the nurse appeared again with the attending doctor.

'Hi there, Vera,' he said as he looked down at the notes.

'Am I well enough now to fly back to the United States?' she asked.

Toddie watched but his face was impassive. He was a hard one to read.

'I think we have done what we can in the short term in order for you to fly. You can be discharged in the morning, but please heed my admonition that you contact your doctor once you're home to have this hypertension thoroughly investigated. I will include a letter with your discharge papers for the attending physician.'

'Yes sir!' Toddie smiled, 'and thank you for your help and advice.'

'Safe travels, Vera,' the doctor said. 'The nurses will organise your paperwork for your discharge tomorrow morning.'

As the doctor and nurse departed, Toddie reached for her handbag to search for her ticket and passport. She picked up the phone at her bedside and dialled the airline reservation number she'd written on a piece of paper tucked into her wallet.

Her seat now confirmed for the following evening's flight. Toddie replaced the phone handset and went out to the nurses' station to discuss the procedure for discharge and settling the hospital account the following day. Then she returned to her room and began to organise her belongings. She reached for a cigarette, then thought better of it, popping the packet back into the drawer with an unread paperback. Toddie unzipped her suitcase to remove the travel attire she'd already set aside for the flight.

Following breakfast the next morning, Toddie began to prepare for discharge. She tried to contain her excitement lest her blood pressure became elevated again. The journey home had begun.

It was after midday by the time the nurses had collected and assembled all of her medical reports. Toddie was already dressed for her flight due to depart later that evening, and sat on the edge of the bed waiting for her paperwork to be completed. The rostered nurse brought her an envelope with her medical records. Toddie packed it into the inner zip pocket inside her suitcase.

'Thank you, dear,' she said with a smile and, with a cursory glance to check she left nothing behind, made her way to the elevator.

Being discharged from St Luke's required payment of a significant bill – fortunately she still had enough traveller's cheques to cover it.

•

Shortly before noon, Inspector Bob Drane received word from the communications team at the bureau's Sydney headquarters that Vera Todd Hays was about to be discharged from St Luke's Hospital. Drane had been involved in the operation from the outset so it made sense he saw it to its conclusion. Drane and Michele Khoury had made the short drive to the hospital and now they waited in the hospital foyer for their target to appear.

As Toddie paid and was tucking the hospital receipt into her wallet, she felt a friendly tap on her shoulder and turned around.

'Why, hello ... what are you doing here?' she said to Drane and Agent Khoury. Toddie recognised both of their faces from their encounters over the recent weeks of their Australian travels. They were the public service couple holidaying, like Toddie and Beezie, in eastern Australia.

It was to be, for Bob Drane, a most awkward arrest; in fact, 'the most difficult in his career', he said.

'I have some bad news for you,' Drane said, and proceeded to show her his identification. 'I am Inspector Bob Drane from the Federal Bureau of Narcotics. I would like you to come with us to our office.' Almost as an afterthought, he asked after her well-being. He was aware of the reasons for her hospital admission. 'How are you feeling?'

'I'm alright, but I would like to know what this is all about,' Toddie replied.

While doctors and nurses had being doing their best for five days to get Toddie's hypertension under control, Drane and his team had been doing their best to bring Operation Genius to a successful conclusion, beginning with the arrest of their other target: Florice Marie Bessire.

•

Two days earlier on 31 January, after farewelling Toddie at St Luke's and taking a taxi to the airport, Beezie had cleared passport control shortly before 7 pm and was idling away the time waiting for her flight by wandering through the duty-free stores, enjoying a cold beer and doing a little reading. While Beezie was torn about having to leave Toddie alone in hospital, she felt better knowing her companion was finally getting proper medical attention. She hoped it wouldn't be long before Toddie was winging her way home too. After taking a seat at the departure gate, Beezie lit up a cigarette. She was already going over in her mind the list she and Toddie had made of what needed to be done on her return to La Pine. The house would need a good airing after being closed up for so long; she'd need to do a big shop to restock the pantry; and she'd get someone in to check the gutters, downpipes and hot water system, although neighbours had been keeping an eye on their home in their absence. There would also be bills requiring immediate attention and her paperwork Social Security had to be lodged.

'Passengers travelling on Qantas flight 3 to Los Angeles via Honolulu ... this is your first and final call to proceed to departure gate 6 where your aircraft is now ready for boarding.'

At the same time, four Narcotics Bureau agents had staked out the airport terminal. Instructions had been issued to passport control to immediately notify the bureau's airport officer-in-charge when the target had cleared the barrier. It was 8.10 pm and the message had come through.

Two male plainclothes agents discreetly approached Beezie just as she was stubbing out her cigarette. Her luggage had already been intercepted, retrieved and placed in a bureau vehicle.

'Excuse me, Miss Bessire,' said one of the agents, pressing his hand toward her left elbow. He produced his badge and said, 'I am Agent Polden from the Federal Bureau of Narcotics. May I see your passport?' Beezie froze momentarily and then handed it to him.

'Miss Bessire, I want you to come with me,' said the agent.

'What's the trouble?' asked Beezie.

'We are going to ask you some questions about a large quantity of cannabis located in the campervan in which you have been travelling,' he said.

'But what about my luggage?' asked Beezie.

'It's already in our car,' the agent said, and with that, the second agent approached and discreetly ushered her away from the lounge.

To the passengers in the immediate vicinity, it was a manoeuvre barely noticed. On first glance it would appear the two well-dressed gentlemen were fellow passengers headed for a drink with an older lady. Beezie, however, was confused; she had made her reservation, paid her departure tax, was in the boarding lounge and only steps away from her US-bound plane.

Her knees were already trembling as she took her first few steps outside the lounge. Flanked by the two agents, she was led along a fluorescent-lit walkway to the bureau's airport operations centre.

The first agent said, 'We are taking you to Customs House in the city where we have some questions to ask you about the campervan in which you and your companion have been travelling. You do not have to say anything to us unless you wish to do so, but anything you do say will be recorded and may later be used in evidence. Do you understand?'

'Well, I won't say anything then,' Beezie replied.

Beezie shared the back seat of the bureau's unmarked car with one of the agents, silent for the duration of the twenty-minute journey back into the city. She was overwhelmed with fear and apprehension, aimlessly looking out of the window but registering only a blur.

Inspector Drane and Agent Khoury had been notified Beezie was in custody and on her way into the city. Agent Polden drove directly to Customs House at Circular Quay, on Sydney's waterfront. He and his partner escorted Beezie through the tiled foyer of the largely deserted building and took a lift to the second floor where agents conducted their interviews. There were two rooms available, but one was often used as a storeroom, and by the time Drane and Khoury arrived Beezie was already seated in the interview room, and lighting the first of what would be many cigarettes. She sat on a chair at a wooden table, two more chairs opposite, waiting for Drane and Khoury to occupy them.

Drane officially identified himself once he'd entered the room and sat down. 'I am Inspector Bob Drane of the Federal Bureau of Narcotics and I have a series of questions I would like to ask you,' he said.

Drane was a professional at interrogation, one of the bureau's best, in fact. He knew the first hour in custody was when a suspect was vulnerable and unguarded. In this case, he was going to begin slowly, and give Beezie 'her head' so she could speak freely if she wanted to.

'You look familiar,' Beezie said to Drane.

'We met at the Central Coast Leagues Club,' the inspector answered, while Agent Khoury began taking notes.

'That's right, now I remember,' said Beezie, coming out of a fog as she began to recognise his face and that of Michele Khoury.

'Miss Bessire,' said Drane, 'we have just taken possession of the campervan that you and Mrs Hays have been travelling in. Do you know that it contains a large quantity of hashish?'

'What's hashish?' she asked earnestly.

'Hashish is a drug which comes from the cannabis or marijuana plant,' said Drane.

'I don't know anything about that,' said Beezie.

'I intend to ask you a number of further questions which will be recorded on paper,' said Drane.

Beezie interrupted. 'Well, I don't know, I'm in a strange country. Aren't I allowed to have a lawyer?'

'Yes,' said Drane, 'You are. Do you know one you would like to call?'

'No, I don't,' Beezie replied.

Drane then explained, 'We have a system here called Legal Aid, something like a public defender. Would you like me to call them?' he offered.

'Yes, please,' said Beezie.

Drane left the room while Khoury remained. The pegboard-lined interview room was filling with cigarette smoke as Beezie came to grips with the situation.

Australian Legal Aid's duty solicitor that evening was Robert Harkins, and after a call from the bureau, he made his way into the city, arriving just after 10 pm. Drane informed him there was a major operation afoot, and that the bureau had been shadowing two women from Melbourne throughout Victoria and New South Wales. The other woman, he said, was in a hospital under 24-hour surveillance.

Harkins then entered the interview room and spoke briefly with Beezie. He ascertained she was well, but tired. These were not ideal circumstances for his client to begin what would likely be an extended period of questioning. Harkins wanted any further matters dealt with the next day, after Beezie had the opportunity of a reasonable night's sleep. He left the room five minutes later to speak with Drane.

'We believe the van contains a very large quantity of an unknown narcotic substance,' Drane told Harkins. 'It's in Gosford at a storage depot and will be searched first thing tomorrow morning. The two major conspirators and heads of the organisation responsible are Vern Todd and Phillip Shine. They are more heavily involved in the offence than the ladies, but they are still at large in Australia and might be arrested at any time.'

Harkins quickly recognised the enormity of the operation. It had the potential to become a major criminal case in the courts, as well as national and international news.

'I am seeking your cooperation in having the women make full disclosure of all the surrounding circumstances to facilitate our investigations of the other persons involved in the offence,' Drane said. Harkins knew this tactic. The inspector wasn't offering any inducement to the women. This was merely code for securing the lawyer's assistance to encourage the women to answer fulsomely and honestly all of the investigator's questions.

It was too late for Harkins's client to participate in any further questioning; it was almost 11 pm. Beezie was complaining of numbness and dizziness, so arrangements were made for her to be detained by bureau agents in a motel overnight and the interview would continue in the morning. Harkins departed the bureau and returned home.

Beezie's diary recounted the event:

After I was arrested, Michele Khoury and Bob Drane came into the room ... saying how sorry they were that first night of questioning. I didn't say too much. In fact, I was so shocked and frightened I really didn't make too much sense and I didn't know what was in the van. Up to that time, they hadn't told me. I told them I was too numb and couldn't think too quickly. They took me out to the last motel Vera and I had stayed at before she went to hospital, and we stayed there the night.

The next morning at 9.35 am, back at Customs House, Beezie was seated before Drane and Khoury. They continued their questioning and, as she had been advised by her solicitor who was in attendance, she cooperated as best she could. She understood it was in her best interests.

Toddie of course was totally oblivious to all of this. For all she knew, as she lay in her hospital bed at St Luke's, Beezie was not only flying back to the United States, but family and friends were getting ready to welcome them both once she had been discharged from hospital and returned home.

Beezie's diary entry on the second day of her arrest continued:

When they started questioning me, they had taken pictures of the trap doors in the floor of the van and had a packet of stuff that Drane said was hash. They both said they didn't want Vera and me, but that they wanted Vera's nephew and the ones who were heading up the whole thing. They said they had been trying to get Vern for four years and if I told the whole story that they would see that we got deported. I trusted both of them, since we had socialised with them on two or three occasions. Both Vera and I liked them and thought they were great fun. Being in a strange country and far from home and being frightened and sick at heart, I felt I had to trust someone and at the time, I thought they were the only friends I had in Australia. They both said that when we were deported they hoped they would be the ones to take us to the airport to buy us a couple of drinks and wave goodbye to us. Michele kept telling me what a fair and great guy Bob was, and that I could trust him. Being on a woman-to-woman basis, I believed her and felt comforted to a certain extent. I tried to tell things in the correct sequence as far as my frightened and confused brain would let me.

At the conclusion of the interview, Beezie was asked to read each page aloud, initial any errors once they were corrected, and then sign at the bottom of each page. In total there were more than one hundred questions and Beezie, by then mentally exhausted and still reeling from the shock of her predicament, merely scanned the words before her, signed and turned over each page. She found it too hard to focus on the content or endure the agony of thinking through it all over again.

As Khoury was putting away the typewriter, and Drane was sorting the records of the interview, Beezie said quietly, 'I'm so sorry I have caused all this trouble. We didn't know there was that much in the goddamn thing. You tell Vera not to protect that son of a bitch anymore.'

A short time later, Khoury took Beezie and her belongings to an unmarked bureau car. They headed west to Sydney's maximum security women's prison, the Mulawa Correctional Centre at Silverwater. Mulawa – an Aboriginal word for 'place of shadows' – was built to house ninety-three female inmates. The accommodation was mostly dormitory and multi-occupancy rooms within Caroline Chisholm House, Margaret Catchpole House and Mary Reiby House.

When Beezie arrived, officers were waiting to receive their new inmate, having been advised there was an elderly American woman who had been charged with drug offences to be placed in the prison's remand section. The bureau requested, owing to her age and her importance to them as a witness, that she be kept for the first night in a segregated room, particularly to protect her from other inmates. At reception, all of her possessions were dumped onto a metal counter, and while one of the guards entered an inventory of the goods, another officer began the task of recording personal details. Within an hour, Florice Marie Bessire had been stripped of her clothes and was clad in a pair of government-issue brown khaki overalls. She now found herself a prisoner among murderers, junkies, thieves and white-collar criminals – all of them women.

The diary entry detailing her arrival at Mulawa was raw:

You arrive at Silverwater (Mulawa) and are hastily moved into reception. You're stood against the wall and an officer yells: 'Take off your clothes and then throw them on the floor.' You are taken to the storeroom and told to pick out some clothes. What a laugh. You would laugh if you were not so damn scared and still in shock. Nothing of course fits. At least you look like everyone else inside. For the first couple of days I couldn't find a bra, and the panties were no-go. This was utter humiliation. So from the beginning, you are stripped of pride and dignity.

For Beezie, a person who didn't frighten easily, every nerve in her body screamed with fear that first night. A sympathetic dormitory officer helped her settle in. Beezie lay awake, wiping away tears and slipping in and out of an uneasy and restless sleep, until finally the first hint of morning light peeked through the cell vent. She could now see her confined quarters but she didn't know whether she preferred the light or the dark. At exactly 6 am, the overhead lights were turned on and almost simultaneously a variety of radios burst into life: hard rock blaring across half a dozen stations in different cells occupied by prisoners. By 7 am, her head was thumping and aching. Instinctively she thought of getting an aspirin from the medicine cabinet, but realised one didn't exist. No longer had she the freedom to simply 'go to the medicine cabinet'.

Beezie was confronted by the starkness of her strange new reality and with no-one to talk to, she continued writing down her thoughts:

The mind rejects the vile ugliness of the words and threats you hear in here. The soul shrivels, your heart grows cold with fear, your stomach cramps and you break out in a cold sweat. You can't truly believe that a human being can act like this. The reek of humanity: not too clean, disinfectant and despair including your own, and the stink of fear. Oh yes, fear has a different smell all its own. I fear for my sanity. I'm in a state of shock and mostly limbo. I feel like I'm treading water, waiting for a big wave to come along and toss me onto the shore.

•

Now formally charged, Beezie remained in prison on remand awaiting a trial date. She could glean no news about Toddie from the prison staff.

Meanwhile the bureau's Operation Genius focused its attention on the second American woman: Vera Todd Hays. Inspector Drane's interception of her at the hospital during discharge went like clockwork.

With Toddie now in his bureau vehicle and Khoury in the front passenger seat, he began a conversation. He didn't mince his words on the ten-minute drive from the hospital back to Customs House.

'The campervan you have been driving has been found to contain drugs,' he told Toddie.

'I wouldn't know anything about that,' she said. 'And anyway, where's Beezie?'

'She's in Silverwater,' said Drane.

'What's Silverwater?' asked Toddie.

'Well, there's a prison there for women.'

Toddie became teary, and asked, 'What the hell for?'

Drane said he couldn't tell her but that she would understand once he had conducted their interview at the bureau's headquarters. Upon arrival, Toddie was escorted into the same interview room where Beezie had been questioned earlier.

Khoury kept watch while Drane conferred with his superiors. Soon after, Drane returned with a copy of Beezie's signed interview, which he handed to Toddie.

'Would you like to read what Florice Bessire had to say?' he asked.

'Yes, why not,' replied Toddie. She spent about twenty minutes reading and re-reading the document. She found it hard to concentrate, but when she had finished, she looked up at Drane.

'Mrs Hays, let me remind you that you do not have to say anything in reply to what you have just read, but anything you do say will be recorded and may later be used in evidence. Do you understand?' the inspector said.

'Yes, I have nothing to say,' replied Toddie.

Drane hoped that she might in fact be prompted by the contents of Beezie's statement to say something ... anything.

Drane pressed on. 'Is Vern Todd related to you?'

'Yes,' said Toddie, contradicting her declaration that she had nothing to say. 'He's my nephew.'

'When did you last see him?' asked Drane.

'Several weeks ago,' answered Toddie.

'Mrs Hays,' said Drane, producing one of the blocks of hashish taken from the campervan, 'I would like you to look at something.'

'I have never seen that goddamn stuff before,' she said, in an almost identical response to the one Beezie uttered when confronted with the plastic-wrapped drug package during her interview.

'It was taken from the floor of your campervan,' said Drane.

'My God, how much?' asked Toddie.

'Almost two tonnes,' said Drane, who had been surprised himself when the total stash had been weighed, recalling that early analysis from the drill inspection aboard the *Straat Luanda* indicated agents could expect to find between 130 and 175 pounds (60 to 80 kilograms).

Toddie burst into tears and said, 'There's no fool like an old fool. All we wanted was the trip and a bit of adventure. He said there'd be "a little" grass in the van and nobody in Australia would worry about it because it was nearly legal. He said nobody would worry about two old ladies because it was the first time, we wouldn't get into much trouble.'

Drane asked her who had said this to her.

'Vern Todd,' replied Toddie.

'Mrs Hays, would you like to tell me the story?' asked Drane in an almost endearing, fatherly tone.

'I will tell you as much as I know,' she replied.

'What you tell me will be recorded on the typewriter in the form of a record of interview.'

'Okay,' she said, and the next stage of the interview process commenced.

Toddie's diary noted:

Upon arriving at the narcotics agent's office, I was informed by Bob that Beezie had made her statement, and in saying this, he handed me same. After I read the statement, Bob said, 'I told Beezie that I would do everything in my power to see that you two are deported and Vera, I sincerely mean this. Cooperate and tell us all you know about the trip, and especially about your nephew, Vern Leonard Todd, as we have been after him for four years. We know he is one of the Mr. Bigs of Australian drugs and I will see that you and Beezie will be deported. Michele and I will be at the airport to have a few drinks and wave goodbye.' Bob said this with deep sincerity and Michele concurred. We were told many, many times that we were not the ones they were after. They wanted Mr. Big, Vern Todd, and the organisation he headed.

At about 7 pm that evening, Khoury repeated the procedure she had followed with Beezie, taking Vera to the Mulawa prison and having her processed before she was assigned a cell.

The trauma of being incarcerated for the first time was an experience to haunt both women for the rest of their lives. Immediately upon entry into reception, Toddie was ordered into a room, stripped of her clothing and told to shower. A guard provided a bar of soap that felt like it burnt her skin and made her hair feel like glue had been rubbed into it. She was issued a pair of ill-fitting overalls made for someone three times her size, and sandals which were too small, all adding to the indignity. She was then taken to the wing where prisoners on remand await their day in court. The other prisoners staring through the cell bars gave Toddie the shivers immediately. Some of the prisoners already knew who she was.

Toddie wept until there was no more energy left to weep, before falling asleep that first night, not knowing what lay in store the next day, or the day after that. She was in a state of shock. She'd read and signed every page of the interview, initialling mistakes which had been corrected. She hadn't really read them again; she was sick to her stomach and couldn't fathom that this was happening to her. And where was Beezie in the jail, she wondered?

Throughout the process she was thinking of her family at home, wondering how she could tell them she was in prison. She was mad, hurt and bitter. She hated her nephew like she had never hated anybody in her whole life.

The next morning – 3 February – at the 7 am muster, Toddie and Beezie saw each other for the first time since their farewell at St Luke's just days earlier. They were initially relieved to see each other, but being very aware of the company in which they found themselves and given the lack of privacy, they didn't say much, except to ask each other if they were okay. They lined up and waited for breakfast. Discreetly scanning the room and being careful not to be caught looking at anyone in particular, they noticed women of all ages and ethnicities: some appeared to be hardened criminals, foul-mouthed, coarse and tattooed. It was very confronting. They felt distinctly uncomfortable, exposed and nervous. They didn't belong here, they thought. It seemed like they'd accidentally wandered onto the set of a movie, but this was not make-believe.

On 4 February, the Australian Broadcasting Commission's public affairs program *This Day Tonight* broke the story about the massive hashish bust nationwide and in the course of that TV broadcast nicknamed Toddie and Beezie the 'Drug Grannies'. From now on they'd be known by that moniker. The story captured the attention of the Australian public immediately, and within twenty-four hours, the world press was buzzing with the news of the two elderly American women's arrest.

The TV story revealed the two had been followed twenty-four hours a day for almost ten weeks, and that their campervan contained 1.9 tonnes of cannabis resin – the biggest haul of hashish – or of any illegal drug – to date in Australian history. The report indicated Narcotics Bureau investigations were continuing, and said the recent arrests of two West Germans driving hashish-filled Renault cars were connected to the same organisation.

The ABC story was entirely accurate, unlike many of the stories that would follow in the next five years. The Australian media was to go through a sensational headline orgasm for weeks after the women's arrest.

The Narcotics Bureau later blamed the ABC for the authorities' failure to catch the masterminds – Vern Todd and Phillip Shine. But it appeared the bureau, while concentrating on the women, may have ignored the cunning and mastery of Todd and Shine, who fled the country several days before the women's arrest.

Investigations later confirmed that Todd and Shine, both using false passports, escaped from Australia with an estimated A$6 million before the women's arrest, and probably fled via South-East Asia to Europe. One report had Todd first sailing to Norfolk Island on his yacht, before jumping aboard a second vessel to exit Australian waters and its sovereign territory.

While Todd had spent at least $A200,000 of his own money on the operation as part of a larger budget of close to an estimated $A1 million funded by a variety of drug operatives, he already had millions of dollars – some legitimately and much illegally generated – behind him.

The banner headlines of the *Sydney Morning Herald* on 4 February read: 'Hashish seized worth $19 million: two men charged'. The journalist didn't check that Toddie and Beezie were in fact two women. The Sydney afternoon tabloids, the

Sun and *Daily Mirror*, speculated whether the 'drug king' had fled the Narcotics Bureau's trap. Photographers and reporters converged on the Neutral Bay marina where the Customs shed housed the seized campervan since its transfer from the storage shed at Gosford.

Commander Tom Mullaly was justifiably proud of his agents' haul of more than four thousand packages, each weighing almost half a kilo (one pound) of top-quality Afghan cannabis resin. It was valued at between A\$12 million and A\$19 million, depending on whose figures were quoted and whether it was the narcs', wholesale or street valuation. In total, eighty-eight green, blue and white plastic garbage bags each containing forty-six slabs of hashish were laid out in the marina compound for the press to photograph.

•

Toddie and Beezie were afforded no favours by the prisoners at Mulawa. Their age, their nationality, combined with their strong American accents, and their crime – Australia's biggest hashish importation ever – made for an uncertain status in the prison's inmate hierarchy.

In the United States, the reaction of the women's families was unvarnished shock. Long-distance calls from the family members were emotional and heartbreaking as Toddie and Beezie wrestled with how to explain their predicament.

On 7 and 8 February, Inspector Drane and Agent Khoury visited the women at Mulawa and took further statements, focusing especially on Vern Todd and Phillip Shine. The women's legal aid solicitor Robert Harkins did not accompany the women during these interviews. Given that Beezie had so far proved an excellent informant against the drug organisers, agents expected similar cooperation from Toddie. The absence of legal representation over the two days made the agents' work much simpler: without their lawyer present there was little chance of objections being raised to the questions posed, and no-one to advise the women when it was better to remain silent.

●

Toddie and Beezie were formally charged with breaches of the *Customs Act 1901* at a hearing in the Special Federal Court on 9 February. Their statements to the Narcotics Bureau investigators were presented. A strong contingent of uniformed and plainclothes police guarded the courtroom and its exterior. As they were quickly bundled inside the courtroom from the narcotics agents' car, the women shielded their faces from the media with copies of *Reader's Digest*. Neither woman spoke during the two-minute hearing.

As neither woman was seeking bail, the matter was adjourned to 27 February. The prosecutor, Greg Smith, told reporters outside the court the women faced a maximum sentence of twenty-five years' imprisonment if found guilty of the offences.

After the short hearing, legal aid solicitor Harkins approached Drane and told him both women were alleging they had specifically been *promised* deportation in return for their cooperation. Drane strongly denied the claim. 'No, I didn't,' he told Harkins. 'I said I would *try to do something* for them.'

Drane and Khoury drove the prisoners back to Mulawa, but not before an unexpected detour to the Ermington pub near the prison where they all stopped for a counter lunch. It was an unorthodox way of escorting the prisoners back, but it was an indication of the captors' relationship with their captives.

Toddie's diary read: 'Bob and Michele took us out and wined and dined us for lunch. There was much laughter, tears and again Bob said we had nothing to worry about as we would be deported.'

Meanwhile, prison authorities were alerted to Narcotics Bureau intelligence warning there could be attempts on the women's lives inside Mulawa. Reports were already circulating on the prison and criminal grapevines about the women's cooperation with authorities gathering evidence against Todd and Shine.

•

By that afternoon, the women's 'walk of shame' into and out of court had been captured by the city's voracious press pack, and in time for the late editions of the afternoon *Daily Mirror* and *Sydney Sun* tabloids. Their faces were front-page news as Khoury escorted them from the court.

As she packed up for the day at Customs House and caught a bus to her hotel during the rush hour, Khoury found herself out of luck getting a seat so held the overhead strap for the short journey. Seated in front of her was an office worker engrossed in his afternoon newspaper, consumed by the front-page headline and photo. Suddenly he glanced up at Khoury with a surprised but knowing look. *Oh shit*, thought the narcotics agent to herself. Sure enough, there she was, photographed escorting the two prisoners from court, occupying the entire front page. Her fellow bus passenger had made the connection. It wasn't difficult given she hadn't yet changed clothes, and she was standing full frame in front of him. Khoury glared back at him and discreetly motioned with a forefinger to her lips with a whispered 'Shhhhhh'. Nothing more was said for the remainder of the ten-minute bus ride.

Around the time of the women's arrest, the Minister for Business and Consumer Affairs Wal Fife, who was responsible for enforcing Australia's tough new anti-drug policy, was touring South-East Asia with Narcotics Bureau chief Harvey Bates. The minister had been briefed on Operation Genius prior to his Canberra departure. He was surprised, but nonetheless pleased, by the 1.9-tonne haul.

•

Over the following weeks, while the women struggled to adjust to the prison routine, they were to read reports from journalists who had visited La Pine to interview neighbours and friends. The town's residents expressed surprise if not utter dismay at the women's quandary and confirmed they were popular, well-liked, honest and upstanding citizens.

One of their hometown friends told of a postcard he had received from Sydney saying 'everything was fine' and to 'expect us home soon'. Others described them as 'everybody's granny'.

Nancy Carter, for whom Beezie had worked at True Value Hardware, said she had come to know both women quite well, especially for the eighteen months Beezie had been employed there.

'There's no way I can imagine them getting involved in anything like that,' she told reporters. A prominent businessman in the town was reported as saying, 'It's hard to imagine them being arrested for anything, let alone drug smuggling.'

Another resident exclaimed, upon learning of their arrest, 'If anyone had told them what was in that van, Beezie and Toddie would have told them to go to hell! They were outgoing and easy to get along with, the kinds of people you could start talking to in a lounge. But they'd be vulnerable to being set up and used because they're so outgoing. I think they got conned without knowing it.'

Thelma Mitchell was another staunch supporter. 'These women were opposed to wrongdoing of any sort,' she told reporters. 'They wouldn't even fish without a licence and let alone catch more than their limit.' Nancy Carter echoed Mitchell. 'Beezie and Toddie would start worrying a month ahead of time if their licence plates were going to be overdue.' Bookending the support was Thelma's husband, Don, who said, 'They wouldn't smuggle a couple of fifths of tax-free booze in from Nevada.'

The small community of La Pine was in shock about their arrest and the news that the women risked a lengthy prison sentence. Residents were unaccustomed to the attention journalists were now paying them. Locals promised there would be red-carpet treatment for the two women when they returned, and that they would throw the 'biggest reception party anyone in the Cascade Ranges had ever seen'.

For the imprisoned women, it was heartening but of little consolation to learn of their community's support. They'd already written instructions to the Mitchells to turn off the water, disconnect the phone, defrost the fridge 'but be sure to leave the door ajar. And we want the outside light left on'.

•

One of the first changes to the women's routine inside Mulawa was the meaning of faith: while both were Christians, they were not regular churchgoers. However, they soon discovered how important this invisible means of support would become. They took comfort each day reading their prison-issued Bibles.

Surrounded by dangerous criminals, prison officers warned Toddie and Beezie to be constantly on guard. Their lives were likely under threat. There was no 'normal' anymore.

The safety and security with which they were familiar in each other's company no longer applied.

CHAPTER TWELVE

ONLY A 'LITTLE ILLEGAL'

Several weeks after their arrest and incarceration in Mulawa, an officer summoned Toddie and Beezie from their cell one morning with news a lawyer had arrived to see them in advance of their next court appearance on 27 February. Both women had already appeared in court to be formally charged on 1 February (Beezie) and 2 February (Toddie), then together for a brief mention on 9 February. There were to be several more court dates before they got through all this, but they realised it was the only way out. The women were given no prior notice of the visit as had occurred on previous occasions when their public defenders met with them. They were escorted to the meeting room where conferences between prisoners and their legal representatives were conducted.

Toddie and Beezie entered the room and sat down opposite a middle-aged, greying man in a suit. He introduced himself as Brian Alexander, took out his notebook and proceeded to ask the women a flurry of questions about their statements to the Narcotics Bureau and details of names and places they had provided.

After a time, it eventually dawned on Toddie that they had already been through all of this same information with their other lawyers. They seemed to be not only covering old ground, but being pressed for details about matters which seemingly had no particular relevance to their upcoming court appearance.

'Who did you say you work for?' Toddie suddenly queried.

There was a pause.

'I have been sent here by Phil Roach who represents Vern Todd and Phillip Shine. They asked us to come and see if you needed any legal representation,' Alexander said.

Both Toddie and Beezie immediately recognised the trap into which they had fallen. Here was someone passing himself off as working in their favour, when in fact he was extracting information from them about their cooperation with the Narcotics Bureau.

'We don't want anything more to do with you, and you can leave immediately,' ordered Toddie. He left without further ado. Assuming he was from the Australian Legal Aid Service, they'd jumped in feet first and sung like proverbial canaries. Toddie spoke immediately to the prison superintendent requesting that any of their future visitors be screened to ensure they were bona fide. They were powerless to complain to their legal aid solicitors, or to the Narcotics Bureau, because they realised they attended the meeting without first checking the visitor's credentials.

After the Mulawa visit, Alexander continued to seek more information from the women through their solicitor, Robert Harkins. Harkins ignored the advances.

What the women did not know was that Vern's lawyer, Phil Roach, was one of Sydney's most 'colourful' criminal lawyers. His staff at one time included legal clerk Brian Alexander, who played a key liaison role between several law firms and some of Sydney's major international drug kingpins. Alexander's function was to provide representation under the code name 'Robert James' to various drug syndicate members when they were arrested and report back on their 'loyalty'. Later, in 1981, Alexander's arrest for conspiracy with two Federal Narcotics Bureau agents was dismissed in court, but it was widely rumoured within criminal circles he had turned snitch. It was reported that by December of that year, members of Sydney's underworld had kidnapped Alexander, taken him aboard a boat into the middle of Sydney Harbour and thrown him overboard, still very much alive. His hands were apparently cuffed behind his back and an old iron gas stove was chained around his waist. His body was never recovered. Other reports among the underworld placed Alexander in Melbourne, where he met an equally horrific death in Port Phillip Bay.

On 21 February, Bob Drane and Michele Khoury again visited the women in Mulawa and had them sign and read all of the transcripts of evidence they had provided during their interviews after their arrest. Once the meeting with Drane and Khoury concluded, Toddie offered an unsolicited further statement to the agents. It was tendered in later court hearings. It read:

> We believed the carnet had power to prevent us leaving Australia because of the simple reason we had been told by Vern Todd that he had contact with somebody in the higher echelons. It could have been in the police department. That was the way he told it. It still could have been somebody else (and even higher) who said he would have all the air terminals checked, and that our passport numbers were computerised and listed, and we were never to leave the country. He said we wouldn't get out at all.

The women appeared again at a specially convened hearing of the Federal Court on 27 February. Khoury attended and first went to the basement cells where she spoke to the watch house officer and requested access to the women. Upon entering the cells, she learned from Toddie that police had confiscated her reading glasses in case she tried to self-harm. Khoury was furious and beckoned the policeman over to the cell.

His explanation: it was policy.

'Well, your policy can get fucked,' said Khoury. 'Give this woman her glasses.' The young constable reluctantly obeyed. In reality, she had no formal jurisdiction here, but she wasn't concerned about formalities. The spectacles were returned to Toddie.

The second hearing was expected to be brief. Both women had been advised by their legal counsel a plea of guilty was likely the lesser of two evils. To plead not guilty in the face of the statements they had already given the Narcotics Bureau was futile, they were told. It might frustrate attempts to negotiate an understanding – such as recommending their deportation – with the prosecution, whatever the trial's outcome. On the other hand, pleading guilty was admitting to the charge. It would be something Toddie and Beezie would have to live with – for the rest of their lives.

The women weren't entirely convinced pleading guilty was the correct decision. However, Toddie had been advised that because the vehicle's registration papers were in her name, there was no way she could deny the charge of having knowingly imported the van (and its load of drugs). Toddie and Beezie had been encouraged to believe in their interviews with and statements to the bureau's agents they *would* be deported – only if they pleaded guilty and were sentenced. Their expectation – without any prior experience with the justice system, in the United States or Australia – was that the court hearing, and any sentence, would be formalities. Nonetheless, the pressure of attending court and the uncertainty of the outcome was still stressful. They believed that if a guilty plea and a judge's rebuke was what it took to get home and put the nightmare behind them, they would follow their lawyer's advice. Thus, they both proceeded with guilty pleas.

During the second court appearance, the two women were again to meet with Inspector Drane. In a small anteroom, he produced two dozen colour and black and white photographs of various locations and settings, some familiar to the women. Most of the photos were of the van with decals the women had affixed, but the collection also included images of the interior of Vern Todd's home on John Street. Those photos had been taken by police after search warrants were executed. Drane finally produced photographs of Todd and Shine, although he said nothing to the women about their whereabouts.

Following the hearing, the two women were transported back to Mulawa by Khoury and another agent.

•

Toddie and Beezie had begun to pray together to maintain some calm. Sleep was hard to come by. They'd lie on the beds in their cells unable to block out other prisoners' noises ... moaning, crying, sobbing, shouting, screaming or just loud conversation. The process of dehumanisation had begun. They felt like they were trapped in cages with a pack of wild animals.

Lights went out at 10 pm, but by 11 pm, the women were often wakened by officers rattling their keys as they marched through the dormitory, conducting the first of many bed checks through the night. Lighting up a cigarette became the default response when sleep eluded the women. Toddie soon discovered prisoners were rationed only seven packets a week, so she tried to reduce her consumption. Any plans to stop smoking, as the doctor had advised, were by now out the window. There was no way she could cope with the stress of jail and the impending trial without her cigarettes.

The first letter home to her family was the most painful. Just knowing the shame and sorrow their situation was going to cause their families was a wrench. And how would Toddie address her nephew's deceit when she wrote to her brother about his son's wicked betrayal? That would be the hardest letter to write; it might take some time to formulate the most appropriate words to make abundantly clear her hurt, without blaming Vernon Sr for his son's deceit and abandonment.

Beezie composed her first letter over and over again in her mind, trying to minimise the full impact of the whole event. Finally, after much anguish, both women completed their letters and handed them in to be mailed. Then began the wait for their families' replies.

Prison life continued to shock and degrade them. They still could not come to grips fully with where they were. While every prisoner was assigned a work duty and expected to perform it in return for their meagre weekly wage, the officers, noting Toddie's ill health, didn't push her. Toddie was mindful that she had to appear to be carrying her weight lest she incur the wrath of fellow prisoners, so she did her best. Both women put their names down for cleaning or gardening work to help pass the time. Beezie also signed up for writing and art classes while Toddie took a pottery class.

One morning, as Toddie performed her chores sweeping out the dormitory block, her left leg gave way. She fell heavily to the floor. Toddie had suffered on and off for many years from sciatic nerve compression, which caused stabbing pain to radiate down her left leg. The ache was becoming constant and it was getting worse. The incident was serious enough to require hospitalisation in the infirmary. Within a few days, she was out of bed and moving about again, but almost immediately the condition returned and she fell heavily a second time.

The precursor to her current health woes could be traced back to 1963 when she underwent a spinal fusion. It was the result of cervical disc degeneration that had prematurely ended her promising athletic career. At Mulawa she was prescribed a course of painkillers, fitted with a leg splint and, as an extra precaution, a board was placed under her mattress.

During Toddie's hospitalisation, Beezie was allowed to visit her for one hour daily. They spent time in prayer, and Beezie would apply her training as a therapeutic masseuse.

At this point in their imprisonment Toddie wrote in her diary:

I made up my mind I would not be a cripple. We knew that with our prayers and the means to help ourselves, that this too, would pass. Our prayers are fervent: morning, noon and night. Here we are, two elderly ladies scared to death, in a strange country with no family, friends – no-one. Are we too late in our prayers? We have always been Christians, even before this nightmare, but like so many, we have taken our Christianity for granted. We are both retired ladies, who have worked hard all our lives and served our country during World War II. In our accumulated driving years, we had maybe six driving tickets. Not that we didn't deserve more, but we were just never caught. What went wrong with our lives? Was it loving and trusting our own blood kin? No, I think not; I believe somehow it is all of God's plan. Like most Americans we have been too complacent; seldom if ever did our eyes look towards the heavens. Now here we are praying as we have never prayed before. Oh, dear God, please give us a sign. We do not know what we are looking for, but there has to be something.

The women wept when reading the letters that began coming in from immediate family members. They read and re-read them, taking comfort from hearing their loved ones' voices as they read their handwritten words. More letters from other relatives and friends began to arrive, as well as other unsolicited letters, from Australian and overseas supporters – complete strangers – in which the writers expressed sympathy and support.

Toddie's loathing for her nephew remained bitter and all-consuming, and it was hurting her. It was a depth of ill-feeling she had never before experienced and it made her sick to her stomach.

'To be victimized by my own flesh and blood whom I loved dearly from the day he was born ... Lord, I still can't believe it,' Toddie wrote to Don and Thelma Mitchell. Upon reading the letter, Don was furious. 'Can you imagine the lack of gumption in a man, letting his aunt and her friend take the rap for something he set up and tricked them into? It's disgusting,' he told a newspaper reporter.

When Toddie marked her sixtieth birthday on 18 March, she didn't feel like celebrating. The birthday cards from both Beezie's and Toddie's families only reinforced the helpless situation in which she found herself, at least until the trial and then the sentencing. After that, she imagined – and expected – they'd finally be going home.

On 11 April, Bob Harkins visited the women once more before their next appearance in the NSW District Court for the sentencing hearing. At the conclusion of Harkins's short pre-trial meeting with the pair, Toddie looked him in the eye and said, 'The Narcotics Bureau is on our side, Bob.' Harkins didn't respond. He left to prepare the finishing touches to his brief, which he would be presenting to Jack Hiatt, QC, the barrister retained by the Australian Legal Aid Service to represent the two women at their next appearance.

Judge James Staunton, the NSW District Court chief judge since 1972, was the trial judge. He was born in 1922 and admitted to the NSW Bar in 1951. He became a Queen's Counsel in 1966.

The word around the legal traps in Sydney suggested there had been fierce competition among the state's judges vying for the Drug Grannies' case. It was to be one of the first major drug importation cases in Sydney in which the accused faced new and harsher penalties under recent amendments to the Customs Act. Drug traffickers now faced up to twenty-five years' imprisonment and/or a A$100,000 fine if found guilty. Soon, if the Australian government's threats were to be believed, these penalties would become even more strict: life sentences were under consideration. The Drug Grannies' case would not only enable the law to be seen to be effective, but because it would generate so much media exposure, it had the potential to act as a deterrent to others considering drug smuggling. After all, the women were pleading guilty – it was now just a matter of the sentence.

Several days before their 14 April court appearance, a female prisoner was admitted to the remand wing of the prison. Though it wasn't known at first, she was there to threaten the Americans, warning them to shut up and not cooperate with authorities. When the ploy was discovered, blanket security was instituted for all future court hearings. The women were no longer taken to and from court in unmarked Narcotics Bureau vehicles, but were transported in secure prison vans.

Previously, the bureau had taken the women by car on account of their age and Toddie's ill health. Their first 'ride' in the rear of the prison van on 14 April was challenging for them as they sat on wooden benches without handles or bars for support, balancing precariously as the truck negotiated the hour-long drive from Mulawa into the city centre.

At 10 am sharp, Vera Todd Hays and Florice Marie Bessire stood in the dock of the NSW District Court for the start of their sentencing hearing as Crown Prosecutor Alec Shand, QC, read out the charges:

Before the court are Vera Todd Hays and Florice Marie Bessire. Both these two persons pleaded guilty before a magistrate on the following charges: that on or about 31 January, 1978 in Sydney, and in the State of New South Wales, each without reasonable excuse did have in her possession prohibited imports to which Section 233B of the Customs Act 1901 applied. To wit: narcotic goods constituting a quantity of cannabis resin reasonably suspected of having been imported into Australia in contravention of the said Act. I hand to your Honour a copy of the committal document which sets out that charge.

With that, the prosecutor handed Judge Staunton the document.

The crowded courtroom was hot, and the air conditioning, only recently installed, wasn't powerful enough to keep the morning sun and its heat at bay. The women's barrister, Jack Hiatt, QC, opened for the defence:

> I am instructed by the Australian Legal Aid Service and I appear for the two punitive prisoners. I use that adjective deliberately for two reasons. The first is that a matter of reassurance, my two clients would like it to come from your Honour if it be, that should they adhere to that plea, that neither has pleaded that either had in her possession $8 million wholesale value of cannabis. Nor has either pleaded to having in possession $19 million worth of hashish, as has already been announced in the newspapers.

Obviously, not only were Toddie and Beezie frustrated by the inaccurate reporting of the media, but so too was their counsel. Right up to the day of the trial, the media continued to report their arrest in Gosford, when in fact both were apprehended in Sydney. While these minor inaccuracies resulted from a lack of fact checking, it was lazy if not sloppy journalism from many quarters.

'I understand they are being held under Section 51A on pleas of guilty for sentence in the terms that Mr Shand has announced,' said the judge. 'It is only to those offences in each case they be required to adhere to their plea.'

Both prisoners adhered to their pleas of guilty, which they'd entered in an earlier hearing before a magistrate in mid-March.

'My instructions are that the charge to which the two prisoners pleaded guilty and that to which we would understand they continue to plead guilty today involves a substance known as cannabis resin, and not a substance called cannabis. It is upon that basis we will be asking your Honour to consider the pleas of guilty,' said the prosecutor.

The opening legal arguments established, the first witness to take the stand was Inspector Bob Drane who, after being sworn in, recounted the details of Operation Genius from 5 December 1977 through to the women's apprehension and arrest.

Drane explained the rationale behind the haul's valuation: 'The total weight of the substance was 1.9 tonnes, and if sold at a wholesale price of $2200 per pound, would realise $9,641,156. If sold on the street at $180 per ounce, would realise $12,557,958. This is the largest single seizure of cannabis resin in Australia to date.'

It was established under questioning of Inspector Drane that warrants had finally been issued that day charging Phillip Richard Shine and Vern Leonard Todd with conspiracy with each other and the two women to commit an offence, namely the importing into Australia of cannabis resin in excess of a trafficable quantity. Those warrants had not been issued until almost ten weeks after Beezie's arrest, and long after the two drug kingpins had already fled Australia.

Drane confirmed the prisoners were not also to be charged with conspiracy. Cross-examination then followed.

'The two prisoners were not your main target, were they?' asked Hiatt.

'*My* main target? Yes sir,' said Drane.

'They were, the two prisoners here?'

'Yes sir.'

'Are you serious about that?'

'Yes sir, *my* part of the operation was the two prisoners,' explained the inspector.

'On 5 December 1977, it was known that they were going or had in fact taken delivery of a Mercedes campervan. That was known, was it not?' asked Hiatt.

'On 9 December, yes sir,' replied Drane.

There was another debate coming up; both men knew their territory, and the rules. The women's barrister was keen to establish his clients were simply 'mules', innocent of any foreknowledge of the 1.9-tonne drug importation. It was a difficult line to walk given Toddie and Beezie were both pleading guilty. However, Hiatt was keen to focus on the drug kingpins – Todd and Shine – and why *they*, instead of his clients, were not in the dock today.

> **HIATT:** And for the purpose of the charge they were then in possession of the vehicle containing the substance.
>
> **DRANE:** Yes, sir.
>
> **HIATT:** Then tell me, if they were the main targets, why was there what your people call 'surveillance'? Why were they surveilled for weeks around Australia?
>
> **DRANE:** Sir, they were *my* main targets. I was in charge of the surveillance units following the campervan, and the two women were the targets of *my* surveillance: the two women and the campervan. Other inquiries were being made by other officers.
>
> **HIATT:** Why did you not arrest them when they took delivery?
>
> **DRANE:** Because other inquiries were being conducted.
>
> **HIATT:** For more important targets?
>
> **DRANE:** For more important people, yes sir.
>
> **HIATT:** Higher up in the affair?
>
> **DRANE:** Yes sir.
>
> **HIATT:** You have seen quite a lot of the two prisoners, have you not?
>
> **DRANE:** I have, sir.
>
> **HIATT:** In your view are they any more involved than dupes?
>
> **DRANE:** I do not know about the word dupes, sir. To a lesser extent than other people, yes.
>
> **HIATT:** This is tremendously important to them do you understand?'
>
> **DRANE:** I realise that.
>
> **HIATT:** If you do not like the word dupes, what would you substitute?
>
> **DRANE:** It is very hard to put into words, sir.
>
> **HIATT:** You asked for their cooperation didn't you, after they were arrested?

DRANE: I certainly did.

HIATT: And you got it to an extent, I suggest, that you have not had before in any arrested person?

DRANE: I wouldn't say that, but they were very cooperative.

HIATT: Can you think of any other people that were as cooperative?

DRANE: Oh yes.

The women were getting the feeling that Drane wasn't going to be doing them any special favours, at least not the favours they had been expecting. He wasn't agreeing they were dupes, and he was hedging on just how cooperative they had been. Harkins sought leave to approach the prisoners to get instructions. Toddie and Beezie let Harkins know that Drane had, *in their recollection*, specifically offered them deportation if they cooperated to their fullest. Harkins returned to Hiatt and passed on his clients' information.

'There is no way in which they could have been more cooperative, is there?' asked the women's barrister.

'No sir,' replied Drane.

'I have to ask you this question, it being on instructions. I do not necessarily suggest that it was to obtain the record of interview which you did, but at some stage did you, at any stage, say to the two prisoners that you would do your best to get them deported after sentence?'

'No sir.'

Audible gasps could be heard from Toddie and Beezie. Toddie felt like shouting out 'that's a lie'. She wanted the court to know they believed they had both been told full cooperation would lead to deportation. She remained silent, however, as difficult as it was – she did not want to jeopardise their future.

'Anything like that?' Hiatt tried again.

DRANE: I was asked from the best of my recollection whether they would be deported.

HIATT: By them?

DRANE: By them.

HIATT: On the best of your recollection?

DRANE: I would have given them the answer of the policy of the Narcotics Bureau.

HIATT: What did you say?

DRANE: That they would *probably* be deported after they had served their term of imprisonment in Australia.

HIATT: That is what you said?

DRANE: Yes sir.

HIATT: On your recollection of the conversation, is there any way in which they could have understood the position to be that you yourself would make some effort to get them deported after sentence?

DRANE: Just going into a bit of detail, I had a bit of discussion with the ladies and I never at any stage told them any *lies* as to what I could do or what I could not do. I certainly could not or would not have the power to have them deported straight after sentence.

Lies? Hiatt had only asked the investigator to test his recollection. He didn't suggest there had been any 'lies'. Hiatt hoped that he had planted sufficient doubt as to what had occurred that the judge would be able to take this into account when sentencing.

HIATT: You may take it that I accept that answer absolutely. I am asking you to consider if you would be so good to listen to another proposition. Can you think of any conversation between the three of you which might inadvertently have led them to think that you could make some effort to obtain their deportation after they were sentenced?

DRANE: No sir. I can only say we did discuss deportation, but not to that extent.'

HIATT: Was it discussed more than once?

DRANE: I cannot recall. I was asked a question by the prisoners about deportation and I told them what the policy was.

HIATT: Because you developed some regard for them, did you not, as people?

DRANE: I did.

HIATT: And quite a deep sympathy for their plight?

DRANE: I had sympathy, yes.

The women felt maybe the pendulum was now swinging a little way back in their favour. Even they knew it wasn't every day a narcotics investigator professed sympathy for his targets. Later, Hiatt pressed the point of Vern Todd and Phillip Shine – their escape from the bureau's grasp, and their eventual getaway from Australia.

HIATT: There was intensive surveillance carried out right throughout Australia following the van in order to achieve the arrest, if possible, and of persons other than or additional to the prisoners?

DRANE: That is correct.

HIATT: It was to that end that you sought the assistance of the two prisoners?

DRANE: That is correct.

HIATT: You have had a lot to do with this case and its successful conclusion and the two prisoners. Are you able to say, and I do not want to press you if you feel that you cannot, but are you able to say from your knowledge of the facts that they were in the first instance assisted to go by the nephew by a small amount of money relative to fares for an overseas trip?

DRANE: Yes sir.

HIATT: And progressively they were caught in the net?

DRANE: Yes sir.

HIATT: Part of the net was to induce the prisoner Hays to go to London and have some papers relating to the campervan put in her name. Is that so?

DRANE: This is what happened, yes sir.

HIATT: And the further it went along, the more difficult it became for either or both to extricate themselves, even had they wanted?

DRANE: They became more involved as they went along, yes sir.

HIATT: Involved by the machinations of the two for whom the warrants were issued this morning?

DRANE: Yes sir.

HIATT: The two persons for whom the warrants were issued this morning are persons who were either known or strongly suspected of having used the same system of motor vehicles and campervans on previous occasions?

DRANE: Yes sir.

HIATT: There is not the slightest doubt is there that these two prisoners had nothing to do with any other offence other than this particular isolated campervan?

DRANE: There is no evidence of that, no sir, and there is no suggestion of it.

HIATT: Because this genuinely was to be for them the one overseas trip that they would have after their retirement?

DRANE: Yes sir.

HIATT: As a result of all of your conversations with the two prisoners, do you have any understanding about what, in a tangible way, in their predicament, would result from this cooperation?

The packed court was getting its money's worth. The nitty gritty details into which the women's barrister was delving – what possible 'deals' were cut in order to get the women to sing – were not always matters raised in an open court. Most judges preferred a more tidy, orderly approach – and to confine this sort of legal argument to chambers.

DRANE: I had an idea of what would happen, yes sir.

HIATT: What was that?

DRANE: That we would inform the Court that they had cooperated, and that the Deputy Crown Solicitor's office and somebody else would probably speak to His Honour in Chambers to inform him, rather than have it said in court.

This was known as 'offering consideration' – not charge bargaining.

HIATT: That of course was only in the extreme case that having lost the two persons once, you did not want to lose them again. That would be right, would it now?

DRANE: You mean to speak about what we know in court, in public?

HIATT: Because there was a lot of material that would have caused these two persons for whom the warrants were issued this morning to disappear for good and permanently if they were put too much on inquiry? Isn't that the position?

DRANE: To the best of my knowledge these persons have already disappeared. My main reason for not wanting a lot of things to come out in court was for the women's sake. No other reason.

Drane was aware the women's lives would be at risk in prison once it was known they had cooperated with investigators.

HIATT: No other reasons?

DRANE: Yes, some things that we are still inquiring about.

HIATT: Because the surveillance after the prisoners took delivery of the campervan was unsuccessful in achieving the arrest of other than the two prisoners, wasn't it?

DRANE: It was.

> **HIATT:** That was after about $300,000 to $500,000 of
> taxpayers' money was conscientiously expended in
> seeking to get more than the two prisoners.

At this remark, the prosecutor jumped to his feet to object. Before he could speak, Justice Staunton interrupted: 'A course of approaching me in Chambers to advise me on any material in this matter was not taken, and indeed if it had been, I should think you would be well aware of the condition such information would have been received if I had considered it relevant to know.'

This was a gentle reprimand Staunton was giving to the defence counsel who was veering close to a charge of abuse of process.

After further evidence was given, including the submission of photographs of the campervan and the presentation of a one-pound block of hashish for His Honour to study, the prisoners' antecedents were read out. Other than unblemished records, their wartime service, and their upstanding status as fine US citizens, the material was unremarkable. With that, Drane retired from the stand and the case for the Crown was closed.

Hiatt requested an adjournment to another date for Toddie's medical evidence to be prepared and put to the court before sentencing. He said Beezie would offer evidence on oath, and dependent on Toddie's health, she would either make a short statement or also give evidence on oath.

The Crown prosecutor countered. He was anxious to have the matter over within a week and inquired about Toddie's condition. The judge granted a short adjournment to enable Hiatt to seek instructions from his clients and prepare them for the proceedings to follow later that day. Hiatt also produced for the judge an itemised list of American character witnesses.

It was decided Toddie would make a statement only, and not give evidence under oath. Her lawyer believed she would become too emotional for an objective offering of evidence to be made. He likely also feared how she would respond to a grilling from the prosecution.

Toddie stood, facing the judge, and spoke quietly, but forcefully: 'Your Honour, people. I am just so ashamed and so sorry for everything – for how everything happened. So sorry for the humiliation of the United States, and not knowing what was going on or anything. I don't think I can testify, I am so ill and sick.' She sat down, bent forward and covered her face with both hands.

Beezie was then sworn in, and Hiatt began his examination of her evidence. She was asked about retirement, where she had lived, what funds she had in the bank, her income, their mortgage, and the True Value Hardware's wages of two dollars an hour. Importantly he asked about her attitude to drugs. Hiatt was careful to tap Beezie's earnest desire to be truthful.

'I don't like drugs at all,' she said matter-of-factly.

No-one was to know the private hell Beezie had gone through as a child when her sickly mother relied on pain medication to provide relief, and when, because there was no money, Beezie would have to keep her company, caring and consoling until her father could scratch together a few dollars to purchase the medication on which her mother relied.

'Have you ever tried smoking grass?' Hiatt asked his client.

'No sir, never have,' Beezie replied.

Having established her character, he pushed on to the matter at hand – the trip.

HIATT: What was it that you understood that you and your companion were to do with that [the van] if he [Vern Todd] merely said he wanted a little grass?

BESSIRE: It was supposed to have been put in the bus at some time.

HIATT: This is what he said?

BESSIRE: No, he just said he was, he might be wanting a little grass.

> **HIATT:** That was all that was said about it before you left the
> United States?
> **BESSIRE:** Yes.

This response firmly established that Vern Todd had said drugs *would* be involved in the trip, a point affirmed in the women's earlier interviews with the Narcotics Bureau agents. That the drug indicated was 'grass' and that the quantity was only enough for 'personal use' was irrelevant in the eyes of the law.

Hiatt's questions continued, establishing how the trip began, including where and how the carnet was arranged in Toddie's name. The luncheon adjournment came and went within an hour. Soon after lunch, Beezie's testimony continued and traced their travels across the Continent, and the near nervous breakdown Toddie had suffered in Lahore when feuding with her nephew.

Hiatt then asked, 'When you got to New Delhi, driven by Vera's nephew, was there some further conference about the trip? Whether you would continue and whether there was some mention of danger?'

> **BESSIRE:** Vern Todd told her [Toddie] that she would have to
> drive on.
> **HIATT:** What did he say?
> **BESSIRE:** She would have to drive on to Bombay because the
> car was in her name. She had the carnet in her name and
> that it was – the organisation was bigger than he [was].
> **HIATT:** Was any enquiry made by either of you as to what the
> organisation was?
> **BESSIRE:** She did.
> **HIATT:** What did she say?
> **BESSIRE:** She asked him what it was all about.
> **HIATT:** What did he say?
> **BESSIRE:** He said there was no need for her to know. Just
> to deliver the van, but there was no need for us to know.

I cannot recall the conversation, there were so many conversations.

It was now clear, however, the women had been coerced into working for a larger organisation. Hiatt's questioning continued.

HIATT: So far as you are concerned, what was it you were taking delivery of in addition to a car?

BESSIRE: I didn't know for certain.

HIATT: Was an elaborate performance going on by people who claimed to be a syndicate?

BESSIRE: I had my suspicions.

HIATT: What was your suspicion?

BESSIRE: Well, I didn't know whether it was hard drugs or gold. I had been reading about quite a bit of smuggling gold through that part of the country. That flashed through my mind also.

HIATT: Getting to the stage where a little bit of grass was a bit out of proportion to what was happening?

BESSIRE: Yes sir.

If ever a prosecutor acquired a cooperative witness, it was at this point, because there was the case on a platter, and he hadn't yet cross-examined Beezie about this aspect. Having pleaded guilty, Beezie proceeded to unintentionally condemn both herself and her companion, Toddie. Her answers in court were forthright and honest. But there was little wriggle room in which she or her defence counsel could manoeuvre to ameliorate an already awful situation.

One might have expected Beezie to minimise the extent of her suspicions, to place less emphasis on the organisation's standover tactics and to cast a more favourable light on the unknowing role she and Toddie had played in the smuggling operation. But this was Beezie's first time in court, and it wasn't for a speeding ticket.

Hiatt questioned the offer of $200,000 made by Vern to continue driving the van once it had arrived in Melbourne. Beezie became muddled and this confusion was to be later played against her by a disbelieving judge.

HIATT: First of all, on the best of your recollection, where did that [offer] happen?

BESSIRE: To my recollection it happened in Melbourne.

HIATT: In Melbourne? Do you appreciate that that is not what your record of interview says? You do appreciate that?

BESSIRE: I do appreciate it. I was pretty frightened.

HIATT: But you were doing your best?

BESSIRE: I was doing my best.

HIATT: And you are now on oath and you are still doing your best to tell the truth?

BESSIRE: I am sir.

HIATT: Tell his Honour then, what were the circumstances in which the $200,000 was mentioned in Melbourne, where was it, do you remember?

BESSIRE: At the Hilton Hotel.

HIATT: At about what time of day?

BESSIRE: As I recall, just before lunch.

HIATT: Who was present?

BESSIRE: My travelling companion, Mrs. Hays, and Vern Todd.

HIATT: Somebody else?

BESSIRE: No sir.

HIATT: Who said what?

BESSIRE: Vern Todd said if this was successful we would receive $200,000.

HIATT: Who said that, what, when?

BESSIRE: Mrs. Hays then threw up her hands and said 'What would we do with $200,000?

> **HIATT:** Did you yourself believe that it was a genuine offer of
> $200,000?
> **BESSIRE:** No.

And then the last question before she was to be cross-examined
by the prosecutor. 'What do you yourself say about your
feelings, finding yourself where you are now?' asked Hiatt,
no doubt hoping his client would respond at some length and
confirm for the court her simple and unsuspecting nature. But
her response was simply that she felt 'pretty remorseful and
pretty stupid'.

Crown Prosecutor Alec Shand, QC, wasted no time in
seeking clarification on several matters.

> **SHAND:** I would just like to get a couple of things clear.
> Firstly, it is the fact that from early on in your travels in this
> campervan, you knew you were carrying some quantity
> of – not any specific quantity – but some quantity of
> grass?
> **BESSIRE:** No sir, I did not know that.

A few questions later, with the witness floundering with
semantics, Shand pushed the point further.

> **SHAND:** You tell us, before Narcotics Officers spoke to you
> or interviewed you, you had no belief that there was grass
> in the campervan?
> **BESSIRE:** I don't know what.
> **SHAND:** I'm asking for your belief.
> **BESSIRE:** Sir that is my belief. I did not know what was in it.
> **SHAND:** Did you have any belief at all as to what was in the
> campervan before the Narcotics Officers spoke to you?
> **BESSIRE:** I believed something was in it. I did not know if it
> was grass, sir, or what.

The cross-examination then moved to the issue of the expense money given to Beezie and Toddie, and at what stage it was supplied in relation to Vern's reference to 'a little grass' being in the campervan. A crucial juncture then arose, with the prosecutor comparing the answers Beezie was giving to the court with the answers given in her record of interviews with Narcotics Bureau agents three months earlier.

SHAND: I want to ask you … whether in fact having completed the interview, you read through the questions and answers to make sure they were correctly recorded. Did you do that?

BESSIRE: I was supposed to. I didn't.

SHAND: You did not do it?

BESSIRE: No.

SHAND: You signed every page of it?

BESSIRE: I did.

SHAND: You did not read it through?

BESSIRE: At that time I was pretty nervous. I couldn't read it through. I have read it through since I've been at Silverwater (Mulawa). It does not make much sense, it is not even good grammar.

SHAND: Do you remember this question: 'You agree it is an accurate record of our conversations?' Did you say yes to that?

BESSIRE: Yes sir.

SHAND: Without meaning—

The prosecutor was interrupted by Beezie whose next words were to sum up in a nutshell her feelings for the narcotics agents who had arrested her and Toddie: 'I said it because I was well, may I say, I trusted Drane.'

As Shand's expert cross-examination continued, he was able to uncover the substance of Vern Todd's conversation with Toddie and Beezie in May 1977 as Beezie had recounted in her record of interview with Drane.

> **SHAND:** Is it true from the time he [Vern Todd] came to the United States in May 1977, you knew that when you took that trip in the van, it would be carrying some grass?
>
> **BESSIRE:** Yes, but only for his own use, not a huge quantity. It was the way he said it, there was not to be any huge quantity. He didn't say he was going to deal it or sell it.
>
> **SHAND:** Did he give you any idea of the quantity at all?
>
> **BESSIRE:** No sir. Just a small quantity.
>
> **SHAND:** So there was a specific agreement between the three of you that there would be no hard drugs, but only grass in the van?
>
> **BESSIRE:** That is right.

Beezie had walked into the trap, and the prosecution knew it. And then, when it had been determined the women were in fact asking Vern Todd in Australia what might happen if they were caught, the prosecutor asked:

> **SHAND:** Did you not believe when you had the conversation in May 1977 in the United States attended by Vern Todd that you would be doing the wrong thing driving the van carrying grass?
>
> **BESSIRE:** Not really. Not the way it was presented to us, no sir.
>
> **SHAND:** You thought there was nothing illegal about it?
>
> **BESSIRE:** Well no; well I guess there is no such a thing as being a little illegal.
>
> **SHAND:** Shades of grey, perhaps?
>
> **BESSIRE:** Yes, but it seemed to be a minor thing, the way it was presented to us.

That just about summed up both Beezie's and Toddie's perceptions of their whole adventurous trip. It never dawned on these two older ladies in La Pine – naive, unworldly – that they were going to be used by a close relative to import Australia's biggest ever shipment of hashish. It seemed Shand, having tasted blood, decided to offer them a chance to diminish some of their responsibility.

SHAND: Why did you think he [Vern Todd] wanted you to take that trip?

BESSIRE: He wanted the van in Australia.

SHAND: And you believe he wanted grass in it, when he was there, is that the position?

BESSIRE: No. It wasn't the way it was presented to us. Several years before, he said he made movies, or wanted to make movies. He wanted a camper made and sent to Australia. He made this statement before we ever heard of making this trip ourselves, about a year before, and he wanted a camper because we had one in the States. He wanted one to carry camera equipment and to make movies. That was the thing we heard a year before. Then later he presented and said he had a camper in Germany that he wanted brought to Australia.

SHAND: You said it was getting to a stage where a little bit of grass was a bit out of proportion.

BESSIRE: That is right.

SHAND: Did you ask Mr. Lange?

BESSIRE: Yes.

SHAND: What did you ask him?

BESSIRE: He said we did not need to know.

SHAND: At all?

BESSIRE: That's right.

SHAND: Did you then think there was nothing wrong?

BESSIRE: That time we did stop.

SHAND: Why did you go on?

BESSIRE: We were being threatened.

SHAND: With what?

BESSIRE: To begin with, we could not abandon or sell the bus. It was in Mrs. Hays' name and we had to continue the trip.

SHAND: Because otherwise it would have been necessary to abandon the bus?

BESSIRE: That's right. He said we would be hounded the rest of our lives until we got out of there, no matter where we went.

SHAND: He said that?

BESSIRE: He and Vern both have said that to us.

Further cross-examination by the prosecutor concentrated on the issue of the offer of $200,000 – whether it had been made in Bombay as inducement to continue to Australia, or whether it had been made in Melbourne. From Beezie's performance when answering questions from her counsel earlier in the proceedings, the prosecutor must have realised she would be a piece of cake.

And she was.

Eventually, Judge Staunton was moved to determine for himself the details of the $200,000 offer. 'Miss Bessire, you said about this matter of the $200,000 that it happened in Melbourne?' queried Judge Staunton in a move of judicial clarification. 'It is your belief that that conversation happened in Melbourne. Is that right?'

BESSIRE: Yes sir.

STAUNTON: You have had pointed out to you that the context in which it appears in Question and Answer No. 93 of your record of interview?

BESSIRE: Yes sir.

STAUNTON: 'If she [Vera] conveyed in her answers that the conversation [about the $200,000] had taken place in Pakistan or India, would that in any way make your belief in your recollection that it took place in Melbourne?

BESSIRE: Well, when I heard that conversation – I never heard all conversations that went on. See, Your Honour, that is the first time I recall hearing it. I said Bombay when

I recalled Bob Lange, he never mentioned money of any
kind or any price, only Vern.

STAUNTON: You did not hear all conversations?'

BESSIRE: No sir.

STAUNTON: There could have been a conversation in
Bombay that you don't know anything about. The first you
heard about it was in Melbourne?

BESSIRE: Melbourne, that is right.

Judge Staunton made several notes on his pad at this stage,
and then turned to Hiatt, who asked two final questions of his
client.

HIATT: When you were in La Pine and before you left, what
was your understanding of the means and financial
position of Vern Todd?

BESSIRE: Oh well, we thought he had a lot of money. He
was in the import/export business as far as everybody at
home knew, he was a big businessman.

Beezie's answer brought a smile to just about everyone in the
courtroom. It was a rare moment of comic relief with the fate of
two lives hanging precariously in the balance.

HIATT: Did he seem to treat your travelling companion, to
use a phrase that occurs in the record of interview, as his
favourite aunt?

BESSIRE: Yes.

Beezie retired from the stand and returned to her seat with
Toddie and the defence counsel. She had been grilled for almost
two hours.

Hiatt, understandably respectful of the fate that awaited his
prisoners, not only because of their guilty plea but also because
of the evidence offered on the witness stand, decided against

making a final address to the court that day. He nonetheless repeated his request to have Toddie medically examined by the NSW Health Commission's medical officer in order to prepare a report that would be furnished at the next hearing when the women would learn their fate.

In his final summation, the Crown Prosecutor thought it best to clear up any doubts in the court's mind about the issue of inducements offered in the expectation of deportation, as alleged by the prisoners. Shand reaffirmed Drane's answers in court and rebutted any suggestion of impropriety on Drane's part. He said Bessire's evidence failed to support any suggestion of impropriety. In response, Hiatt indicated he had no instructions other than to accept the integrity of Inspector Drane.

'I will stand this matter over for the prisoner to be sentenced on a date to be fixed. I indicate that it appears to be desirable for the prisoner Vera Todd Hays to be medically examined ... I would suggest that the examination be conducted at an institution within control of the Department of Corrective Services,' instructed Judge Staunton.

And with those words, the court rose shortly after 2.50 pm and the matter was adjourned until 21 April when the women would be sentenced.

CHAPTER THIRTEEN

HASHISH AND OLD LACE

Mulawa officers were required to continue keeping a careful watch on the two American prisoners upon their return. There was reliable intelligence that Todd and his associates were making threats against them via the inmate grapevine. After Beezie's evidence, the pair would be potentially even more vulnerable to swift prison justice.

'I won't be seeing you girls anymore because I've got to get back to my office in Melbourne,' Agent Khoury told the prisoners at the reception area upon their return from the day's court proceedings. 'Have a wonderful flight home and if I get to the US next year, I'll look you up.' The only unfinished element of Operation Genius was the women's sentencing, but Khoury was returning to her base in Victoria as her work was done.

Both Toddie and Beezie believed a true friendship had developed between them and the agent, not dissimilar to the bond they believed they had with Drane, whose testimony in court referred to feeling 'sympathy' for the women.

Their diaries shared their increasing impatience with the process. Prison life was wearing them down. Beezie wrote:

I want to feel solid ground under my feet again; to make decisions and use my own judgement; to be able to answer 'no' if I mean 'no'; go to bed when I wish to; rise when I want to; eat when I want, not just because the clock says it's time to muster. I'd like to mow our lawns, work in our garden, work in our flower beds, be able to see the people I wish to be able to. We've got to get out of here soon because we are becoming institutionalised.

The media reporting had, as expected, seized on the sensational elements of the day's proceedings in court. The newspapers, like the radio bulletins and TV news reports, focused on the substantial financial inducement Vern had offered the women. It was the women who had revealed the details of the offer, and they thought they'd made it clear in their statements in court that they didn't believe it was genuine.

Toddie recorded their frustrations in her diary:

The Press has crucified us. They treated us like criminals and twisted everything around, making out we're greedy. They don't understand Vern only used the $200,000 as a ploy because we were getting mad at him. He couldn't very well put a gun to our heads, so he instead used money as the ploy. The Press don't seem to understand we told him we didn't need, or want the money – all we wanted was to get out of this thing and go home. They have tried us and convicted us even before we've heard what the sentence would be. Even before we went to court, we were crucified.

The women's diaries and correspondence with family and friends were to form an important part of their survival strategy. Rarely did a day go by without letters being written to family.

One of Toddie's poems reflected her feelings about their predicament.

The Los Angeles Times *called it*
Hashish and old lace,

Humiliated, degraded, we can't
Save face.
The Australian papers called us
Two greedy old women,
Without checking our past they
Sent us to prison.
The only speed we know is the
Speed of a car,
To our loved ones we flew
Near and afar.
The only Grass we know is the
Kind you mow ...
We sit here now on the edge
Of our beds and
Only see tears far, far
Ahead.
For every month here we feel
We've aged ten, but if
There is a beginning, there
Is an end.

As 21 April approached, the women prepared themselves for their final day in court. They often spoke long into the evenings, comforting themselves that they had cooperated with the authorities, been befriended by the arresting agents who took them for drinks and a meal after some of their court appearances, and that their character references showed them to be good American citizens.

They believed their guilty plea indicated they were prepared to take the verdict on the chin, though they would continue to assert they hadn't set off for this 'trip of a lifetime' with any idea of its true intent.

•

On the morning of the sentencing, Queens Square in Sydney was heavily blanketed by more than thirty uniformed and plainclothes police at the courthouse, inside and out. The prison van carrying the women accelerated past the waiting press and through the gates into the yard where the prisoners were processed before being dispatched to holding cells to await the start of their trial.

Toddie and Beezie were escorted into the courtroom at 9.55 am to await the judge's entrance at 10 am. Judge Staunton entered the court from his adjoining chambers and eased himself into his chair as his associate called the court to order. The first instruction given in recognition of the prisoners' health and age was that they were permitted to remain seated until otherwise ordered to stand. The session was to last approximately thirty-five minutes.

Judge Staunton read from his script, meticulous in his choice of language and authoritative in his delivery.

Each prisoner has appeared before me to a plea of guilty ... each prisoner is an American citizen and their involvement in these offences commenced in May 1977, when Vera Todd Hays was approached by her nephew Vern Todd at her home in Oregon, and invited to go with Florice Marie Bessire to Germany to collect a motor van and drive it to Bombay. All expenses for the trip to and from America together with $25,000 were offered as inducement. The prisoners were told that they were being paid to take a small quantity of 'grass' (marijuana) and that it was not a load of 'hard stuff'.

According to the prisoners, on arrival in Bombay they were asked to ship the vehicle to Australia and fly there and resume possession of it. I am satisfied that at this time they were offered the sum of $200,000 to carry out this additional part of the operation.

Staunton went on to summarise the details of the women's case, before outlining the considerations he took into account when deciding on the women's sentences.

Each prisoner made and signed lengthy records of interview and the prisoner Hays gave a very long account of the matter which was tape recorded. The contents of these records clearly enough show that the prisoners were willing participants in an operation which, from its outset, concerned the illegal dealing in some large quantity of drugs.

The material placed before me relating to the offences and to the personal position of the prisoners gives rise to a sentencing problem of unusual difficulty. On the one hand, the nature and circumstances of the offences called for sentences which expresses the determination of the courts to accept the responsibility of giving effect to the grave view taken by the legislature – by the penalty provided – of offences of this kind; on the other, the previous good character of the prisoners, the nature of their involvement in the offences, their age, state of health and other relevant matters require that the Court gives adequate and proper weight to the subjective features of the case.

Dealing first with the offences, it is clear that an illegal operation of very great magnitude was being undertaken. It was very carefully and exhaustively planned, the obvious intention being that it should appear that a vehicle being used for an extensive world trip had arrived in Australia from halfway around the world in the course of that trip. To add conviction to this impression was the engagement of two elderly American women as apparently adventurous travellers arriving at yet one more continent in their travels, there, no doubt, being the hope that these people and their vehicle would receive less Customs scrutiny than, say, two young hirsute males. To what extent were the prisoners privy to this scheme? The explanations of each that they were to be paid $25,000 for taking the van to

Top left: Toddie unashamedly declared her first-born nephew, Vern Jr, to be her 'favourite'. She'd often use her military leave to visit him and the family. Top right: Vern Todd Jr was known to keep up with current fashions and trends. His wedding day attire and mode of transport (dune buggy) were no exceptions. *Fairfax Media*

Toddie (third from left) was a member of the semi-pro softball team The Croonerettes, which was sponsored by Bing Crosby (at the piano).

Toddie (left) and Beezie attended the Colgate International Women's Tennis Championships at White City while in Sydney in November 1977, witnessing Evonne Goolagong Cawley's return to tennis after a break to have her first child.

Top left and right: The van was the women's home away from home for their 'trip of a lifetime' through ten countries, including Australia. They decorated the exterior with decals from the US.

Left: Beezie's natural warmth meant she made friends no matter which country they were in. Here she is with the mechanic in Jaipur who got them back on the road after another breakdown.

Below: Another day, another border control post: the women wait in line at the Pakistan passport control on their way to pick up Vern.

The inside of the van was stripped out to reveal the secret compartments and sub-flooring in which the 1.9 tonnes of hash had been concealed. *Fairfax Media*

More than 4000 individually wrapped one-pound (half-kilo) blocks of hash were removed from the floor cavities. Even the narcotics agents were surprised by the record size of the haul. *Sydney Morning Herald, Fairfax Media*

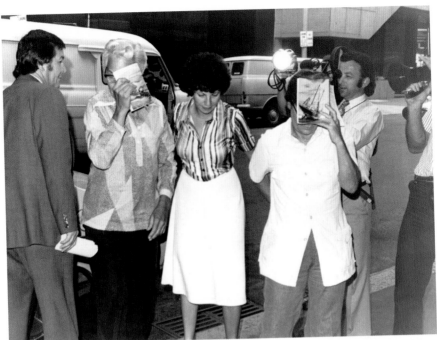

Narcotics agent Michele Khoury (middle) escorts Toddie (left) and Beezie (right) to the Special Federal Court hearing in February 1978 as Inspector Bob Drane (far left) runs interference. The women shield their faces with copies of *Reader's Digest.* Julian Zakaras, *Sydney Morning Herald, Fairfax Media*

After their sentencing, the women were shell-shocked. Toddie required a helping hand for the perp walk and Beezie couldn't bear to look into the eyes of the journalists and photographers. *Fairfax Media*

Toddie and Beezie relied heavily on written and audio correspondence (via cassettes) with friends and family in the US during their incarceration. Photos and cards pinned to the wall also helped bridge the distance and kept their loved ones' faces fresh in their memory.

Mutual respect, dignity and trust were the foundations of the women's twenty-year relationship. They welcomed the opportunity on weekends to 'dress up' for the evening meal.

Beezie (second left) and Toddie (second right) enjoy a break at the Norma Parker Centre with their guards, including deputy superintendent Shirley Goodfellow (far right). The women's relationship with the prison officers was based on mutual respect.

In an effort to draw attention to the women's plight – their languishing in prison at the mercy of an indifferent federal Attorney-General – the ABC's *Four Corners* was permitted to talk to and film Toddie (left) and Beezie (centre) in their room at the Norma Parker Centre.

On one of Toddie's hospital visits for her multiple eye surgeries, she celebrated Christmas as a patient. Away from the monotony of prison, she was reminded of the freedoms she had lost.

Top left: When Toddie and Beezie were released from prison, they had only hours to pack before running the gauntlet of journalists and TV crews. Wayne Lock, *Sydney Morning Herald, Fairfax Media*

Top right: The author, Sandi Logan, briefs the media outside the prison after the women's release and deportation. The Drug Grannies requested that in the event of their sudden departure he front the press pack for them. Philip Lock, *Sydney Morning Herald, Fairfax Media*

Beezie (left) and Toddie (right) left the Norma Parker Detention Centre in a government vehicle, the excitement and anticipation clearly on their faces: at last they were going home. *Fairfax Media*

Toddie (left) and Beezie (right) with the author inside their mobile home shortly after their long-desired return to La Pine, Oregon. Steve Boyer, *The Bend Bulletin*

Free at last, Beezie (left) and Toddie (right) celebrate outside their La Pine mobile home. 'Be it ever so humble, there's no place like home.' (John Howard Payne) Steve Boyer, *The Bend Bulletin*

Bombay carrying a small amount of 'grass'– it being said that the drug was merely for the personal use of one individual – is unacceptable if this is intended to mean that each did not appreciate that she was taking part in a major drug smuggling operation. Further, the evidence of Miss Bessire that they were offered $200,000 in Melbourne to drive the vehicle to Sydney is rejected. It is inconsistent with her account in her record of interview ... I regard Miss Bessire's attempt to remove the occasion of the offer of $200,000 to Melbourne as a very real recognition of the fact that a finding that they had pressed on with the operation having been offered such a sum overseas would, or might, weigh heavily against them. It seems to me to follow that the prisoners not only willingly entered into an arrangement whereby they carried drugs of a substantial value but were prepared to continue with the arrangement – certainly at a vastly increased inducement – after they became aware that they were to bring into this country a large shipment of illegal drugs.

Such conduct of itself would require a very heavy sentence. The personal position of the prisoners is to some extent unusual. Each is a person well on in years and of previous good character. The latter fact is perhaps not surprising; the employment of such persons, for obvious reasons, would be the hope of those organising the operation. In addition, each appears to have led worthy, blameless lives and to have attracted the esteem and respect of their relatives and friends. It is sad to find two women with this background prepared to commit major crime for greed of money.

I accept that Vera Todd Hays has a serious medical problem. Each has cooperated with the investigating officers. However, when all this – and perhaps more – is said, the fact remains that each was prepared to play a vital role in the importation of this large quantity of drugs into this country.

I believe it to be my duty, in all the circumstances, to impose sentences which will reflect the dismay and abhorrence of the community for these offences. It is highly unlikely of course that the prisoners will ever again be involved in such offences, nevertheless, it must be made clear to others that the courts are determined to punish severely those who lend themselves to the illegal importation of large quantities of illegal drugs. As a result, hopefully, the principals will be unable to find carriers prepared to take the risk.

With that said, Judge Staunton ordered the women to stand. The women rose to their feet, faced the bench and awaited his verdict.

Florice Marie Bessire, I sentence you to imprisonment for fourteen years; this sentence to date from 31st January, 1978.

Vera Todd Hays, I sentence you to imprisonment for fourteen years, to date from 2nd February, 1978, and I draw to the attention of the Department of Corrective Services your need for medical attention.

And then, the sting in the tail which no-one had expected, Judge Staunton added: 'In respect of each prisoner, by reason of the nature of the offences and the antecedent character of each prisoner, I refrain from fixing a minimum term of imprisonment. My reasons for doing so will be given in writing.'

The women remained standing impassively, open-mouthed and speechless. They were still trying to come to grips with the words 'fourteen years' echoing in their heads, unable to make sense of it ... and what was that bit about 'refrain from fixing a minimum term'?

For the women, it was an unthinkable outcome. What had brought about the severity of the sentence handed to them? Throughout the judicial process they had expected their cooperation and their guilty pleas – as recommended by their legal representatives – would ultimately lead to deportation. The judge didn't refer in his sentencing to any such possibility.

Toddie wrote in her diary:

The gavel came down. We were told to rise and face the Bench. Now we knew this nightmare would end. Yes, it ended alright and so did our lives with a sentence of 14 years without parole. We can't believe it. We are in a state of shock. That's it; we heard it wrong, but no, the words keep ringing in our ears. 'I will make an example of you ladies: 14 years without parole.' Example for what? We've been blameless down through the years, serving our country during WW2, working hard all our lives, both retired. The hardest thing we had to face in our life was when we heard the sentence. The doors of the court and the world were closed to us. Aliens in a foreign land. No loved ones, no friends, nothing. There was nowhere to turn.

Judge Staunton, having administered the final body-blow of justice with a jaw-dropping sentence, now calmly set about gathering his papers, preparing to leave the courtroom for his chambers. The courtroom came to life.

Reporters raced from the courtroom after the judge's final delivery to file their copy. Fourteen years' jail. No minimum term of imprisonment! If the copy typists taking down the journalists' stories were quick enough, they might make a 'front five' page in the second edition, and if the copy was good enough, editors would likely delay the paper to replace the front page with the Drug Grannies' sentence.

The prosecution team and Narcotics Bureau agents were delighted. As they gathered around the table, the buzz of conversation worked itself to a crescendo of excitement as they traded their endorsements of the outcome. The sentiment was that at last they had secured an outcome that reflected the crime: Australia's biggest drug haul to date and fourteen years' imprisonment without parole. Australia was now well on the way to making it known to the world's drug kingpins it would not tolerate drug smuggling.

Meanwhile, also in the courtroom, Toddie and Beezie were slumped on their chairs, in shock, devastated by the severity of the sentence they'd just been handed. They heard no conversation, no laughter or euphoria from the prosecution table – it was just noise. With a shuddering intake of breath, Toddie turned to Robert Harkins, who had been with them almost from the time of their arrest, and was one of two solicitors instructing Jack Hiatt, QC.

'What happens now, Bob?' she asked in a voice barely audible.

'We will talk about it later, Vera, but all I can say at the moment is that I'm very shocked by the sentence,' said Harkins. He swallowed, finding it difficult to know what to say when their eyes met. Suddenly he was all too aware of how old the women looked, and momentarily wondered what the effect fourteen years in prison would have on them.

'What happened?' she asked. 'Where did that decision come from? Why was he so harsh on us? Did he not read our evidence? After what the narcotics agents told us and you, it seemed certain we'd get some sort of deportation arrangement as well.'

Toddie's voice was trembling. She was beginning to shake. Beezie, seated beside her, was trying to regain some sort of composure. Harkins tilted his head back and stared at the courtroom ceiling. He still had no words to adequately address the moment.

Two policemen and a policewoman approached the defence table, a task they had carried out countless times before when a trial concluded and the defendants were readied for transfer. The prison van was waiting to transport Toddie and Beezie back to Mulawa.

The women felt numb with confusion and bewilderment; they were desperate for an explanation that would help make sense of the past thirty minutes of their lives.

They were later to reflect in their prison diaries on their reaction to the handing down of the sentence. Toddie wrote:

Our world dropped out right there and then. We couldn't have felt any worse even if we'd been shot. In fact we might have felt better; when you're shot, you're in shock, you don't actually feel the pain of the bullet hitting you. Well, it was probably the same thing, it just didn't register. We were both stunned. It's not a feeling that's very easy to describe because the first thing that flashes past is not so much you, but what you're doing to your loved ones. Most individuals can handle what's handed to them ... it's the other people it affects which you can't handle.

Toddie, whose bad back and ongoing hypertension were persistent concerns, was helped from the courtroom and out a rear door of the court. With a cane in her right hand, she allowed a burly policeman to take her by the left elbow; for her it was support, for him it was a standard operating procedure when escorting a prisoner. Beezie walked unaided, except for the policewoman's hand she felt discreetly fixed to her belt loop. It seemed that everywhere the women looked there were cameras, flashguns, microphones, cords and feet as the media pack converged upon them. The women bowed their heads to avoid the scrum's attention on their short perp walk to the van. They dared not look at the faces belonging to the feet. That would mean looking into the eyes of the journalists, photographers and camera operators who, for the past three months, had painted them as 'hardened-drug traffickers without a conscience' and 'with a lust for money'.

These were the very same journalists who day after day after day attempted to secure 'exclusive' interviews with the women in prison and who, in some cases, upon being refused permission, proceeded nonetheless to file their copy, which was often based on speculation, rumour and 'unnamed sources'.

The journey from the court back to the prison was largely shrouded in silence, punctuated with the women clearing their throats in attempts to stifle their sobs. They were lost in their own thoughts. Each felt as though they were in another dimension, that they were in fact a third person, situated somewhere else, observing the chaos but not actually participating.

Beezie spoke first: 'Why didn't the judge order our deportation? What made him decide against a minimum period of sentence?

Toddie just shook her head. 'Maybe Bob Harkins can give us some answers.'

Press cars sped past their van, racing to the prison to get a last photograph for the afternoon newspapers. The women were locked inside the same bullet-proof prison van which had collected them that morning. Four guards rode shotgun with the driver in the twin cab, while two armed guards occupied a smaller rear cabin. Three police cars escorted the van on its journey to the western suburbs. As the prison vehicle entered the gates at Mulawa, there was another burst of camera flashes. The assembled media shouted questions at the women, protected from the crush by the sanctuary of the van. The main gates opened in time for the vehicle to advance uninterrupted onto the prison grounds, and then the gates quickly closed behind it.

The Drug Grannies were by now well-recognised inmates among the other prisoners at Mulawa, both in the remand wing and in the prison itself. Originally an old public hospital set well back from the main road in sprawling grounds, it was once described by a former head of the state's prison system, Dr Tony Vinson, as 'one of the most ill-conceived prisons imaginable'.

He said of it:

Prisoners ranging from murderers, heroin addicts, white collar thieves, prostitutes and even shoplifters or traffic violators, all shared common dormitories, with about half a dozen solitary confinement cells in two double storey buildings. Several smaller structures on the ground were either unusable, or in the process of renovation, ostensibly for prisoners and their newborns. Cyclone wire fencing surrounded the grounds but for the experienced criminal, foolhardy with desire, it took only a blanket or some clothing draped over the barbed wire fence and it was 'home free'.

For Toddie and Beezie, nothing would ever be home free until they were back in La Pine. Today – 21 April 1978 – they were beginning their fourteen-year sentence for drug smuggling, the start of a sentence which, if they were to survive, would keep them behind bars for 5110 days and nights. They had spent almost eighty days in remand awaiting sentence and it already felt like they were beginning to lose their sanity.

As the women emerged from the prison van, they were escorted straight to the cells they had occupied in the remand section. The officers would wait until the next morning to commence the formal process of transferring them and their possessions to the main prison wing, which housed convicted prisoners formally serving their sentences.

Inmates were preparing for the lunchtime muster, and bulletins over radios in the prison's work and recreation areas were broadcasting news of the American women's sentence. The Drug Grannies had learned soon after their initial incarceration on remand that there was a code: inmates did not ask fellow inmates why they were serving time. With the Americans, though, the code didn't need to apply; the media coverage was so intense that not only all of Mulawa knew of the Drug Grannies and their two tonnes of hashish, but by now all of Australia had heard the news.

Back in their remand wing, the women faced familiar surroundings but it was then that the real shock of the day's proceedings set in. Toddie sat on her bunk. Beezie was with her.

'My God, what's happening to us?' Toddie asked.

Beezie fought back tears and kept wiping her eyes. She went to say something that might console Toddie, but no sooner did she open her mouth than she began to sob; they both began weeping openly. Each understood the hopelessness, the shock and the grief the other was experiencing.

Toddie recorded the women's reaction to their sentence in her diary:

> I kept telling myself this wasn't happening to me. But sadly to say, on awakening, it was for real. I thought to myself: 'Am I too late to pray?' Where did I go wrong, trusting and loving dearly my nephew. Well, that couldn't be. We all came from a very close-knit family and there was no end for our love for each other, but again, it was he who put us here. Lord, I am full of hate and bitterness towards him. This, in turn, won't affect him I am sure, but it is slowly destroying me. I hated my nephew Vern with such a hate that – well, it's hard to explain unless people hate. You don't know what the word really means. You can say you hate someone but when you actually do it, it tears you apart as an individual. It hurt me deep inside; it was such a deep hurt that I couldn't eat, I couldn't sleep, I found myself deteriorating mentally, physically and in every way, and I had to stop. I must stop my hating and turn to love and forgiveness, even though I'm in a place where I should not be. I had to forgive.

That first night after their sentencing, after the lights were out, four officers accompanied by the duty superintendent suddenly appeared at the women's cell. In hushed tones, Toddie and Beezie were told to get up quietly as they were being quickly removed and transferred to the relative isolation of the hospital annexe.

Outside, it was raining steadily. The two Americans, dressed only in their nightclothes, were ushered across yards and open walkways. Both of the women had taken prison-issued sedatives before lights out and were groggy. Toddie needed assistance from two of the officers and hobbled along. She barely registered what was going on around her.

By the time they reached the annexe, they were soaking wet. The hospital had single cells, and the women were separated. The duty superintendent explained they were moving them because they'd become aware of a serious threat to kill them. The hospital cells were the safest place to be inside Mulawa; they could be closely watched and secured in a smaller, confined section.

For the next three days, tranquillisers were dispensed by the prison's nurse and the women remained in the hospital cells for their own safety. The first change to the post-sentence hospital lockdown was the freedom to walk 30 yards (10 metres) to the foyer and back.

•

By now the news of the women's fate had sped around the world, including to Toddie's family. Her younger sibling Hazel phoned on 22 April, acutely aware she might not be able to talk to her sister for long. Toddie wrote in her diary:

> Sister Hazel called from the States. God, what a blessing. For at this point we are both being sedated because of the trauma we have been through. It seems funny to say but the officers here at Mulawa are also in a state of shock as much as we are. No-one can believe it. Hazel's call could not have come at a better time. Sure, we cried a helluva lot, but just to hear my sister's voice lifted our morale 100%. Bless her.

After two weeks of confinement Beezie was moved into Dormitory 1, while Toddie remained in the hospital annexe. Both women had been fearful of the day they would be moved into the prison 'proper'. When that day came, Beezie was anxious. She had heard while on remand that the crims, the heavies of Mulawa, ran Dormitory 1. Theirs was unquestioned authority. If you didn't do what they told you, then you could expect to be beaten up. Word was informally passed by one of the senior guards to a prisoner in Beezie's new quarters to keep a 'look out' for her – to protect her. To that unnamed guard, Beezie was forever grateful.

The Mulawa routine overwhelmed the women. Once lights went out at 10 pm there were often fights, bashings and even rapes, and for Toddie and Beezie it was terrifying.

On the outside, the legal argument for the women continued. Harkins filed notices seeking leave to appeal to the NSW Court of Criminal Appeal. Strategy and planning meetings were to take up much of his time as he prepared the case.

Harkins was, however, mindful the women potentially faced an *increased* sentence of up to twenty-five years' imprisonment if their appeal failed. He believed, as did most of the legal and law enforcement fraternity familiar with the case, the fourteen-year sentence was intended to send a message that Australia was 'getting tough' on drug traffickers.

Though Inspector Drane and Agent Khoury may have viewed the prison sentence as severe, they believed the crime was too. It was the biggest mobile surveillance carried out by the bureau since inception and the seizure reflected the enormity of the operation. It reportedly chewed up between A$250,000 and A$300,000 in staffing and overtime alone.

Had Vern Todd and Phillip Shine been arrested, it would have been a coup of coups for the bureau. However, Drane later claimed there was insufficient evidence to arrest Todd and Shine during Operation Genius. Surveillance on the two men in Sydney – including intercepts on their telephones – had secured valuable evidence. Until legislation was introduced years later, though, phone intercepts were inadmissible as evidence in court. Drane believed Todd had become aware of the surveillance of his home and business premises in Woollahra. Investigators were relying on physical contact to be made by Todd and Shine with the 1.9 tonnes of hashish to be able to make their arrests.

Although the bureau and other police jurisdictions knew from at least four years' intelligence gathering that Todd was a drug kingpin in Australia who imported hashish secreted in vehicles into Australia, he had yet to be seen ever physically taking delivery of even a gram of the drug from any of those importations.

Todd was already a convicted drug criminal. He was not only well known to the Narcotics Bureau, but also to the NSW Police drug squad and numerous overseas law enforcement agencies. As Drane told the women during their interviews, they'd been trying to catch him in the act of an overseas drug importation for years.

In fact, police *had* caught Vern Todd in Australia: twice. Once in June 1974 then again in October 1975. His first arrest, along with Illu Speech and David McDougall (also spelt MacDougall), related to a 20-kilogram (43-pound) cannabis haul. The marijuana originated from Griffith, one of New South Wales' prime cannabis cultivation centres. As was Todd's practice when distributing his local shipments in the early seventies, he would have a small-sized lorry – a one- or two-tonne truck – which had transported the cannabis to Sydney, parked near his office in John Street. Some of his associates' responsibilities were to divide the loads into smaller consignments for dealers in his vast network. One of those dealers was Illu Speech. It was, according to Speech, a wonderful period when there was a lot of money to be made, as well as a lot of fun making the money.

In this particular matter, when the trio was arrested, Speech drove a car containing the 20-kilogram load, headed for the inner-city suburb of Burwood, where his orders were to park in front of a pre-determined kerbside stationary vehicle; he would know it was the right target because the signal was that both front windows would be wound down. The marijuana, in compressed bricks, was in the trunk of Speech's car and after parking, he was to remove the load and discreetly place the bricks through the open windows into the parked vehicle.

As was entered in evidene in the trial at the Waverley Court of Petty Sessions when Speech, McDougall and Todd appeared, both Todd and McDougall were allegedly overseeing the entire operation from the relative safety of a taxi. Unknown to Todd and McDougall, the drug squad was also closely monitoring the operation, and as Speech removed the marijuana bricks, police officers pounced. They arrested all three men, charging them with possession and supply. At the time, Todd had also been suspected of supplying marijuana and hashish to yachts in Sydney Harbour which doubled as floating illegal gambling casinos. Several croupiers who dabbled in prostitution had been arrested and charged, and in their statements to police they all pointed the finger at Todd as a drug supplier to the casinos. Police were keen to apprehend him given the intelligence they were amassing about his criminal activities.

Todd should have appeared before Waverley Court on 27 August 1975, represented by the law firm headed by Phil Roach. But he didn't front the court. His barrister at the trial, Adrian Roden, was in the unenviable position of having to explain why his client had failed to appear on the day. He said it was because of a mix-up in dates, and for this he apologised. It was a committal hearing, where a decision was to be made whether the case should proceed under the jurisdiction of the District Court. Todd's bail – a paltry $200 – was forfeited and the matter was given brief mention.

While a bench warrant was issued for Todd's arrest, an adjournment was sought and granted, allowing the case to be held over until 13 January 1976, when it would once again come before the Waverley Court of Petty Sessions.

While dealing with this matter during the debacle of adjournments and date confusion, Todd was arrested a second time, this time by the Federal Bureau of Narcotics. Agents charged him on 24 October 1975 with being in possession of a prohibited import – cannabis resin from Pakistan. But it was only a small quantity.

At the time, Todd was appearing in an Australian TV soap opera produced by Reg Grundy Productions. When he was arrested, he signed promotional pictures of himself for several of the arresting female narcotics agents. He appeared before a special Federal Court soon after and was fined $250. However, Todd was kept under surveillance because intelligence analysts were beginning to chart vehicle imports and their relation to overseas tourists flying in to collect them. The common denominator was Vern Todd. It appeared, on the face of it, the holidays being taken by these 'tourists' were costly and of only a short duration. Todd and his associates interacted with the 'tourists' on many occasions. Something didn't add up.

When Vern's trial date of 13 January 1976 on the NSW Police charges of possessing and supplying twenty kilograms of cannabis came around, his defence counsel argued that the accused were not suppliers just because of the quantity of marijuana allegedly in their possession. Under the *Poisons Act 1966* section 45C, this quantity was considered a trafficable amount and therefore was considered 'supplying'.

Legal argument ensued, through several courts over several months, on the technical definition of 'supply'. Todd, McDougall and Speech's trial was finally set for 12 May 1978 – almost four years from the trio's original date of arrest.

During this busy period of drug importation and business development, Mr X, Vern's international drug ring partner, arrived in Australia. He stayed in a luxury apartment in Randwick from 1976 to 1977. His rent, electricity, gas and telephone bills were paid for by Todd. It was Mr X who had met Toddie and Beezie in Stuttgart on the pretext he, his wife and their baby would be joining the women on their campervan odyssey. Vern and Mr X travelled extensively around Australia planning drug importations, checking disused airstrips in the Northern Territory and Western Australia, and generally mapping out Australia's likely future consumption patterns of cannabis and cannabis resin.

They were businessmen with an eye on the future.

When Todd's trial finally came up in May 1978, David McDougall was acquitted. Illu Speech took the rap, pleaded guilty and was sentenced to twelve and a half years' imprisonment. Todd failed to appear. Of course the Drug Grannies' bust a few months earlier, in January, had hastened his imperative to abscond.

Vern Todd enjoyed spectacular success avoiding judgement day any time he was called to answer the bell.

McDougall continued to be a leading figure in the original business that Todd started, which had been renamed Tubby Infant Products Ltd. When the original company name was registered with the NSW Corporate Affairs Commission, Todd's occupation was listed as that of actor, and his business partner's as student. In March 1973 McDougall, a manager by occupation, was appointed to the board of directors as the replacement for Todd. He also took up full-time employment with the firm as its manager.

Todd as company secretary held 1500 ordinary shares and so did his partner. By 1977, Todd had an additional fifteen shares. While coordinating the Drug Grannies operation, he also found time to conduct the company's annual general meeting on 30 December 1977. But in 1978, with the case of Vera Todd Hays and Florice Bessire drawing public attention to his name, the company had to protect its profitable trading position. The increased Tubby Bath profile in the United States and Europe couldn't be jeopardised by a director and company secretary connected with an international illegal drug importation business.

On 11 May 1978, Todd's resignation – in absentia – as both company secretary and director was accepted. The accountant, who was also a shareholder with the company since inception, was appointed secretary. David McDougall resigned as the alternate director to Todd, but was immediately reappointed to one of three full-time director positions the company now boasted.

At an extraordinary general meeting on 22 June, a special resolution was passed that the company drop any reference to Vern Todd and its name be changed to Tubby Infant Products.

Curiously, serious media investigations into Vern Todd were largely non-existent at the time of the women's arrest. While there was extensive material on the public record about him, and he was after all a well-known and popular man about town, no journalists seriously pursued his role in the Drug Grannies' case.

•

Prior to the hearing of Toddie's and Beezie's matter before the Criminal Court of Appeal, Bob Harkins arranged a meeting with the Narcotics Bureau, and the Crown Solicitor's Office. Attending the meeting were Harvey Bates, director of the Narcotics Bureau, who flew up from Canberra especially for the session; the NSW regional commander of the bureau, Inspector Tom Mulally; and Greg Smith, of the deputy Crown solicitor's office, who had successfully prosecuted several similar cases. Harkins's objective at the meeting was to ensure that the bureau's hierarchy recognised the seriousness of the allegations of Drane's undertakings on deportation Hays and Bessire were continuing to make, including in their forthcoming appeal.

During the discussion, Harkins highlighted what he considered was the severe head sentence (fourteen years), and the lack of a non-parole period. This of course was not the bureau's doing; it was a judge alone who had come to that decision. Harkins pointed out the Americans' sentence exceeded even a life sentence. Most lifers only served eight to ten years in New South Wales and were then paroled. He said if Hays and Bessire continued with the appeal, the court would be told of the alleged inducement by the bureau's agent.

Harkins also shared with the meeting attendees the possibility the women might withdraw the appeal and instead throw themselves upon the mercy of the Governor-General to release them on licence at an appropriate time. Release on licence was like parole, but it relied on the disposition of one person: the federal Attorney-General. He could either recommend a Commonwealth prisoner's release on licence to the Governor-General, or not. There was no standardised system for this form of early release – as there was for parole for most prisoners charged under state and territory laws – so it was a long shot for any prisoner.

Reassuringly, Bates said the bureau would not interfere if a non-parole period was secured on appeal. The meeting lasted almost an hour.

Following the meeting, Harkins met with the two women and told them the decision whether to appeal was now up to them. While they considered their options, the 1.9-tonne haul of hashish from the women's campervan went up in smoke at a specially supervised destruction the bureau conducted. The media attended but was kept at a safe distance.

Commendations from the federal government to Inspector Drane and his team members who apprehended the women soon followed.

•

The women were reluctantly adapting to their new routine in the convicted prisoners' wing, which began each morning at 7.10 am. Toddie and Beezie would have their breakfast and be ready to leave on the prison bus at 7.30 am for the short ride to the Parramatta Linen Service (PLS). PLS serviced all of the public hospitals as well as all of the prisons in metropolitan Sydney. Roll call before and after breakfast enabled a quick head count to ensure there had been no escapes. A third muster at the main gate followed before the prisoners boarded the bus. The women had opted to work at PLS partly because it took them off-site to give them a change of scenery, and because it paid the best wages. Sweepers, dorm cleaners and gardeners earned a meagre $2.50 per week; kitchen helpers, laundry workers and reception staff received $5.50 each week; PLS women were paid a relatively handsome $14.70 weekly.

There were usually between forty and forty-five women prisoners at PLS each day. Half of them worked on sewing machines in a sub-basement producing and repairing sheets, pillowcases, tea towels, nappies, pyjamas, dressing gowns and uniforms. The remainder worked upstairs where the industrial washers, dryers and sorting tables were located. Toddie and Beezie were assigned to a sorting table handling the washing after a first cycle, determining whether it was ready for drying, or needed further attention. Toddie noted in her diary:

> The stuff comes to us on dollies that hold 16 bags, and each bag weighs from 30–75 pounds. It's really too heavy for us but we manage. It's better than running a sewing machine day after day and making the same thing day in and day out. I know I ran a machine for a while making damn pillow cases. Now I'm happy on the job I'm on. HAPPY? My God, what am I saying? I'm supposed to be retired and here we are working six and a half days a week for $14.70 per week. We thought slave labor went out with the turn of the century.

As they further surrendered to their prison life, they began to look forward to diversions to their daily routines: appointments with the doctor, or dentist, or their lawyer. This offered them the hope that something – anything – might break the monotony and keep them in touch with the real world outside the confines of the prison.

On 9 June 1978, Vera was referred to a neurosurgeon for an opinion on her back condition. In May she had been fitted with a brace and special orthopaedic shoes. Spasms continued to affect her left leg until she fell again and was bedridden for three days before the specialist referral.

Later in June, US Consul General Ralph Jones contacted Bob Harkins to say he was considering lodging a démarche with the Australian government to protest the women's sentence. Harkins offered to prepare a draft including points to raise. Writing in the name of the ambassador, Jones would likely seek confirmation that his nation's citizens had not been disadvantaged compared with local offenders facing the same charges. It was important to the US government that its citizens were not being discriminated against in an Australian court simply because of their foreign citizenship. The fact a non-parole period was not imposed was a key point of discrimination. This was not a matter of interfering in a sovereign nation's laws; rather, it was an issue of just and equal treatment before the eyes of the law. Ambassador Philip Alston in Canberra opted to hold off lodging the démarche until after the appeal outcome. He didn't want to appear to be seeking to unduly influence the court.

Toddie's examination – the medical attention Judge Staunton had ordered be afforded the prisoner when he handed down the sentence – was undertaken by a visiting neurosurgeon at Lidcombe Hospital in Sydney's western suburbs. Unexpectedly, it was performed in the presence of a class of interns. It was an unconventional consultation for Toddie, the likes of which she had never experienced. She was undressed to her undergarments facing the group while they studied her x-rays and compared them to her aged spine. The specialist sent his report to prison authorities, and a copy to Harkins.

The report was lukewarm and skipped over most of Toddie's extensive medical history. The examining doctor wasn't particularly convinced of Toddie's ailments or of their claimed impact on her quality of life. This was to be the start of a string of medical interactions with doctors and specialists whose competence Toddie questioned. But she was discovering very quickly that as a prisoner she had few, or at times, no rights; she certainly didn't have the right to choose her own doctors.

Harkins's strategy to argue an appeal primarily based on the alleged inducements the Narcotics Bureau agents held out to the women was not fully supported by the women's barrister, Jack Hiatt, QC. He feared that publicly accusing the bureau of offering inducements – after the matter had been denied and resolved in the original hearing – could backfire. The women's lawyers finally agreed not to use alleged inducements but, rather, to focus the appeal on three other cases – and the length of those sentences handed down – where the accused were foreign citizens, had committed serious offences, but whose sentences *had* included a non-parole period.

The argument Harkins planned to take to the Criminal Court of Appeal was that Judge Staunton had erred in law by failing to impose a non-parole period on the basis of the women's US citizenship. Owing to Hiatt's heavy case load, the earliest he was available for the appeal hearing was not until 9 September.

By now, Beezie had reached her 62nd birthday. It was no different to the anticlimax of Toddie's 60th. There was no celebration.

On 5 July, almost three months after their sentencing, Toddie's brother Vernon Sr – father of the nephew responsible for his aunt's and Beezie's predicament – wrote a letter to Tubby Bath director David McDougall. Vernon Sr and his wife were shareholders in their son's company.

The handwritten letter read:

Dear David,

I am sure you are aware that my sister, Vera and her friend Beezie are in the Sydney prison. I was wondering if possible you might contact her for me and see if there is anything we might be able to do to help them. It would be most appreciated, and I would be most grateful to you. They are in the Silverwater Prison. Hope you can see them in person.
P.S. Please let me hear from you.

When McDougall received the letter he contacted his lawyers. They advised he contact the women's solicitor, Robert Harkins, and forward it to him. When the letter from brother Vernon Sr turned up at Mulawa, Toddie read it and then filed it away. She was still fuming about her nephew's ruse that had put her in prison, but at the same time she was torn by the painful realisation that he was her brother's own offspring – he was family.

•

When finally the women's appeal came before Justice Yeldham of the NSW Court of Criminal Appeal, the women were to surprise not only the media – expecting another field day filled with sensation and intrigue – but also their family and friends in the United States who were hoping they would be released. Jack Hiatt, QC, formally withdrew the appeal, after anxious consideration and conference with the women. The prisoners had decided, he said, 'to appeal to Caesar'. Subsequently, notices of abandonment of the appeal were signed and the matter was dismissed.

The decision to drop the appeal was a difficult one. There was always the risk of a lengthier sentence being imposed and/ or that an inordinately long period of non-parole would be set. There was also the risk of whipping up further abuse targeting the women in the hostile Australian media. Conversely, the women's legal team believed there was as good a chance an application to the Governor-General seeking their release on licence might succeed. The reality, however, of intervention by the Queen's representative in Australia was that it always relied on advice from the relevant minister – the Attorney-General – whose government's anti-drug laws were what Judge Staunton so effectively utilised in his sentencing of the women.

In fact, in late 1978, Harkins was already exploring the best timing for an application to the Governor-General for the women's early release. In December, he wrote to the women explaining that it could be detrimental to their cause if an application was lodged prior to a date where there was the prospect of success. The Attorney-General's Department's policy on such applications was for Commonwealth prisoners to serve at least one third of their sentence – in Toddie's and Beezie's case that would be four and a half years – before they should even *consider* seeking early release, unless there were exceptional circumstances.

Harkins wrote: 'However I am of the view there is *a good chance* release may occur after one quarter of your sentence is served.' It was something to which they could cling, but only eight months into their fourteen-year term, that strategy seemed at best tenuous, at worst untenable.

It had become clear to Toddie and Beezie that they faced a unique set of challenges. They were foreigners, and Americans; a nationality with which Australians shared a complicated love/hate relationship. They were tarred by their association with their drug kingpin nephew, and they faced lengthy non-parole sentences as federal prisoners in a state-managed prison system without the protections and community release provisions afforded state prisoners. They were women with complex health needs due to their age.

Was it any wonder they felt vulnerable and abandoned?

Before the decision not to proceed with their appeal, a surprise visitor turned up at Mulawa one day: Narcotics Bureau agent Michele Khoury. The three women had a good cry together. Khoury kept telling the pair she was sorry for the way things had turned out. 'It wasn't supposed to be this way,' she said. Toddie reassured her that after months of hell, she had begun a lot of soul-searching:

First I know I have to rid myself of the hatred I feel for my nephew Vern before I can bow my head in prayer. This accomplished, I will begin to feel better, but the walls are closing in on me, with the riots, screaming, women sexually assaulting and attacking women. This I cannot comprehend and I may lose my sanity soon. The only way I can cope is to completely shut it all out of my mind.

It seemed Toddie was also telling Khoury, and indirectly Drane, that she no longer harboured resentment towards them either, for putting them behind bars. In order to preserve her sanity, she couldn't allow any hate to occupy space in her heart.

'I can only begin to be free if I forgive,' Toddie said.

CHAPTER FOURTEEN
KILL THOSE DAMNED YANKS

The names Vern Leonard Todd and Phillip Richard Shine (as well as any known aliases, including Vern Anthony and Bob Lange) were circulated among Interpol member countries following the arrest and imprisonment of the Drug Grannies. Both names were especially well known in West Germany, and Todd had already come under the scrutiny of the Federal Bureau of Investigation (FBI) in Los Angeles following his 1975 drug conviction in Australia. Similarly, the US Drug Enforcement Agency (DEA) had Todd flagged as a 'drug smuggling suspect' and noted he was possibly residing in Australia or South America.

A major break in the Todd–Shine organisation came through a tip-off to Interpol from an overseas law enforcement agency in 1978. Intelligence sources carefully guarded the exact origins of the tip-off because of the informant's ongoing value to them. The source had been suspected of being involved in a major shipment of drugs to North America. The haul of several hundred kilograms of hashish ingeniously packed inside forklift wheels – a tell-tale sign it was one of the preferred modus operandi of the Todd–Shine syndicate – originated in Bombay and was detected by a Royal Canadian Mounted Police narcotics officer. During the investigation, information came to light which resulted in police being directed to someone called 'Shane' or 'Shine' residing in Paris.

Telex messages from Canadian intelligence reached French police and the first major breakthrough tracking the organisation's ringleaders came with Shine's arrest on 21 December 1978 in Paris. He was living under a false name and carrying a fake Australian passport. He had been a well-known figure among Sydney's entertainment and nightclub set for the high-quality hashish, cannabis and sometimes even cocaine he supplied in the early seventies. He was also Vern Todd's right-hand man in Europe and at times in Australia.

West German authorities succeeded in a French extradition hearing securing Shine's return to West Germany to face charges there of drug smuggling. Information that narcotics police in Frankfurt and Berlin had secured, which was later supported by evidence from the Drug Grannies, bolstered the West Germans' confidence of a successful prosecution.

Mrs X, daughter of a wealthy Berlin doctor and wife of Vern's confidante Mr X, had also been arrested six months earlier, on 13 June 1978. Her trial uncovered important evidence in relation to the entire network. Before West German authorities, led by prosecutor Dr Harald Körner, could secure a conviction of Mrs X, she was able to delay the trial through a 'medical absence'. Her lawyers secured an adjournment and Mrs X, at the time approaching her 26th birthday, was released on bail.

When Shine first came to trial in Frankfurt on 22 May 1979, Mrs X was summonsed to appear as a prosecution witness. Her evidence against what the West Germans described as the 'Drahtzieher' (drug boss) Shine was important. She, however, fled midway through the first week of the hearing. Her defence counsel produced a medical certificate stating she was ill in Nepal receiving specialist treatment for dysentery. They said she could not travel back to Germany, and required constant medical attention to overcome her illness.

Meanwhile in prison in Sydney, the Drug Grannies began meeting other inmates who claimed they too had been duped – by relatives, boyfriends or even husbands – into unknowingly carrying items loaded with drugs, often heroin, as its availability increased and demand for it in Australia grew. Ignorant of what they were carrying into Australia, they were similarly intercepted, arrested and jailed for many years. Toddie recorded in her diary:

> There are a lot of funny incidents and a lot of sad ones, and a lot of scary ones when we look back at what's happened to us since we left La Pine. There is a lot of stuff we hope we can offer to help other people – especially at our age – or even youngsters to watch out for which they're doing with their loved ones and kinfolk or anybody for that matter, so as not to be duped. We are seeing now so much of this happening in jail. There are plenty of young girls to testify to the stories about carrying a suitcase for someone, not knowing there was anything illegal contained inside, and all of a sudden being picked up. The big man has vanished in the meantime. It's very heartbreaking to see.

Also heartbreaking were the incidents occurring around the pair inside jail. They were becoming more and more aware of the rapes among women, of bashings, of women having their hair viciously pulled or forcibly shaved, of others being attacked with scalding water. The victims' injuries were hard to ignore. The language was the foulest they had ever heard – from men or women – and Toddie and Beezie thought they'd heard some pretty colourful epithets in their time in the services and on assembly lines. The invective and menace of many of the inmates' language shocked the women to their core.

Most prisoners didn't quite know how to react to the Americans. The reason for their incarceration was impossible to conceal; their accents, their size (especially Toddie's height) and their likeability meant the Americans weren't easy to pigeonhole. They certainly were never able to fly under the general Mulawa prison population's radar.

Their age, maturity and prior experience in positions of authority equipped them with the skills needed to handle the personalities of some of the prison guards. The older and more mature officers treated the women in a respectable manner, unlike many of the younger and inexperienced guards who mishandled the Americans. Toddie and Beezie quickly told the latter what they thought and, when required, where they should go, leaving the guards speechless.

The women's lives were still in danger, and they all – guards and the Americans – had to be ready for anything. On several occasions, gangs established outside the prison continued to maintain their cliques inside the jail. They tested the women's mettle several times. On one occasion, Beezie – all five foot four (1.6 metres) of her – was cornered by several women, but, unbowed, she picked up a shovel and swung it high in the air, inviting any and all of the gang to make the first move.

The next time Beezie met one of them alone, she suggested to the gang member that now they were one on one, she might like to settle her differences. Beezie's fists were clenched, and even though she was sixty-two years old, she still felt she could sock a punch if she had to. Her opponent declined the offer, and quickly left the scene.

Toddie described Beezie in a diary entry: 'Beezie is small, but dynamite. She is given a wide berth. They won't fight one on one; they fight in wolf packs but she's not foolish enough to enter their brawls.'

On another occasion, Toddie described the horror she had witnessed after prisoners had been bashed:

The results of the bashings are horrible. They are cut with broken glass, teeth knocked out, black eyes and broken bones. The officers are never around when this happens. The victims never inform on the ones responsible which is understandable as you might not fare so good the next night.

Other prisoners had already threatened to bash the two Americans. Toddie described one experience she had early in their time at Mulawa to a US reporter:

Beezie and I were standing there when we were fronted by the prison heavy. I said, 'Look, if you're gonna hit me, you'd better make it a good one because if I get up off the floor, you won't know what happened to you. When I get through with you you'll never get off the floor. I've got a black belt at home and being in the services two years and in the police academy in Los Angeles, I have learned judo and karate. But don't tell anybody else. Don't let it get around.' And in less than five minutes, over 100 women all knew. And they sort of walked around us from then on.

It didn't stop Toddie from often sleeping with a screwdriver under her pillow – as a trusted prisoner, she had access to tools. However, on one occasion Toddie got into a heated argument which almost erupted in violence. She wrote:

Well it was bound to happen. I finally got into a big verbal fight with the ex-representative of our dorm. We both eat at the same table and she sits opposite me. Next to her sits her lover that looks and acts like a man. If you didn't know better you would wonder what in the hell a man was doing in a women's prison. Everyone here is afraid of this big butch, but I couldn't care less. Then she says to me: 'One of the old timers has just returned and I advise you to be careful. You and Beezie are the heavies upstairs in the dorm and I think they'll put her up in your wing.' I told her she was wrong about Beezie and me being 'heavies'. She came back at me with the foulest language: 'You fuckin' cunts are always complaining about the loud noises and running to the officers with everything.' By this time our voices are getting louder and there was complete silence in the dining room. I told her she was 'a God-damned son-of-a-bitching liar'. She gave me a thumb up gesture and in return I gave her the good old middle finger Yankee salute.

The argument carried on for another five minutes, but without any physical confrontation. And not a single prison guard intervened. It was an example of the prisoners' code in action.

The only visits the women had in the first year of their imprisonment were from members of church-affiliated prisoner support and fellowship groups. Toddie and Beezie were hesitant about the media but an interview with a visiting American TV crew which arrived without notice was to provide them with the opportunity to recount their experiences and explain how their lives had changed. They told Oregon-based reporter David Jackson they were now doing 'God's work in jail'.

There was also an unannounced visit by US newspaper columnist Eric Robinson, a retired pastor of the United Methodist Church, who wrote in the *Oregonian*:

> They said that although they feel discouraged and depressed at times, they were treated well by the authorities. They told me there were a few hard cases in with them – bossy types trying to rule the roost and take over leadership. The women said 'We've learned a lot here. First, we're learning patience.'

Some of those hard cases were to be the cause of tension and later a riot during Toddie and Beezie's incarceration at Mulawa.

The first Christmas in jail was, they both agreed, a farce. No-one knew or understood the true meaning of the day, the women felt. Forced to remain in the dining room for three hours after lunch and dinner to listen to hard rock and 'watch idiots dance', with terrible food to boot, the Americans were unimpressed.

There was no shortage of 'insider' information. Toddie was to hear one day from a fellow inmate of her nephew Vern's reputation. 'You're the thirtieth person who has told me they knew my nephew,' Vera said to a young woman, 'and all of you can thank him for being inside.' More than once there was talk of a rumoured contract out on his life because people were doing *his* time in jail.

The lows far outnumbered the rare highs, but Toddie's second birthday celebration in 1979 wasn't as bad as her first in jail; by then she and Beezie had fostered some camaraderie among other inmates who organised a celebration. There were cards and small presents. They set up a table in the dormitory with food and gifts: cigarettes (they were like gold), hand-crocheted mats, pillows and macramé. It helped Toddie appreciate the number of friends they had made inside. She and Beezie were confident they could pick the 'good guys' from the 'bad guys', as they called them.

On one occasion, Toddie was held back late in the day to offer evidence in defence of an officer accused of assault, whose supervisor was seeking a quick resolution. Toddie's explanation of what she saw, which supported the officer's version of events, was accepted. This sort of action often led to the women being labelled 'screw lovers' by some of the hardened inmates.

The lows they experienced didn't always involve the pair directly, but were nonetheless deeply distressing. Two days after Toddie's birthday, a young prisoner was raped by three other inmates. It was the third such attack in a year. Some of the 'bad guys' were animals, Toddie said. Following the attack, sympathetic guards approached Toddie and Beezie and asked them to take under their wing two young women – aged only eighteen and twenty-four – who had just arrived.

Beezie wrote about the law of the prison jungle in her diary:

The heavies, the toughs try to run the jail within the system to enforce their way of thinking on the other women. They run in wolf packs, and are evil women. Think filth, talk filth, smuggle in drugs – then have the junkies make their beds, clean their rooms, do their washing, buy things for them on their buy-ups, gang rape weaklings who dare to defy them. The woman who has been attacked usually winds up in the hospital in pain, and hysterical, and left with a deep-seated fear. The terrible part of this whole situation is that the women never inform on the inmates responsible; they know they can't stay in the hospital forever and once she has been returned to her respective wing, the danger of being attacked again is more than doubled. Toddie and I have escaped this treatment even though we have been threatened countless times. Because of our age, they are afraid of reprisals by the other women and officers in the system. We've never backed down from them or acted afraid, so they go find another victim.

It was always a low when bad heroin surfaced, usually smuggled by visitors into the jail. Toddie and Beezie knew immediately that a bad batch of smack was in circulation when the junkie inmates began vomiting at random – on beds, footpaths, and up and down the stairs.

Gradually the Americans earned the respect of other prisoners and officers and had their pay increased in recognition of their skills. They cleaned old isolation cells which needed to be used for difficult prisoners; they hacksawed through bolts to refurbish grilles and wire mesh ... and they continued to be called 'screw lovers' by the bad guys.

Time and experience quickly taught the women that outwitting the junkies and befriending the officers was the safest form of survival. When the first drug raid was made on the prison, the women realised how serious the heroin situation had become. Specially trained officers with sniffer dogs from the NSW Corrective Service tore through each room. It looked like a tornado had hit the dormitories. They didn't find any drugs.

After separating the prisoners from Dormitory 1 and 2 into their groups and resettling them, the superintendent hoped the tense situation in the overcrowded buildings might defuse.

But shortly after 10 pm that night, when the lights were out, a riot erupted at Mulawa. The inmates on the second floor broke a window above their door and crawled through to the hallway downstairs, and soon were outside Toddie and Beezie's dorm trying to break out. The Americans peeked through their overhead window and could see women were escaping into the yard. One of the prisoners was armed with a long shard of glass. The rioters seemed clearly intent on causing maximum destruction and stabbing or slashing anyone who tried to stop them.

Toddie later made detailed notes in her diary about the event:

We had the biggest riot of all time. At least five inmates were involved. They had broken out of the upstairs dorm and had broken the window above the door downstairs and one of the inmates escaped. They thought they had blocked out our vision on the small window on our door where Beezie and I observed the goings-on. I reached over and switched on the alarm. Now when the alarm is turned on, the officers come running as it is usually because someone is very sick and the first thing they do is open the dorm front door. We could see what was going to happen. One inmate had a piece of glass about 10 inches long and three inches wide. She had gloves on and was holding it like a knife, ready to slash and stab. The other inmate had unwound the fire hose and the nozzle, and she was swinging it like a mace. We immediately went to Beezie's room and stopped the first prison officer, Mrs Lopez, who was running by and told her to stop the other two officers Mrs Brain and Ms Campbell, who were approaching the door, because the girls were waiting there to kill them. We told her to get male officers from the adjoining complex at Silverwater. They returned to their posts and put in the alarm for back up. Beezie and I returned to the door to hear the rioting inmates say 'it was probably those God-damned Yanks and we will kill them for this'. What we did was simply because there were fellow human beings whose lives were endangered.

Several of the rioters were high on heroin. The male prison guards were unable to regain control so a police SWAT team was also called in. It took until 3.30 am for the heavily armed contingent to force its way through the dormitory's front door. The rioters had returned to the second floor and could be heard smashing furniture. With a heavy dose of pepper spray combined with the waning effects of the heroin on their stamina, the group of hold-outs was restrained and placed in single high-security cells. Four had already passed out. A doctor was called but no intervention was required. It had been a black Friday – 13 July.

Toddie and Beezie were credited with saving the lives of the three prison officers, but never received formal recognition, other than from within the small circle of those who knew of their bravery. The women were immediately reclassified by the state prison service and considered for remissions. The reclassification was endorsed by the superintendent, and the department's head office agreed. However, because they were Commonwealth offenders, any reclassification or offer of remission was meaningless. The federal Attorney-General's Department had no policy or program which recognised federal prisoners' acts of bravery.

At about this time, plans were underway to open Tomago women's detention centre, almost 150 miles (240 kilometres) north-west of Sydney, where only the state's best-behaved female prisoners would be transferred. Tomago is an Aboriginal word that means 'away from the tribe', and each inmate was to have their own room contained within a row of cabins. Nothing but bush surrounded them.

Before Toddie and Beezie were even considered for transfer, they faced yet another element of prison 'justice'. An inmate standing at the back of the dining room aimed and then propelled a home-made knife a distance of about thirty feet (nine metres) at the Americans. The blade whistled past Toddie's left ear, just missing her head. Toddie and Beezie were unnerved by the attack. Their actions foiling the riot apparently had not been forgotten.

The first attempt to transfer the women to Tomago in late July 1979 was cancelled at the last minute. The women's bags had been packed in readiness for the trip and two new prisoners were already in the process of being assigned Toddie's and Beezie's quarters at Mulawa when the order inexplicably came to halt the planned relocation to their new digs. The women were returned to their old dormitory, but a week later, on 5 August, they were again told to pack their bags for the transfer north.

They learned from their jail escorts that during the first attempt police and prison intelligence had become aware of a plan to kidnap the women during the four-hour drive by car, much of it through winding, slow-moving country roads. The authorities weren't going to take any chances. Toddie had recently provided assistance to a West German narcotics investigator who had covertly travelled to Australia to speak to her at Mulawa. There were rumours that word had once again leaked of her cooperation with the overseas investigators. Nothing was ever secret inside the jail, between the loose lips of officers and the inmate grapevine-fed gossip from the outside.

While the women were not suspected of being involved in any kidnap plan, information gleaned through intelligence sources led authorities to believe Vern Todd had learned about the women's transfer. He might not have been in Australia, but his tentacles reached far and wide. The authorities feared he or his associates might see the transfer as an opportunity to arrange an ambush of the prison vehicle in order to kidnap the women. It was not as far-fetched as it sounded, and concerns of the distinct possibility Todd was not only intent on, but capable of, successfully pulling off such an attack were to surface again in the coming months.

Toddie and Beezie's move to Tomago was a positive step for them in many ways. The prisoners at Tomago were all first offenders, none had committed crimes of violence, and in most cases were mature women who respected the jail system and what it was trying to do for them. The change from the harsh confines of maximum to minimum security brought great relief.

The two women wrote home of their surroundings shortly after arriving at Tomago, and Toddie summed it up this way:

> Tomago is just beautiful – for a jail. It's in a rural area and the most important thing is we can see out, there are no other buildings around. It is free and country clean air, the front gate is open all day! In fact I work out on the highway and it's just beautiful. The boss's office is outside the gate, and I tend her flower bed and keep the front area looking tidy and respectable. The dining room and kitchen area are also outside the main gate and the perimeter fence. It's hard to describe, but it's just a good feeling.

On arrival, they joined twenty-one other women prisoners already in place, and were assigned adjacent rooms, which featured no carpeting on the floor and thin curtains with no backing. They went to the stores area to pick the right size of prison-issue clothing comprising three floral dresses in different patterns, three pairs of cotton underpants, three cotton bras, a petticoat, floral nighties, denim slacks, pinafores, t-shirts, shoes and sandals.

They shared communal showers and ablutions. They could work in the kitchen and earn $3.50 per week, or in the stores and earn $5 each week. And they were allowed to make one phone call weekly.

Tomago was kind to the Drug Grannies, both mentally and physically. They said they could be fooled into thinking it was almost a motel. The big difference was that once booked in, they could never leave. They did not have their freedom.

The women wrote in their diaries that following the brutal and confronting daily behaviour at Mulawa, conditions at Tomago were a huge contrast. The women were still well aware they were incarcerated, but they were treated in a more humane fashion – most likely due to the fact the women there were model prisoners. Beezie said it gave her a sense of being out of jail.

> It's unreal. We have our privacy. This is so important and one thing we never had at Mulawa. The food is much better and HOT and we have both put on weight. We can wear our own jeans, underclothes, shoes etc. On weekends you can take out from your locker more of your personal clothes if you're having a special visit or you just plain wish to dress up. Toddie and I get $4.50 per week each … the areas we maintain are huge but it keeps our day full and active and as long as we are busy we are happy – well, as happy as can be expected under the circumstances. The biggest hardship is we don't have our family or loved ones here, and we can't go home.

The pair – New South Wales's oldest female prisoners – enjoyed a well-earned reputation as being the best-behaved and hardest-working of all female prisoners, but their positive disposition and attitude masked a darker, underlying homesickness that changed their outlook on life. It wasn't always easy to stay motivated and committed to the mundane tasks assigned to them. They lived each day hoping and praying to return to their beloved United States, and the posters, pictures and memories from home which adorned the walls of their rooms in some ways both distracted them from the horror of incarceration and yet fostered their angst.

But Toddie and Beezie were keen to help make the Tomago Detention Centre a success. The local Tomago Progress Association had gathered 1000 signatures for a petition against the jail's establishment before it opened, but a proactive superintendent and head office hierarchy decided engagement head-on was their best strategy. So in addition to providing a kitchen and prisoners-as-cooks for the local community's ever-expanding Meals on Wheels Service for Raymond Terrace–Medowie–Tomago, they also hosted a 'dining in' evening for about sixty guests from the local community, local government and social services. It was the first time the centre had been opened to the public since it had become fully operational with a full complement of prisoners and staff.

'We are just normal people, we have done wrong, and we are now paying for it,' one of the inmates told the dinner gathering before they tucked into the smorgasbord on offer. 'The worst thing for us is to be separated from our families, but this is our home for the time being. We can't do it without your help. Please give us a chance,' she said.

Toddie's love of sport led to the prisoners also forming teams to compete in the local soccer, netball and softball competitions.

In September 1979, an American art curator, Allison Ann Kuliman, was transferred to Tomago after a stint in Mulawa. She was convicted of possessing seven kilograms (fifteen pounds) of hash she had smuggled into Australia in suitcases. Kuliman, who was only twenty and single, was given a non-parole period of eighteen months.

The fact the new prisoner had been given a non-parole period irked Toddie and Beezie. It further reminded them of the unfairness of the Australian legal system. They didn't begrudge Kuliman's 'good fortune', but here was a foreigner committing a drug offence and being granted a non-parole period.

US consul officials in Sydney in conjunction with Jack Hiatt, QC, and solicitor Claude Bilinsky, were meanwhile working on a submission seeking early release for the women, through official channels in Canberra. Harkins had taken twelve months' leave to travel overseas and was no longer officially on the women's case though he maintained a watching brief.

•

It was around this time – nearing the end of 1979 – that I made my first contact with Toddie and Beezie. At the time (having returned to Australia from living and working abroad), I was freelancing for local and overseas news publications, and my first request, by phone, for access to visit them was refused because of the women's specific instructions, scrawled in bold capital letters on their files: NO PRESS. So I wrote to them at Tomago, introducing myself, offering to drive up and visit to at least get the facts. Persistence paid off when the women granted their first interview to a local journalist since their arrest.

The timing of my approach to the women coincided with the announcement that the Federal Bureau of Narcotics was to be disbanded and its law enforcement work transferred to the Australian Federal Police. Toddie and Beezie showed little concern at that development, although they followed with cursory interest the findings of an interim report of the Williams royal commission of Inquiry into Drugs which named a raft of drug kingpins, including Vern Todd.

In reality, the women's curiosity in Vern and his criminal activities had waned. While Toddie had dealt with her hatred of him by moving on, she found it was best he no longer occupied any real estate in her thoughts, or her emotions. He simply didn't matter anymore.

As a journalist, my initial contact with the women was out of professional curiosity, but as time passed our relationship grew and their trust of me, and mine of them, developed. They welcomed my regular visits. Our interactions grew to become a close, personal friendship with shared objectives: justice and freedom. The women began to share their doubts regarding the legal advice they had received and were continuing to receive; about 'promises' they believed had been made to them that if they didn't rock the boat they would be released soon; and about their fears for the future given their advanced age.

With the women's encouragement, I contacted Bob Harkins, who told me he believed the women faced a difficult time ahead because overseas pressure was now being brought to have them testify against Phillip Shine, who was on trial in Germany. This was something which could be arranged far more easily if they remained in custody in an Australian prison.

The women didn't know what to think. Toddie's diary entry reflected this uncertainty:

> We have been promised from one month to the next we would be released. That's why we didn't fight too much because every month that came around, our solicitor said they would be putting in for our release on licence and we should sit tight and wait. I hate that term 'sit tight'. In 1978 then, they said it was too early to apply for release on licence and we'd be wasting our time. It was not to be until 1979, they said. Then in 1979, both Hiatt and Bilinsky came to visit us at Tomago and told us we could expect to be home by the summer of 1980 – and they meant our [American] summer which was, we thought, around June some time. So we didn't push, we tried to do our best and stay within the scope of things. The system has built us up and then dropped us back down with a heavy thud. They have promised us things and then jerked the rug out from underneath. You're almost scared to have hope in anything anymore.

On 8 December 1979, Mr X, accused by West German authorities in their pursuit of Shine and Todd for masterminding attempts to smuggle hashish, appeared in a Bombay magistrate's court. It was alleged he had bought several Mercedes-Benz campervans in Berlin in which he planned to hide and transport the cannabis resin. Indian, West German and Australian police were interested in interviewing him because of his international drug-smuggling connections. West German authorities pressed for his extradition to face charges in West Germany.

If West German police were looking forward to the prosecution of one of the Todd–Shine kingpins, they were disappointed, for within a fortnight Mr X had slipped through the Indian authorities' well-greased palms and escaped. The Drug Grannies were the West Germans' best bet to nail the leaders of the drug ring. 'Keep them in jail' was the unofficial policy of the Australian government.

•

Christmas 1979 was approaching. It was the women's third Yuletide away from family but it turned out to be an unexpected opportunity to enjoy the delights of American delicacies which had arrived in a specially vacuum-sealed parcel from a family member in Virginia. The regular correspondence from the women's siblings and friends, as well as 'letter cassettes', were a constant lifeline for them. Writing letters home was like having a personal conversation. They cherished the time they spent writing as they could, if they tried, feel like they were in the company of the loved ones with whom they were corresponding.

The jail's superintendent bent the rules normally prohibiting food gifts to prisoners and allowed the women their Christmas present, especially as the items were wrapped and sealed. The only condition he set on the package's release was that the women share the contents among all of the inmates at Tomago.

Toddie and Beezie were more than happy to spread the joy of their unexpected Christmas bounty.

PART FOUR

THE FIGHT FOR FREEDOM

CHAPTER FIFTEEN

AN EYE FOR AN EYE AND A QUEEN'S AMNESTY?

Beezie was assigned the position of head gardener at Tomago. Several other younger female prisoners worked with her, helping to maintain the grounds. Both Beezie and Toddie took pride in their work and the 'if you do a job, then do it properly' ethic by which they were raised was ingrained in their characters. Neither were strangers to hard work and long hours during their many years of employment.

On one afternoon in mid-January 1980, while working in the garden, Beezie noticed a row of healthy seedlings with serrated leaves, about four to six inches (ten to fifteen centimetres) in height. They weren't of a species Beezie recognised and they were certainly not something she had planted. But she had her suspicions, so without saying anything she left them there, but for the next few days she discreetly observed the small patch from a distance to see if anyone was tending it.

Approaching dusk one evening a week later she noticed one of the prisoners move in the direction of the plot and bend down, appearing to tend the suspect patch. After the inmate left the garden area, Beezie joined up with her and fell into step as they headed across the lawn back to the buildings. Beezie casually approached her to find out what was going on. 'They're my marijuana plants, Beezie; don't you know that?' said Allison, the recently arrived American prisoner.

'You're taking quite a risk growing that in jail, aren't you?' Beezie said. This was the first time in her life she had seen the actual plant for which she and Toddie were now serving a fourteen-year sentence.

'Well, they don't know what it is, and even if they only get to grow to half their height, I'll be able to pull them up, dry them, and have something to smoke without the guards even knowing,' Allison explained. Beezie simply shook her head and said, 'Allison, don't risk that sort of foolish behaviour – you have a lot to lose if you get caught.' Beezie hoped her admonishment would best resonate if she said nothing further; it was not her business.

Two weeks later, Beezie heard on the rumour mill an alert officer had seen the now well-established marijuana patch. She was apparently monitoring the garden plot too. The prisoner was eventually busted, hauled before the superintendent and severely reprimanded.

One morning in February 1980, without warning, Toddie and Beezie were told to prepare for a trip to a Sydney jail for a legal matter at which their presence was required. They had no idea that there was to be a court hearing at which they would be expected to give evidence.

The drive to Sydney gave them time to find out more from their escorting officers. Apparently they were headed to a specially convened West German court, hearing charges against Phillip Shine. Australian authorities had given the Germans permission to convene the special hearing to take Toddie's and Beezie's evidence. But the authorities had neither consulted nor informed the women or their lawyers.

'We have been shanghaied,' Beezie whispered to Toddie in the car. 'They can't do this, can they? They've given us no warning about this hearing and we have no legal representation or anything. We have been led up the garden path before and screwed; we can't afford to let anything like that happen again. We should at least be able to speak to our lawyer or the US Consul first.'

West German judge Dr Claus Hoheisel presided at the hearing, conducted in the Mulawa prison's solarium. Upon arrival the women demanded to speak by phone to their lawyer, Claude Bilinsky, and shortly afterwards, on his advice, they handed a scribbled letter to the judge stating they would not participate without their legal counsel present.

The West Germans were blindsided – it was possibly not what they had been led to expect by Australian authorities. They had been assured by the Australians that all of the necessary arrangements had been made and consents processed. In fact, nothing of the sort had occurred. It was typical of the lack of rights afforded the women as Commonwealth prisoners – they had no control over their own affairs and were not seen to be worthy of consultation.

The judge and his assistant, Dr Rolf Opitz, spoke with their interpreter and adjourned the hearing so as to confer with Canberra and the women's legal representative about a way forward. This was an expensive undertaking and not an opportunity the West Germans could afford to waste. The women were returned to a holding room in the Mulawa hospital annexe away from the main prison population while the negotiating behind the scenes continued.

During the adjournment, the female interpreter narrowly escaped injury as she entered a staff toilet reserved for the hearing. A rock was thrown at her through a louvred glass window. Fortunately, though it smashed the glass and shattered onto the interpreter, it missed its target. She was uninjured but shaken.

Did other prisoners know the Drug Grannies were back at Mulawa? Was the rock sending them a message to remain silent about Vern Todd and Phillip Shine? If so, who was the messenger? Or was this perhaps a sign the Americans' actions that saved the lives of prison guards during the Mulawa riot in mid-1979 had still not been forgotten? Either way, the incident was unnerving, for Toddie and Beezie, and was a further reminder they always had to be on their toes.

Unsurprisingly, the Germans returned to Frankfurt the next day when no progress could be made with either the Attorney-General's Department or the women's lawyers about the specific legality of the hearing, and what – if any – benefits would accrue for the prisoners. The women were, after all, risking their lives by participating but the authorities didn't appear to be concerned about possible danger or repercussions from within the prison that the women might face.

Claude Bilinsky, an experienced Sydney solicitor who had now been formally retained on the advice and in the absence of Bob Harkins, wanted the women to be offered something concrete in return for their testimony – say, a recommendation from the West Germans to the Australian authorities for their early release. Furthermore, Bilinsky didn't like the underhand way in which the hearing had been suddenly sprung on his clients by government authorities and without the courtesy of their legal representatives being advised.

Around this time, the Australian government, through Immigration Minister Ian Macphee, announced tough new measures – including automatic deportation – targeting foreign drug traffickers arrested in Australia. If only the women could be deported now, they thought. The decision came too late to be of any benefit to Toddie and Beezie, who were by now two years into their fourteen-year sentence.

In West Germany, the press was following the Drug Grannies' case with interest. It was known there as 'Haschisch-Grossemuttern' translated to Hash Grannies, and in the *Frankfurter Rundschau* on 3 March it was reported 'the 30th criminal court of the Frankfurt Assize Court was trying to interrogate witnesses in Australia to throw more light onto a very confused case of international drug smuggling with which an Australian antique dealer (Phillip Shine) and a woman from West Berlin (Mrs X) are charged'.

Australian judges had established, said the news report, 'the two "grandmothers"' worked under the instructions of an international organisation operating in Frankfurt and West Berlin. The two accused [Shine and Mrs X] belonged to the international organisation which consisted at times of 25 people'. The hurdle the West Germans faced was Shine's silence: he exercised his legal right to say nothing, which left the onus of proof on the prosecution's shoulders. They therefore were relying heavily on Toddie's and Beezie's evidence.

In the following months there were to be three more special West German court hearings at which the women did consent to appear and provide evidence, but only because the ground rules had been clearly established in advance and the prisoners had legal representation each time. There were no promises or inducements, just an understanding by authorities the women were placing their lives in jeopardy by cooperating. It was hoped their assistance this time would be appropriately recognised – unlike the indifference with which it was treated by Judge Staunton – when it came to formal consideration of any request for release on licence.

The eleven months' incarceration at Tomago provided the women with not only greater freedoms but also opportunities to meet local community members who made regular weekend visits. The local churches were a great source of support and three dedicated parishioner families – the Wheatmans, Thornleys and Manbys – became friends and solid advocates for Toddie and Beezie's cause. It was not uncommon for me to meet with the local supporters on my regular trips to Tomago – often a four- or five-hour return journey – where we shared information and the results of our independent lobbying efforts to bring forward the women's release.

In February, Toddie and Beezie decided to write directly to the Governor-General, Sir Zelman Cowen, with an application for their release on licence. They made a case for compassion on the basis of their age, their health and the time served, including as model prisoners. They also hoped that their willingness to give evidence against a Vern Todd associate facing drugs charges in West Germany would be favourably looked upon. Ever hopeful their patience and the advice regarding timing would pay off, they waited for a reply.

Reverend Stan Wheatman, a former prison superintendent turned preacher, wrote at the same time to the Governor-General pleading for his intervention to free the women. There was no immediate response.

Frustrated by the absence of any reply from Government House to their or Reverend Wheatman's submissions, but aware of the upcoming royal visit to Australia by Queen Elizabeth and Prince Philip, Toddie devised a plan. She would write and seek the Queen's indulgence: an appeal directly to Her Majesty for amnesty. She submitted her case in writing via Government House in Canberra:

Your Majesty. We are American citizens serving 14 years' jail. We were given this sentence for unknowingly bringing into this country prohibited drugs. We have always been law abiding citizens. Never in all of our years were we ever confronted with misbehaviour of any kind. I served two years in active duty during World War II. Florice worked on the Manhattan (atom bomb) Project. Not being of the criminal sort, we find ourselves deteriorating both mentally and physically. With each passing day our loved ones, like us, are getting into the twilight of their years and the separation from them has taken its toll on us all. Please see attached copy of doctors' reports. We are going into our 27th month of imprisonment. We feel we should be reunited with our family and loved ones. They along with us feel the pain and anguish. Before it's too late we pray with all our heart you will find it in your heart to grant us amnesty. Since our ancestors all came from the mother country, we feel we are part of your great nation. Vera Todd Hays and Florice Bessire.

That night, Toddie wrote in her diary: 'Wouldn't it be a miracle if we were granted an amnesty and be home within the next couple of weeks.'

The Queen *did* visit Australia to officially open the High Court in Canberra on 26 May. But Her Majesty did *not* grant the Drug Grannies an amnesty. In fact, it is highly unlikely her attention was ever drawn to the women's plea seeking her support.

•

The near year-long stint the women spent at Tomago provided me with an informal and friendly atmosphere to get to know them, learn about their backgrounds, families and friends, and appreciate how much their nephew's deception had led them into this crime. They valued little things such as American newspapers or magazines to which I had easy access, books to read, or even imported foodstuffs such as American ketchup or relish which were unavailable inside the jail. Both women were smokers so a visit always included a fresh supply of cigarettes. The more I learned about their court case, the advice they were given, and the sentence without a non-parole period they received, the more convinced I was they'd been betrayed or let down every step of the way. I wasn't sure I could make much of a difference, but I wasn't going to turn my back on them now that they'd reached out to trust me and were seeking my help. It was a time when the concept of 'conflict of interest' – between being an objective journalist on the one hand, and an activist campaigning for their release – was not yet fully appreciated. At least not by me! Short of their legal counsel, they had few trusted advocates. Toddie and Beezie were no longer a mere 'story' for me; they were human beings who were facing what could be a death sentence if they spent the entirety of their fourteen-year term in prison. I wanted to change the narrative of their story.

While their lawyers had made references in conversations with the women – after their heroism during the Mulawa riot – to the possibility of an early release in time for the American summer in June, July or August, those months came and went with no announcement and no explanation.

In late May 1980, an American friend from Toddie's World War II military service suddenly arrived to see her. On my visit that weekend, Toddie was simply bubbling about her surprise visitor. It was the first face-to-face contact for the women with anyone from their past – family or friends – and it lifted their morale tremendously. The pair had not seen each other in more than twenty years and Toddie's diary entry reflected her buoyant mood:

> I feel like I'm on cloud nine. My morale, if possible, was boosted 1000 per cent. She will be here for three days and I know they will be too short for me. She was allowed to stay for lunch and this will be for every day she is here. Never thought I could be this happy here. I had the best sleep since leaving home in August 1977. These two days have flown by but I still have one full day tomorrow. I know the terrible void that will set in after she has gone, but at least these will have been three of the most beautiful days of my life. What fond memories we re-lived.

In July 1980 the New South Wales government decided to close the Tomago women's prison. It required the relocation of its inmates to the site of a former delinquent girls' reformatory in Sydney's western suburb of Parramatta. The building had been remodelled to house adult women prisoners.

Beezie wrote to friends about the impending move, but the matter uppermost in her mind was a cataract which had been detected in Toddie's right eye. It was causing considerable pain and continuing impaired vision.

'It will be much better being transferred to Sydney because it's close to Westmead Hospital so now maybe Toddie will get some much-needed medical attention,' Beezie said.

Norma Parker Centre, as the new prison was called, was originally built as an orphanage. For more than a century it housed parentless children, and in 1943 it became an 'industrial school for female delinquents'. In its latest configuration, it could hold forty-five prisoners, each with separate rooms. It also had a swimming pool, albeit unused and in a state of disrepair.

As Toddie and Beezie had found physical activity helped them endure their incarceration at Mulawa and Tomago, they weren't about to change the strategy, so they put their names down for gardening and pool work at their new jail. Toddie knew from once having had her own pool in Los Angeles that this one on the prison grounds was going to need a lot of work re-sealing, replacing tiles and painting, which she was told male prisoners from nearby Parramatta Jail would undertake. It was just the sort of role that suited Toddie, and Beezie was easily satisfied with gardening duties, which included lawn mowing and edging, as well as tending the flower beds.

Due to their age and maturity, Toddie and Beezie were better able to cope than most with the psychological pressures of internment. Their companionship and problem-solving helped them to develop strategies to try to manage the ever-present gloom. There was a yin and yang to their companionship, one up and the other down, although in Norma Parker that often became noticeably one-sided as Toddie battled significant deterioration in her health on several fronts. Their diaries revealed how they were always on the precipice of being unable to cope. There was no hiding the fact that they were getting older.

As the doctors had previously observed, the anxiety and stress of a long sentence would run them down faster as they aged, and with that, they would become less agile and prone to illnesses. Not only was Toddie's health getting worse but her mental condition was deteriorating. Her letters to her sisters and brothers couldn't hide her unhappiness and distress, although she tried to spare her family from it. Toddie was now being prescribed a cocktail of medications for various ailments. Over time, the medication was also beginning to take its toll on her internal organs. Her reliance on Beezie was now not just emotional but also physical as she was losing her strength and balance.

Toddie wrote in her diary shortly after the pair was transferred on 10 July to Sydney:

> Since I have come to Norma Parker Centre, the feeling of claustrophobia is getting worse. Everywhere I look there are buildings … no open spaces like in Tomago. Whenever I look there is also the big wall that surrounds the centre. We are in a community next to a mental hospital and the officers say they have to keep the front door locked to protect us from mental patients wandering in. Even though an unlocked front gate such as at Tomago isn't anything physically different from a locked one, it's the psychological effect that makes a difference. I may appear to some to be the stronger of the two women because of my size and height, but I am still, in fact, the weaker. I don't know; if it hadn't been for Beezie, I think I probably would have lost my sanity. I truly believe this.

Because the women were now in Sydney, my access to them was easier to balance among my various work and sport commitments. Weekend visits were sometimes augmented with a weekday drop-in when a surprise bottle of hand cream, flowers or a package of new cassettes for them to record 'letters' for their families always brought a smile and a heartfelt thank you. At times Beezie would meet me first with a warning that Toddie was in a bad mood, or worse, to say she would not be joining us for the visit because she was too depressed. I placed no conditions on my visits, and understood only their freedom could ever change the reality of imprisonment. Similarly, the women had the right, and exercised that power when they wanted, to decline a visit if company was simply not desirable. They wrote to me on a few occasions to suggest I change a Sunday visit to a Saturday if they had other weekend jail commitments to attend. To the senior officers' credit at Norma Parker Centre, they remained flexible about visiting times and never refused my entry into the prison, aware the women had no family and few close friends in Australia.

•

Back in West Germany a legal argument in the Philip Shine case arose over the admissibility of the Drug Grannies' testimony, while in the United States a former senior aide to disgraced President Richard Nixon was planning a trip to Australia. The purpose of the visit was to establish his organisation's new field of operations in Sydney.

The presidential aide – Charles 'Chuck' Colson, a conservative, ex-Marine captain, ex-millionaire lawyer, and ex-convict as a Watergate-related felon – arrived in Australia in September with officials from his Christian outreach organisation, Prison Fellowship. He had established the group after his conversion to Christianity following his conviction for obstructing justice in the case of military analyst Daniel Ellsberg, who had leaked a top-secret Pentagon study.

While in Sydney, Colson had heard of the women's incarceration so a visit to Norma Parker Centre was arranged. It helped lift Toddie's and Beezie's spirits immensely when Colson told them he was committed to helping their cause. A new spark appeared in both of the women's hopes to be released.

Nonetheless, Toddie's physical health continued to worsen. Her visits to Westmead Hospital became weekly events –

sometimes she was taken several times weekly – and doctors recommended that the cataract detected in her right eye be removed sooner rather than later. The plan was to operate and then implant an intraocular lens which was designed to return her vision to close to normal. Toddie didn't want to consider the alternative: permanent blindness in her right eye.

Just before the fourth and final hearing with the West German court in late August, a further submission by their solicitor to the Attorney-General, Senator Peter Durack, argued for their early release. It presented to even the most disinterested observer a compelling case for freedom. It invoked a mixture of legal argument and common decency. It would, after all, be Senator Durack who would advise the Governor-General on how and whether to exercise his powers under either the *Crimes Act 1914* or under an even older set of remissions instructions from 1900 in relation to the numerous petitions he had received but upon which he had not yet acted.

Not a visit I made with the women went by when their hopes for a positive outcome weren't the main conversation point. I could only agree with their sentiment, but always tried to be careful about not raising their expectations.

The final West German hearing was consumed with going over points of evidence the women had offered in the earlier sessions. The women's participation was largely a formality, as the arguments were legal and technical in nature. Where there was any cross-examination on evidence Beezie and Toddie had previously provided, it was Beezie who shouldered the responsibility answering the questions.

Toddie played little part in the final sittings due to her poor health. She was by now downing as many as ten prescribed painkillers and sedatives daily in order to manage the pain she was suffering from her eye and back, and other ailments. Visitors began to notice a marked decline in her physical and emotional well-being, only weeks after the uplift generated by the unexpected Chuck Colson visit. Toddie's sometimes mercurial temperament and emotional swings led to times she would stay in her room because she felt too moody to be among people. Her Christian network was understanding and supportive, and sought to limit their contact at those times. She would lash out at Beezie or sometimes direct her wrath at me during visits – venting her frustration over her health and continued incarceration. While she mostly tried to grin and bear the physical and mental agony she was experiencing, it was imprisonment that was killing her slowly and surely.

A reply from Colson, now back in the United States, to a letter of thanks the women wrote immediately after his visit offered little succour. He said in part: 'If it took imprisonment for Alexander (sic) Solzhenitsyn to come to understand the spiritual quality of life, then he could say "bless you prison". I suspect you girls will feel that way as well, I am sure out of all this.'

Activities designed to keep the prisoners mentally active and engaged were introduced at Norma Parker Centre. Beezie took advantage of these new opportunities. A debating team and a drama society were established involving both male and female prisoners. Inmates from Malabar Training Centre – a prison in eastern Sydney – were transported by bus to Parramatta to join with the women at the Norma Parker Centre to produce plays and participate in debates. They hoped to eventually stage events with weekend visitors forming part of the audience. By late August Beezie was a veteran of three debates. The supervising officers were encouraged by both the success of the debating sessions and the high levels of cooperation and interaction between the male and female prisoners. It was a first for the NSW prison system.

While the debating teams continued their scheduled program, two more prisoners at Malabar set about writing and scripting a play to be performed by a cast of prisoners from both jails. Thus *Powder My Nose*, a comedy in three acts, was presented by the prisoners under the direction of the Ensemble Theatre director Gary Baxter, with several TV stations providing free make-up and the Elizabethan and Ensemble theatres providing the wardrobe and lighting. Attended by almost 125 friends, relatives and prison officials, the comedy was a success. Beezie starred in the lead role as Lady Gaye Clutterbuck, whose husband operated a 'fast funeral parlour'. Beezie felt it was important for her physical and mental well-being that she was continuing to throw herself into work and activities to keep her upbeat and on as even a keel as possible while Toddie languished. Beezie's support to her companion was vital.

At Norma Parker Centre where they shared a large room, Toddie had little privacy in which to deal with her emotions. Her constant pain didn't help. Beezie employed a non-traditional approach to snapping Toddie out of her moods. 'Lots of times when Toddie felt down and depressed and sorry for herself, I'd deliberately get her mad at me,' Beezie told an American journalist. 'She'd get so mad but at least it'd change the emotions.'

•

On 10 October Attorney-General Senator Peter Durack responded to the women's submission requesting their release, prepared by Bob Harkins, who had by now returned from overseas and was informally working with Claude Bilinsky. Senator Durack wrote that even after careful consideration of the case and other letters received in the women's support, he was unable to recommend their release. It was for Toddie and Beezie, who had held out for the slim possibility they'd be home for the American summer, another crushing disappointment.

Senator Durack wrote:

I have had the benefit of an indication from the trial judge as to the non-parole periods he would have specified in a like case with the offenders being Australian citizens of similar age and character, and the period he indicated was one of not less than four years. I would therefore ordinarily first review their cases in March 1982 with a view to their possible release on licence in April 1982. However in view of the age and medical condition of the prisoners and the matters raised in your letter, I shall make my first review of their cases in February, 1981.

On my next visit to the prison, the women and I sought to analyse Durack's words, to read into his somewhat obtuse expression. If we understood it correctly, the Attorney-General was doing two things: first, he was nominally acknowledging a non-parole period now of (not less than) four years, when there had hitherto been none. Second, and better still, Durack was acknowledging their age, medical condition and exemplary conduct. He would review the possibility of their release in four months' time – a year before they might have otherwise expected in light of the sentencing judge's indication of an appropriate non-parole period.

This seemed too good to be true, yet it was the Attorney-General himself making the concession that 'age and medical condition of the prisoners and the matters raised' (which among other things referred to their cooperation with Australian and West German authorities) convinced him to bring forward by a year a release on licence review. The women were buoyed by the letter.

Senator Durack's office also replied to Reverend Wheatman's petition along similar lines.

The judge at the sentence hearing, Judge Staunton, had declared in subsequent correspondence with the Attorney-General that he had refused to specify a non-parole period strictly on the basis of the defendants' nationality – in other words, because they were American. His logic was that once released from prison, the women – as foreigners – would be deported and therefore not be governed by local parole conditions. His logic puzzled many barristers and legal experts because there was substantial case law which unambiguously rejected such a proposition. Surely as the chief judge of the NSW District Court, Staunton knew this.

A few days after the Attorney-General's letter, the women received advice from the Governor-General's official secretary, David Smith:

> I refer to your petition dated 17 February 1980 addressed to His Excellency for release on licence which was transmitted through the diplomatic representatives of your country. In a letter dated 19 May 1980 you also petitioned Her Majesty the Queen for an amnesty and this further petition was referred to His Excellency for his attention. His Excellency regrets the delay but you will appreciate that in such matters, His Excellency acts on the advice of the Attorney-General. I regret to inform you that after consideration of all those circumstances, your petitions and several letters received in support of your applications for release on licence, the Attorney-General has advised he is unable to recommend to His Excellency the grant of a licence to you at this stage.

What Toddie and Beezie found difficult to reconcile was that around the same time of their knockback a fellow Norma Parker prisoner, 29-year-old Michelle Ashton, was freed. She was sentenced on 27 November 1978 to seven years' imprisonment for importing drugs into Australia. A Commonwealth prisoner, like them, she was fortunate to have had a three-year non-parole period imposed by her sentencing judge. However, her parole officer submitted a request to the Attorney-General in mid-1980 for her release on licence. Less than two weeks before Christmas, Senator Durack released Ashton – almost a year *before* her non-parole period even came into effect.

It seemed that being American and/or being old were sufficient grounds to be discriminated against by this attorney-general.

The women asked themselves over and over – as did many of their supporters – why the injustice and discrimination?

As much as the faith and support from Christian friends was helping the women to bear up with the pressures and pain of being inside prison, by the end of November Toddie was again admitted to hospital. Toddie and pain were fellow travellers: her medical history included an appendectomy, cervical spinal fusion and two lumbar laminectomies (major spinal surgery which is both painful and risky). Incarceration was exacerbating her health problems and making recovery harder. Toddie despaired that she was now becoming addicted to legal drugs.

On 1 December, Toddie was wheeled into theatre where Westmead Hospital's specialist eye surgeon prepared to extract Toddie's compromised intracapsular lens, and then implant a new intraocular lens. The hope was that Toddie would soon be able to see with her right eye once again. Complications, however, could arise.

In Toddie's case, serious complications *did* arise. Two weeks after the operation she developed pupil flaw and subsequently her intraocular pressure rose. Doctors monitoring her progress in hospital after the operation had detected marked inflammation of the uveitis (the pigmented layer of the eye) and a condition known as fibrinous exudate. She was treated with steroids and mydriatics, agents that dilate the pupil, in the hope of resolving the problem.

Although Toddie was confined to a hospital bed, this was the first time since her arrest she was able to move about at will. She didn't take for granted simple decisions and personal freedoms such as eating her meals when she chose and selecting what she ate from a daily menu offering. She could even refuse to eat if she didn't feel like it. She could wake up, and return to sleep, as she pleased – and not be governed by the clock or prison muster. These basic liberties had been removed from Toddie the prisoner, but now as Toddie the hospital patient, equal among the other patients, she was rediscovering what a difference it was to be a 'free' person again.

Her time spent in hospital also revealed another aspect to Toddie's complex persona. She had been watching over a young man and longer-term patient, aged in his twenties, who, due to his medical condition – which included an acquired brain injury – was restless and wandered the wards. Before his admission to hospital he had been found in a gutter with a fractured skull, suffering severe disorientation. One day when he was cruising the ward he entered Toddie's room and proceeded to lie down beside her on her bed, then promptly fell asleep. Toddie put her arm around him to keep him from rolling off the mattress. Eventually with her free arm, she was able to buzz for the nurse. The attending nurse summoned the rest of the ward's carers to witness the sight before rousing him and then walking him back to his own room.

The prison authorities at Norma Parker Centre were sympathetic to Toddie and cognisant of the fact she had no family nearby who could visit her in hospital. They were able to facilitate special visits from Beezie, often escorting her only as far as the hospital entrance. Beezie would make her own way to Toddie's ward and after the visit return to meet her guard for the journey back to the prison. It was a unique privilege.

Toddie's eye remained covered with a patch for the first two weeks post-surgery. She was popular among the hospital staff, very few of whom were aware of her notoriety. Christmas cards from family and friends were brought in by Beezie to brighten up Toddie's hospital room.

By the end of December, Toddie's eye showed little improvement; the steroid drops were not clearing up the problems she had encountered post-operatively, and the constant pressure caused by the build-up of fluids behind the implanted lens was excruciatingly painful. It was three days into the new year and Toddie found herself in theatre again for emergency surgery.

Surgeons found the original lens implantation had failed. Toddie's body had rejected it. They decided then and there to remove the implant, and at the same time performed additional surgery. Toddie was wheeled back to her room several hours later, groggy from the effects of the general anaesthetic. She was informed of the surgeons' course of action the next morning. She reconciled within herself that there had always been a risk – and she knew that before she went in for the operation. Further, the pressure build-up had become so painful that if removal of the implanted lens was going to end the constant ache, then she would have to settle for blindness in one eye. Still, Toddie hated losing her sight and it added to the sense that she had been on the losing end of life long enough over the past three years.

The pressure on Beezie, who was by now approaching seventy days without the close company and support of Toddie, was beginning to take its toll, as her diary reveals:

> Wish Toddie were here. I'm so damn concerned for her. But no-one seems to care. Sure miss her. The lens was removed and a drain put in, and now from the infection and rejection, she has self-induced secondary glaucoma. What else can happen to her? Damn I wish she'd get better and get back here. She's lonely, I'm lonely. What a hell of a life. It's very frustrating not being able to have a conversation with her. We'll have to get acquainted all over again.

On 6 February, Toddie finally returned from hospital to the Norma Parker Centre. The guards and inmates had arranged a welcome 'home' celebration. Their efforts did not go unappreciated. Toddie wrote in her diary:

> Sure good to leave hospital and on entering the prison gate there's this beautiful big yellow ribbon around the big tree that faces the gate – also a sign reading 'Welcome back, Toddie, it's been a long time!'. Most of the girls are strangers

to me except my dear Beezie and wonderful friend, Glen. Tonight I sleep in our room and in my bed!

It was now February 1981. That was around the time when both the Attorney-General and the Governor-General said there would be an early review of the women's case with a view to granting them a release on licence. After all they'd been through, they were clinging to the most recent encouraging words they had received from the Attorney-General.

Who would oppose their release?

CHAPTER SIXTEEN

BEATEN NOT BOWED – US SUPPORT GROWS

There were three distinct strategies in play to get the women out of prison. It was not an orchestrated campaign as such, more a collective effort by different cohorts with a common goal combining empathy with humanity, founded on a strong legal sensibility.

The legal team comprising Toddie and Beezie's lawyer, Claude Bilinsky, and their former Legal Aid representative, Bob Harkins, pursued the course of a release on licence, utilising case studies, legal precedents, the women's ages, their deteriorating medical condition, and their assistance during the Mulawa riot. Importantly, the wealth of evidence about Vern Todd and Phillip Shine the women had provided to Australian and West German investigators was considered a strong element in their favour.

The women's Christian supporters – friends such as the Thornleys, Wheatmans and Manbys, as well as the Salvation Army's weekly visitors and the Prison Fellowship – initiated international chain prayers, wrote letters to politicians (including in the United States), and lobbied their local members of parliament. They were both a visible and invisible means of valuable emotional support.

As a journalist, I exploited my full toolkit of contacts, getting in touch with fellow journalists, ministers (as well as shadow ministers), backbench politicians, staffers and bureaucrats, as well as exploring story opportunities. The women's case was my personal commitment to right what I believed was a wrong. We became very close. The deeper I dug into the case the more I felt aggrieved on their behalf that the system was continuing to let them down – they were mere political footballs. As a human being, I felt for these two women who were a long way from home and their family, whose emotional and physical strength was, at times, precarious. They were being spun like yo-yos on the whim of the Attorney-General. There were occasions when it could be perceived I had crossed the line between my role as a journalist and that of an activist, but I was blind to the conflict and my supervisors didn't seem particularly bothered. Times were different then.

I initially made visits to the women fortnightly after I first contacted them in November 1979, when they were in Tomago. By the time of their transfer to Norma Parker Centre in July 1980 we were in contact – in person, by phone and even by mail – at least weekly, often several times each week. Our conversations ranged between me providing emotional support – I was now close enough that they could vent, rant and rage – to giving strategic advice on their next steps in the effort to achieve freedom. They had lost any faith in the Australian justice and political systems. They felt completely betrayed.

The women needed human crutches and advocates whom they trusted, and despite being let down at times, they were willing to forgive. There simply was no alternative. They had let go of the hate towards Vern and in order not to be crippled by the repeated disappointments, they tried to keep a focus on the future. It was a rollercoaster ride from day to day, year to year. It didn't mean they weren't angry, but their age and maturity and the fact that they had been with each other by now for more than twenty years meant they were able to keep their heads above water – if sometimes only just. I tried to keep abreast of their states of mind and help them feel empowered – if only in discussing what wording they wanted in submissions, letters, articles – and they could sound off with, or at, me as their temperaments and moods required them to let off steam. When the going was good and they were feeling upbeat, the visits were happy, convivial get-togethers and they would tell me that for a while the prison walls disappeared as we talked about things not prison or early-release related. Instead, we reminisced and talked of home and often of sport. I honed my repertoire of jokes for (nearly) every occasion. We shared a good sense of humour – an international language all to itself – and the women needed to have opportunities to laugh, especially given their circumstances.

It was difficult to manage expectations. The women tried their hardest not to get their hopes up, but they couldn't help but clutch at straws and fervently wish that what was dangled before them *would* come to fruition. They tried not to get ahead of themselves, but some things just had to be done if they were counting on the Attorney-General to say 'yes'. As much as I sought to temper those expectations during my visits, I was not walking in their shoes. More often than not, I bit my lip and kept my own counsel. They packed up boxes of clothing, books and personal effects to mail ahead of their planned departure, or wrote and passed on instruction manuals to other inmates regarding their chores in the garden and swimming pool at Norma Parker in anticipation of a positive decision for release. It was not for me to tell them not to be planning ahead, given it was their freedom we were all fighting for.

Bob Harkins visited the women on 8 February 1981. He informed them he believed that if their submission to be released was to be considered only as a pair, their chances were fifty-fifty. He also told them if considered individually, he was confident Toddie's prospects alone were very good, mainly because of her poor and declining health. But it could come at a very personal cost.

Toddie's diary entry about leaving Beezie behind was unambiguous:

> He told us there is a possibility of BZ having to stay another six months. All I can say is this better not happen. What's happened to all those damn promises? German court proceedings, etc. – the original time from the onset was 3–3 ½ years – so where's the remissions, good behaviour, saving of three officers' lives. Shit on this judicial system. Know I must keep positive thoughts, but at times it's damn hard. I won't go without her!!!

At the same time as the women awaited their most recent bid for freedom, I was employed as a researcher at the ABC national public affairs TV program *Four Corners*. I proposed the idea of covering the women's plight to the executive producer, Paul Lyneham, who agreed it was an important story that needed to be told. Ideally it would be cut and in the can in anticipation of their possible release. Or knockback. Toddie and Beezie were in full agreement with the idea and hoped it would highlight the injustice of their case. I was assigned to work with reporter Peter Ross and we began planning the episode.

●

Beezie undertook the roles of nurse, doctor and full-time carer with Toddie's return from hospital. She administered eye drops, guided Toddie to the bathroom and back to bed, and regularly checked her eye for any marked changes. Regular treatment and check-ups at the Westmead Hospital out-patients section often meant long and tiring waits, but Toddie wasn't going to give up. She would remind herself of her father's wise words of advice: 'In your lifetime, you're going to get knocked down many times, but don't ever stay down 'til the full count.'

Toddie was still grappling with her return from the normalcy of the hospital to the confinement and restrictions of the Norma Parker Centre; she told me it 'felt like the first experience of entering prison: shock, trauma, the works'. She had not fully recovered from her two eye surgeries and feared if she wound up back in hospital, it could jeopardise her and Beezie's possible release.

The women's diaries, however, revealed they were feeling confident – encouraged by the Attorney-General's letter that seemed to support a review of their case earlier than he'd previously suggested. They were excited and planning for the future, unable to ignore the numerous cautions not to let their expectations get too high. Toddie's diary entry didn't hide her optimism:

> Every second is an hour; every hour a day; every day a week. Sure hope to hell this is our month! We got a couple more boxes of stuff packed to ship home. Thank God we're getting that out of the way so when the good word comes through, at least we won't have to mess with that. When the time comes we will have like 10 minutes to pack. Sure hope this isn't a BAD omen on our part – in other words, jumping the gun. The situation now is different and we hope to be home within the next two or three weeks. Sounds too good to be true, and hope it's not wishful thinking on our part.

As February segued into March, the diary entries made no attempt to hide Toddie's fragile emotional state. She seemed ready to explode and give up entirely.

> We started to play cards, but I blew – no apparent reason, but took out my emotions on Beezie. Could have bit my tongue off, but it's always too late and damage is done. Most of frustration is over my eye, and I don't want her to know that it's bothering me, but again if it isn't the eye, it's some other

stupid thing and she's the brunt of all my pent-up emotions. Sorry as hell for Beezie as I know I'm no fun to be around. She never knows from one day to the next what my disposition will be like; in fact, neither do I. Truthfully, I'm about ready to give up; can't take much more of this. Still sick in bed and sick to death of ME. Don't know how the hell BZ puts up with me. But with any luck, I could get my calling any time. Yes, I'm afraid that's the way I feel. Good riddance. There are days, damn few, I feel pretty good; others very depressed and cry all the time. Poor BZ sure would be a helluva lot better off without me. I hate myself.

Beezie was sworn to secrecy that under no circumstances was she to share with other inmates that it was Toddie's sixty-third birthday on 18 March. Toddie was adamant. Beezie was good to her word, although it didn't feel right. Respecting her companion's wishes on this occasion was contrary to all they'd ever done for each other in the past, but she understood Toddie's feelings at the moment. Beezie never complained about Toddie – she was a steadfast mate and the strength of the relationship was that she was so. Beezie noted in her diary she would find a way to make up for the lost celebration:

Well, I kept my promise to Toddie. She didn't want a birthday card and she didn't want me to mention her birthday to anyone, so I didn't. This is the first time that she hasn't had a cake. We'll make up for all birthdays, Christmases etc. when we get home.

The waiting game dragged on into April. Their patience grew thin, their tempers fiercer and their patience with Australia all but exhausted. By now I was never sure what to expect on my weekly visits. Toddie would alternate between sobbing, shouting at me, apologising and then having to absent herself, leaving Beezie and me alone for the rest of the visit. We would then discuss how fragile Toddie was, and I would take my cues from Beezie that letting Toddie blow her top was a healthy release that kept her from spiralling into deep depression. Beezie always remained polite to me. It was all I could do to support her when Toddie's temper flared, as it was doing on an increasing basis. What was reserved for Toddie's diary would also spill out at times into some of our visits:

Shit, I'm sick of this place. Sick of this stinking stupid asshole country; a really dumb shithead country. Good mood, huh? You might just as well be dead as exist like this. You can sure tell my mood is no good. Well finally the end of this month. Now we can start really being hopeful, nervous, jittery, uptight etc. Now I just hope they get on the ball and give us an answer soon. Wish they would send us home. I would love to die peacefully, with dignity, surrounded by my loved ones. Son-of-a-bitch if we don't go home soon I'll go mad. I'm pissed off at this stupid country, and I'm getting madder by the day. If someone doesn't get off their ass I'll really blow a gasket. Why in the damn hell do we have to suffer so??? I'm so damn sick of the ass-hole place, I could scream. Got into it with one of the young punks at the breakfast table. These punks come in for three or four weeks and think it's a fucking school. Play time all day while we do all the yard work, and naturally the officers couldn't care less. Yes, I'm good and mad today and just might take a swing at the one I had the fight with. Sorry for my language. I've been institutionalised after being here three years plus, and I hear those words continually, day in and day out.

Daily chores were expected to comprise part of all prisoners' daily routines – both to help them to save some money for when they were released, and to promote good physical and mental health. For Beezie, daily chores were also an important way to burn away the time. The women continued to attend muster and put on brave faces for their visitors. They also coped with the demands of numerous filming visits by the ABC crew who were interviewing them.

In early April I was told in a phone conversation with a senior official in the Attorney-General's Department that the agency's latest brief to the minister recommended releasing the women on licence. In fact, he told me the release was likely to be announced within three weeks. The important principle I had always been so careful to follow in my dealings with Toddie and Beezie, to take care of managing their expectations, was on this occasion completely ignored. I almost immediately called them to share the news. Any caution that the advice was not yet in writing, and that it was merely a bureaucrat's recommendation, I overlooked. It was such positive news that I felt compelled to share it without delay.

Toddie's diary entry was naturally full of enthusiasm:

Sandi called. He had just talked to Canberra and that we would be going home in about three weeks. God I hope he's right. I'll believe it when I see it in writing. I thought I was going to faint!! Kept asking him if he was sure – I couldn't believe my ears. For a change, HAPPY HAPPY TEARS!!! Couldn't wait to share this. Our tears flowed together. Still won't believe it until we see that signed paper. Oh, happy day!!! Even though we both don't feel 100%, this is the best news ever. Peter Ross also in touch with Canberra and he says our leaving is within three weeks, 100% positive – or it could be sooner. We are surely on Cloud Nine. We want to yell to everyone about our going home at the end of the month, but afraid to do so until we receive written confirmation and set date; even though we know it's 100% go, unlike last year when we were told we would be home for our summer in the States 1980! Will write my last letters today and tomorrow and tell family the news and ask them not to write to us here anymore. Yes, we know we are going home. I hope we haven't gotten our hopes up too high and end up shot down again. Think also today will try on clothes I purchased last year for our return to the States for our summer 1980!

I didn't need to trade places with the Drug Grannies – aching for their freedom – to fully comprehend their eagerness to grasp at anything, no matter how slim a chance it offered. Irrespective of being let down before, when all the odds seemed in their favour, they still dared to hope that maybe this was their time. They clutched at any sliver, any skerrick of news about the possibility of getting out.

Soon after this diary entry, their world collapsed again. Their release on licence was inexplicably knocked back by the Attorney-General.

The situation was all the more shattering since the advice had come from me, the trusted advocate who had reported the possibility, and who misread the bureaucratic tea leaves. I decided that the devastating news was not something that I should convey to Toddie and Beezie over the phone – the mea culpa would have to be done face to face, and I would deal with their frustrations and the repercussions in person. I owed them that. My pain would result not so much from what the women said, but from the fact that based on a telephone conversation with a bureaucrat, I had been too quick to raise their hopes. It was only fair that they be able to vent in person. I drove straight to the prison and requested a small interview room to meet privately with them.

'I have some news for you both which you are not going to like,' I told Beezie shortly after I arrived. 'It's going to hurt you just as it is already hurting me deeply to have to tell you this, but your release has just been knocked back by the Attorney-General. I don't know why. It had seemed all but in writing. I've jumped the gun and my lesson has been at your expense. I am so sorry, and I wish I knew more.' This was not the news either prisoner was expecting to hear from me on this visit.

The date of the Attorney-General's decision – 23 April 1981 – would never be forgotten; not by the women, their jailers, their legal team, their family and friends, and especially not by me. It was a difficult and distressing episode and exposed the naivety of my twenty-four years' life experience. Peter Ross was also mortified, as he had been told independently their release was all but a done deal. How wrong we were. I resolved never to put the women in that position again.

Beezie was devastated. She kept sighing, but had few words. Eventually she took a deep breath and asked the question we all wanted answered: *Why?* Why had the Attorney-General done this to them?

Graciously, she told me that she knew what it was like to make a mistake, and she understood that passing on the advice of a bureaucrat came with good intentions. What upset her most, she said, was the bigger issue of the reasoning behind the Attorney-General's decision.

Senator Durack's decision this time felt particularly personal, and it was. Unambiguously, at senior levels within the Attorney-General's Department, the advice to the minister had been to release the women. These senior public servants had told me so and, further, they confided that they didn't expect any pushback this time.

I could offer an explanation, but there were no immediate answers. After Beezie and I had worked through the issue, she said, 'I'd better go and get Toddie'. I prepared myself for the worst.

When they came down together, Toddie was visibly shaking with rage, something I expected and to which I believed she was quite entitled.

'Look, hit me, hit me hard if you want to hit something because if it's anyone's fault for getting your hopes up, it's mine ... I told you to be prepared for your return home, and now I have to bear the responsibility and disappointment for us all,' I tried explaining to Toddie. But she just screamed, then suddenly grabbed a chair, raising it over her head and made to smash it through a window. The superintendent had been standing outside the closed door waiting for an appropriate moment to enter, aware the effect of the news would likely trigger an uncontrolled outburst from her. He may also have thought I might need his protection. It was the worst outburst I'd ever encountered from Toddie, but it underscored the women's vulnerability and fragile state.

Beezie helped to restore calm. Toddie lowered the chair and with her immediate rage vented, sat down sobbing. We remained together and I apologised again and again. She said she understood that I had not intended any harm, but that I could never really know how painful their situation was.

One of the cruel twists of their predicament had always been that there was never a set date to measure their incarceration – other than a head sentence of fourteen years. It didn't escape their attention that they had far more yesterdays than they had tomorrows left. We talked briefly about not giving up and the importance of remaining steadfast. Emotionally drained and weary, the women hugged me and pledged their continued trust that I'd continue working tirelessly on their behalf. They then headed back to their room.

Toddie's diary entry reflected her sense of hopelessness:

> Well, we got the answer. I really blew my cool and for a while thought I would lose my mind. I have lost faith in everything and everyone. I just plain don't give a shit! I feel dead and they just haven't buried me yet. We've taken this shit for 39 months and once more to have your nose rubbed in it is more than we can stand.

Some days later and after numerous conversations with several intermediaries associated with the matter, I was able to speak to the bureaucrats in the Attorney-General's Department who had recommended the women's early release. They had believed their recommendation to free the women was essentially a fait accompli. After all, it was Senator Durack himself who announced in October 1980 that he would be reviewing the women's case a year earlier than expected. There was more at play here, but only the Attorney-General knew what that was.

Was it rank politics? Was it foreign pressure to ensure ongoing access so as to prise further evidence from the women against the Mr Bigs of the drug world? Was it simply anti-American sentiment? Were the locked-up Drug Grannies too valuable a symbol for law enforcement's campaign against drugs? Or was it personal, a cause célèbre for Senator Durack?

The valuable lesson I learned from mistakenly raising the women's expectations so high was to never assume anything again. I learned the hard way that in politics – and the decision *not* to grant the women early release was now all about politics – there are multiple layers in the decision-making process. Ultimately, until the fat politician sings, nothing is guaranteed.

More than 1.5 million viewers around Australia watched the *Four Corners* program on 2 May, and the repeat on 3 May. On 4 May journalist Caroline Jones, the presenter of *Four Corners*, featured an interview I had conducted with the women on *City Extra*, the daily Sydney ABC public affairs radio program she hosted and which I had recently joined as a producer. It had been recorded following the Attorney-General's rebuff.

Introducing the interview, Jones said:

Today we follow up on *Four Corners'* report ... Florice Bessire and Vera Hays ... say their physical and psychological health is failing and they have made a request to be released on licence and deported home to the United States. The federal Attorney-General says – not yet. He will review the case again before next April [1982] ... the women say they did not know that the campervan was packed with concealed compartments under the floor ... with cannabis resin ... the nephew, the mastermind, Vern

Todd, escaped as did his accomplice, Phillip Shine. Vern Todd was a well-known marijuana distributor, his name and activities surfaced in the Williams' royal commission into drugs. He is still free.

The following day, 5 May, Jones commented on listener feedback to the previous day's interview with the Drug Grannies:

We have had quite a strong reaction to yesterday's report on Vera Hays and Florice Bessire, the two elderly American women sentenced to 14 years for the importation of an illegal substance. Several callers complained that we appeared to be championing the women's cause … and this was improper. No, that's not what we were doing; we were reporting to you an unusual case. Perhaps I didn't spell it out clearly enough. Let me do so. The sentence was unusual in that it did not make any provision for parole. The trial judge said this was because the women were American citizens who, if paroled, would then be deported and so not subject to the normal supervised conditions of parole. Therefore he deemed it inappropriate to set a non-parole period which would have opened the way for possible parole. He later reported that had parole been appropriate, he would have been thinking in terms of a four-year non-parole period. They have now been in prison three and a half years and they had given the authorities a good deal of assistance with information. The elapsed time of their sentence, plus their assistance with authorities, plus their deteriorating health, make this an appropriate time to raise the subject of their future, and the possibility of their release on licence, which is why we did so. The situation now is that the federal Attorney-General, Senator Peter Durack, will review their case again before April, 1982.

She then posed the question no-one in authority was prepared to, or knew how to answer:

> Perhaps the most outstanding feature of this whole story concerns the man who was *not* caught ... Vern Todd, the nephew of Vera Hays, the man who initiated the venture, the man who somehow escaped a strong network of narcotics agents who were on constant surveillance for 10 weeks on the case and who eventually arrested the women. Vern Todd was named as a major marijuana distributor in the Woodward Royal Commission into drugs. Today he is still free. And the reason for that is not yet fully explained, but there are some alarming possibilities.

The strong listener reaction was perhaps instructive for the women's supporters: the community's view about the women was not necessarily all sympathetic, and in fact some of it was not only negative but nastily so. What was the government hearing through its own MPs' offices? What were constituents' telephone calls and letters telling them?

The lawyers, Christian supporters and I continued pursuing new but complementary strategies to lobby the Attorney-General for the women's release on licence. The dejection we all felt following Senator Durack's shock decision in April quickly gave way to a renewed fighting spirit.

As Claude Bilinsky arranged new medical reports for submission to Canberra, the church supporters ramped up their community engagement efforts. I began a letter-writing campaign targeting influential Australians and Americans: politicians, bureaucrats, journalists and non-government organisations. There had to be a way to demonstrate to the decision-makers how unjust it was to keep the women locked up. The costs associated with their imprisonment and medical bills (especially Toddie's) amounted to many tens of thousands of dollars annually. We needed to garner community support, both in Australia and the United States.

While the Christian supporters' strategy relied on a mix of prayer and presentations to decision-makers, I largely maintained my distance from their activities so as not to be perceived to be a captive of their approach. Deep down I was a humanist who cared for and about people, and who believed ultimately it would be 'people power' which would make a difference.

By mid-1981, Toddie's failed eye operations had reached the point of no return. This was her surgeon's first such implant failure and it was exacerbated by a persistent infection.

The women were swinging from extreme lows to less extreme lows; depression had set in like a long, cold winter. They still dreamed of freedom and cleaved to anything remotely hinting at a return to La Pine. Toddie wrote in her diary:

> In the back of my mind, for some unknown reason, there's this feeling of being released near the end of July this year. There has been no indication, but still we haven't received an official explanation as to our knock back. Maybe the Attorney-General has decided to hold off for another three months. Well I can dream, can't I? Damn how you grasp at every little straw.

Beezie on the other hand found it hard to lift herself from the encroaching depression. Her diary entry from 29 May reflected this: 'I guess it's true that after the three year mark you start changing. I know I am. My faith is lagging. I'm becoming bitter, anti-social and dreadfully homesick. Praying doesn't seem to help any longer. I'm not receiving the peace that I used to.'

Correspondence I helped them write to US President Ronald Reagan, Oregon Senator Mark Hatfield and Prison Fellowship's Charles Colson implored the recipients to help muster support to pressure the Australian government to review their requests for release on licence. The women's letters said:

> It has become colder now with the winter onset and although it doesn't snow in Sydney, it does get cold. What

we desperately need is support from the American people. Without it, the Australian Attorney-General, Senator Peter Durack, is probably counting on the ability to wear any local criticism of his decision to refuse our request for release on licence. We believe that the American people's support is one aspect which could not be countered.

The letters written were posted and the women could only wait for the responses.

•

Meanwhile in Frankfurt, West Germany, on 13 June and with two Australian Federal Police drug squad detectives in attendance, Phillip Shine was convicted of drug smuggling and sentenced to the maximum term of imprisonment under German law – ten years. The Drug Grannies' testimony before the West German court hearings convened in Australia as well as Toddie's evidence shared with a West German narcotics investigator were instrumental in the prosecution's success. The West Germans credited the women's cooperation as being the key to securing Phillip Shine's ten-year prison term.

Under the heading '10 years' imprisonment for hashish smuggler', the *Frankfurter Rundschau* newspaper reported:

> The 29-year-old antique dealer Phillip Shine was given 10 years' imprisonment and Mrs X, a 28-year-old housewife from West Berlin was committed to seven years' imprisonment in her absence. The judgement today brings to an end the 18-month court case which is one of the most expensive cases in the history of Frankfurt's District Court.

Toddie and Beezie were justified in expecting their cooperation with the overseas trial to cast a favourable light on their case for early release. Here was proof their statements had been vital in securing convictions. Surely the Australian government could not fail to recognise, if not reward, this.

•

An inmate doing time for drug possession had recently been transferred to Norma Parker Centre and struck up a conversation with Toddie one day. She said a friend of hers knew her nephew Vern and had stocked his Tubby Bath product in her store for years. The friend and her twin boys had even been renting Vern's Woollahra house for the past six weeks, she said. Toddie made a diary entry to ensure she didn't forget any of what she'd been told. It was too important.

> She volunteered all the information with no prompting on my part. I was told Vern had left Australia for a while, but had returned, sold all his property and purchased a home on Sydney's north shore. We don't know who in the hell we can trust with this information. The girl also told us if we had stayed in Gosford much longer, Vern had plans of getting rid of us. A lot of things are falling into place: for instance, why he wanted me to take it out of Gosford, get rid of us and the van.

It didn't bear thinking about, Toddie said, reflecting on her nephew's efforts in December 1977, trying to convince them not to place the van in storage, or sign over the registration with a solicitor and depart Australia.

Did her own nephew want to have them killed?

In the United States, public support – beyond their friends in La Pine and family members – for the women's release was beginning to grow. Prison Fellowship leader Chuck Colson told the women in a letter he recognised what a 'bitter experience' it was but assured them he and 'some of the key people on my staff will try and come up with some ideas that will be helpful'.

Colson wrote a note to his staff:

We need to discuss this case as soon as possible. It is a heartbreaking story. I am convinced they were railroaded, and they will do another 10 years, probably in Australian prisons if nothing intervenes ... I really think they were duped. I wouldn't mind writing a letter to the American Ambassador to Australia and get Congressman Don Bonker involved. Perhaps we could generate some pressure for them. There must be some things we can do.

Senator Hatfield, who had received the women's letter, sent a telegram to them:

I have contacted the American officials in Sydney as well as the Australian Ambassador in the United States. I am very sorry to learn of your poor health. Please be assured of my desire to assist you in any way I can. I will be back in touch with you as soon as I receive word from either American or Australian officials.

Charles Colson followed up in Washington, DC, sending a letter to Australia's ambassador there, Sir Nicholas Parkinson:

I understand you are familiar with the case of Vera Hays and Florice Bessire. I visited these women when I was in Australia. They are elderly and in poor health. I hope and pray that your government will conclude that justice has already been done through their 44 months of confinement and that your government will temper justice with mercy. We would respectfully request that our petition for release be granted.

Congressmen Bonker made a representation to acting US Secretary of State Walter Stoessel who, Bonker said, 'seemed anxious to help'.

And in Sydney, Claude Bilinsky continued to coordinate a raft of independent medical consultations, x-rays and reports on both women with which to arm himself in his next submission to the Attorney-General. The common thread through all of the specialists' reports was that ongoing incarceration would effectively shorten their life expectancy. For example, the consulting psychiatrist wrote that Toddie suffered from an anxious depressive condition that was 'due to her incarceration and the fact that she is distant from her family who have not visited her as she could not stand the thought of saying goodbye to them'.

On 12 November, a lengthy submission was sent to Senator Durack, arguing the case for the women's release in time for them to be home at Christmas. Bilinsky emphasised the Shine sentence and the women's invaluable role:

> We further believe that an important factor for your consideration is that Phillip Shine has been sentenced in Germany ... his conviction would not have succeeded without the assistance given by our clients to the West German authorities. We would suggest ... you consider ... our clients' release ... with a view to having them back in the US by Christmas.

So for the fourth year running, the Christmas cards from family, friends, well-wishers and Christian supporters arrived, but they could do little to lift the women's flagging spirits.

Not satisfied with the brush-off he received in a pithy response from the Australian Embassy, Senator Hatfield then dispatched a personal note to Australian Prime Minister Malcolm Fraser. He copied in Governor-General Sir Zelman Cowen and Attorney-General Senator Peter Durack. He requested urgent consideration of the women's release, and their return to the United States before Christmas. It was dated 16 December and read:

Dear Prime Minister. Warm holiday greetings to you. I am writing to seek the compassionate release of Vera Hays and Florice Bessire. It is my understanding the judge in the case said in subsequent court papers that had the defendants been Australian nationals, he would have recommended parole after four years, which would be January, 1982 for one defendant, and in March for the second. Both ladies are in poor health and Vera Hays on a high level of prescribed drugs risking the possibility of drug dependency due to the severity of her physical condition. I respectfully request a compassionate release prior to Christmas for these ladies, from my State of Oregon. I can think of no more compelling reaffirmation of the warm relations between our two governments than to have Mesdames Hays and Bessire home for Christmas. Thank you very much for your thoughtful attention to my request. I look forward to hearing from you.
Kind regards, Sincerely,
Mark O. Hatfield, United States Senator.

It was hoped the weight of American political support – the acting Secretary of State, a former White House special counsel, the US ambassador to Australia, and Republican Senator Mark Hatfield – as well as the strong backing of the women's supporters in Australia might underline the injustice and unfairness of their continued imprisonment.

Would the Attorney-General expedite his consideration of their 'next' scheduled release-on-licence review at the four-year mark (as suggested by Staunton) in early 1982 and relieve the women's suffering of uncertainty as they wasted away in jail?

There was no choice for everyone but to wait. And wait.

CHAPTER SEVENTEEN

DAMN THEIR POLITICS AND INJUSTICE

Christmas 1981 came and went without a word from the Attorney-General. At short notice, I boarded a US-bound flight, heading eventually to Washington, DC, to continue the campaign in the United States. Along with the women, their families and their American supporters, we agreed personal engagement with key US decision-makers and influencers was essential. My trip was also to include a brief visit to Europe to meet with West German investigators, the prosecutor from the Phillip Shine trial and, if possible, the prisoner Shine himself, now serving his ten-year sentence. We needed as much help as we could muster, and with Shine I had in mind securing a tape-recorded statement, with his consent. I hoped he might absolve the women of any responsibility for the campervan and its drug haul, and confirm they were dupes in his and Vern Todd's larger machinations. It was worth a try.

Toddie promised me she would maintain her will to live for as long as it took to personally corral support from the Americans. Genuine fears were held that Toddie would not last much longer behind bars. She was sapped of life; her hopes to be home for Christmas had been dashed. Waiting for the scheduled review in April 1982 seemed too far away, especially for Toddie.

After my departure, she wrote in her diary:

Sandi has been gone a week today – it sure feels like it's been months!!! He called from the States and said the campaign for our release was coming along great. Once more we wait with bated breath. You try so hard not to build your hopes up, but that's next to impossible. We are holding up, but just barely. It seems forever and I'm getting more depressed with each passing day. This waiting game is killing us. Sick to death of politics, red tape etc. – and of course, feeling sorry for myself.

Upon my arrival in Los Angeles, Toddie's family members were desperate not only for news of her condition but to help in any way possible. Recent photos from the jail Christmas gathering were shared, audio cassette tapes and letters handed over, and questions answered until late into the night.

Vernon Sr did not attend the family gathering. Toddie loved all of her siblings dearly and said she could never bear to go into the details of her incarceration with her brother, Vernon Sr – for his sake. The Drug Grannies' saga was only one strand of his son's massive web of drug importation operations. Toddie told me it was not only distressing being deceived by her own kin, but it also pained her knowing how devastated her brother would be if he knew the truth about his son's extensive criminal activities.

I then flew from Los Angeles to Washington, DC, which was experiencing one of its coldest winters ever. The US capital was not well prepared for snow or icy roads so the city's streets were relatively empty, with few vehicles about. Prison Fellowship operations were based within the highly secretive but influential C Street Fellowship, also known as The Family, and they provided me with a handy base. They helped me arrange meetings with members of Congress, senators, a member of a US Senate Inquiry into Drugs headed by Senator Sam Nunn,

Interpol, the Drug Enforcement Agency and a courtesy call on the Australian Embassy. Upon arriving at Capitol Hill for a breakfast meeting with Washington state congressman Don Bonker, I was ushered into what appeared to be a huddle of men, hands joined, with a prayer underway. The young staffer who signed me in and walked me to the first-floor office had warned me a new 'Christian influence' was taking over to do 'God's work'. I quickly gleaned from this group, as I joined in prayer, that there was clearly an underground of 'God's people' throughout the US government, across the political divide, at work. It was a surreal experience for this young journalist who did not believe in a 'god' and had never done any 'praying'.

While in the capital, I also made preliminary plans for the American public affairs ABC network program *20/20* – which had an audience of 25 million viewers – to travel to Sydney to interview the Drug Grannies.

Senator Hatfield said in our meeting he was troubled – even mildly offended – by the lack of a response so far from Australian Prime Minister Malcolm Fraser to his recent letter. He expected his personal friendship with Fraser as well as the historically strong bonds between Australia and the USA would have been good enough reasons to, at the least, prompt some sort of response by now – a fortnight having passed since Hatfield had written. With the value of hindsight, his comments could have been a hint about what was to come.

Prison Fellowship undertook during its golden jubilee that month to collect up to 100,000 signatures on a petition, ultimately to be sent to Senator Durack, calling for the women's release.

Both women's diaries recorded the US effort as it was being reported back to them. Toddie wrote:

> Sandi reassured us his main concern was getting us home.
> We sure have a wonderful busy boy, and oh how we miss
> him. Feel like he's been gone months. He is pushing for an

early release date and we pray that it will be the latter part of January or around the first week in February. Bilinsky called. Figures we should hear something within the week. Wow! We can't believe it. Tense time.

While the feedback from all of the Washington interlocutors was encouraging, it was impossible to sense whether diplomatic pressure from 16,000 kilometres (10,000 miles) away would have any positive influence on the women's plight.

My side trip to Europe to meet with the lawyers in the Shine case was delayed as flights on the US eastern seaboard were suspended, then cancelled. The weather was so severe a domestic flight taking off from the city's downtown Washington National Airport on 12 January failed to gain sufficient altitude and crashed into the capital's 14th Street bridge. Services eventually returned as the winter storm passed, and flights to Europe resumed.

In West Germany, my interviews with the prosecutor heading the case against the Todd–Shine syndicate, and separately with the defence counsel who had represented Phillip Shine, were conducted respectively in Frankfurt and Darmstadt. The West German prosecutors were genuinely surprised the two elderly American women were still in jail.

Shine's lawyer arranged for me to meet his client in Darmstadt prison. Shine was gaunt, bearded and carried a small Canadian Roots bag containing his possessions to our meeting.

My intention was to secure on tape a vindication that the women had no knowledge of the illicit haul, but Shine wasn't prepared to do any such thing. Silence had been his defence during his trial so he wasn't going to say anything about his 'crime' now, let alone to me.

But he did express, it appeared, genuine concern for the women. 'I don't hold a grudge against Vera and Beezie even though it was their testimony which has got me in here,' he told me. 'I can't justify what they've done, but I can understand it. If they were in a position facing 14 years with an offer of cooperating in return for an early release, I can understand them offering evidence.'

He certainly had that understanding wrong because no such offer ever existed.

'It's very sad that Vera's health is so bad and yet they're keeping her in jail,' Shine continued. 'Tell those two poor old ladies I honestly hope they'll be released soon, and that Vera's health improves.'

All in all, little if anything was gained from the meeting, although I undertook to convey his sentiments to Toddie and Beezie, and to contact his mother on my return to Sydney to reassure her of his well-being.

•

On 21 January 1982 yet another hint of the possible resolution of Toddie and Beezie's future emerged when a Department of Immigration official phoned the prison from Canberra. The caller wanted to know whether, in the event the Attorney-General decided to grant the women a release on licence, they would be willing and able to pay their own airfares to the United States. The women assured the official they were able to and would be more than willing.

This on face value was a hint, the women believed, that their fortunes might be turning. However, they had been in this position too many times before to not still be apprehensive that it was going to be yet another false alarm.

On the same day the Immigration official made contact with the women, Australia's newspapers, TV and radio news bulletins led with a story detailing US Senator Hatfield's direct approach five weeks earlier to the Prime Minister.

Was this leaked by Senator Hatfield to 'embarrass' Australia into action? Was it dropped to a friendly press gallery journalist for domestic political purposes – a ploy to generate support for the women's continued imprisonment? And if it was a Canberra leak, was it from the Prime Minister or the Attorney-General?

Either way, the result was disastrous for the women's cause as it produced a significant public backlash. The *Newcastle Morning Herald*, in an editorial entitled 'Politics in the Drug Trade', suggested an American politician's overtures sounded like political influence at work. 'Senator Durack,' read the editorial 'should put aside all considerations of age, nationality and political advocacy and approach the case for parole strictly on its merits.' The editorial further asserted that releasing the women in April 1982 might be 'too soon, to show them lenience for reasons relating not to the crime but to politics'.

The Australian said in its 23 January editorial:

> Senator Mark Hatfield('s) ... opinions are well worth attention but the Australian Government will make a serious error if it heeds his request to release from jail two of his former constituents who are serving prison terms for smuggling drugs into Australia ... While it is open to the government to decide, while it frequently does, that because of their health or mental state of prisoners, it is proper to release them before they have finished their terms of imprisonment, Senator Hatfield's intervention should not be a relevant factor in arriving at a decision.

Labor Party shadow Attorney-General Senator Gareth Evans backed that position in a press release, saying, 'If a new regime of leniency for drug offenders is about to dawn, it should apply universally and not just because an American VIP snaps his fingers'.

Ouch.

'Hell they are beginning to tear our guts out again,' wrote Toddie in her diary.

> The editorials about us are terrible and you keep wondering why these so-called editors, journalists etc. who know

nothing about us say we deserve what we got and should serve our full sentence. Everyone is anti-American. Both very depressed and feel this will be another broken promise. Damn, why can't the media leave us alone?? How much more do we have to take?? On the news this morning was Jack Birney MP from Canberra saying we should not be released. BZ real down today, not that she hasn't been before during the past four years, but today she really showed it. Know she has been strong for me all these years. Damn this place and their politics and injustice.

Jack Birney was a former barrister and eastern Sydney backbench Member of Parliament lobbying the government to keep the women in prison. Newspaper coverage described Birney as having waged a 'hard campaign'.

'I received scores of complaints from constituents when there was word that the two Drug Grannies may be released,' he said. 'There is a lot of concern about drug penalties being too light and after all, they've only been there [in jail] almost four years.' By sheer coincidence, it was likely Vern Todd was one of Birney's constituents.

Beezie diarised:

Our Sandi came out this AM. We had a good visit. It was so good to see him. We had a lot of news from him. Only four weeks gone, but like I've said so many times, seems like years. Doesn't seem to be anything concrete. True, Sandi made wonderful contacts and the move is on, but again, are we damned if we do and damned if we don't?

Towards the end of March 1982 and with no indication from the Attorney-General of his likely decision, the women, their lawyers and supporters weren't sure what the next move should be.

The Norma Parker Centre superintendent told the women he believed any direct pressure from the Unites States wouldn't help the women's cause, while Claude Bilinsky was furious with his clients' home-state Senator Hatfield's 'interfering'.

Toddie's diary entries at this time reflected the misery they felt:

> I feel like too much pressure was put on by our government to Australia. Canberra is not going to be told what or what not to do. Again we listen to everyone and not trust our own judgement. I've had it. I'm getting to the point where I take my wrath out on Sandi and of all people, he and BZ do not deserve it. Know it's all this medication I'm on – addicted, depression, suicidal thoughts etc. Got into a terrible fight with BZ this morning. Wouldn't blame her at all if she would leave me when we got home.

Although Beezie had followed Toddie's instructions the year before not to acknowledge let alone celebrate her birthday, for her sixty-fourth she quietly arranged for the prison cook to bake a cake. I visited them the following day and Toddie was grateful for the good wishes. She wasn't cross that I came bearing a birthday bouquet of roses and she had even saved me a piece of her cake.

There was still no word from Canberra as April rolled around. The women spent their evenings playing Yahtzee, which Beezie had received on her birthday in 1981 and played on a daily basis, and watching sports on television, especially cheering on any American teams. They celebrated 29-year-old San Diego–born Craig Stadler's Masters Tournament win in a sudden-death playoff in early April. How Beezie yearned to play one more round – even just nine holes would do, she thought.

The women and their supporters continued to pray, lobby and search for signs of a likely decision. The Williams Royal Commission report produced from hearings conducted between 1977 and 1980 had included testimony from the Attorney-General's Department that a foreign offender liable to deportation was considered for conditional release 'at the time an Australian offender would be considered for release on parole'. Surely, their supporters argued, if this applied to the Drug Grannies, they would soon be considered for release.

It was encouraging news when convicted foreign-born drug smuggler and Commonwealth prisoner Trudie Palisa, a 28-year-old woman sentenced to four years' jail with a non-parole period of one year, was released after only nine months' imprisonment. Senator Durack offered no reasons for his decision. Palisa was a fellow inmate of the Drug Grannies and while they naturally focused on their own predicament, they nonetheless viewed Palisa's release as a good sign.

In another development arising from evidence before the Stewart Royal Commission which ran from 1981 to 1983, police divulged that Australia had arranged for British authorities to grant immunity to three Australian female heroin couriers. The deal ensured the women's return to give evidence against the Mr Asia syndicate, a notorious heroin importation operation headed by Terry Clark, who moved his shipments to Australia, New Zealand and England in the 1970s. One of the couriers, Allison Dine, carried a written indemnity from the Australian government wherever she travelled. The collective view was that hopefully the importance of the Drug Grannies' testimony that led to the conviction of Phillip Shine in the West German trial would be recognised in the same way as was the heroin couriers' testimony to the Mr Asia trial.

But the real surprise was the case of Kenneth Derley, a 31-year-old right-hand man to the infamous drug smuggler and former NSW Police detective Murray Riley. He had been released from Berrima prison after serving only thirty-four months of an eight-and-a-half year sentence. Maybe this was finally a sign the Attorney-General would rule in the women's favour, even though he had been criticised in journalist David Halpin's story in the *Sun-Herald* on 15 April:

The Federal Attorney, Senator Durack refused to say last week why he had ordered Derley's release, as a matter of privacy, Senator Durack's spokesman said. The Attorney-General's Department kept Derley's release very quiet. The New South Wales Department of Corrective Services confirmed they had released Derley at the express request of the Federal Government ... a number of senior drug investigators, federal and state, said they were stunned and amazed Derley had been released ... the Attorney-General's spokesman refused to compare Derley's early release with the recent refusal by Senator Durack to grant parole to the two American Drug Grannies.

As the women anxiously awaited further word on their possible release, Superintendent Wal Thompson at Norma Parker Centre shared with me his hopes for Toddie and Beezie.

You've heard me say it before and I'll say it again: it's not doing any good keeping these two old women in here anymore. Jails are supposed to be for people who are bad and who have been criminal, and the idea is in some way or another to rehabilitate them. These women have paid the price for their crime and alongside the murderers who are getting released from jail early, it's almost a crime in itself keeping the Drug Grannies in any longer.

Deputy Superintendent Shirley Goodfellow, who had known the women since their imprisonment on remand in early 1978 at Mulawa, was dismayed at their continued incarceration. But she had a job to do and carried out her work dutifully. Goodfellow's and Thompson's sentiments were shared by several commissioners of the Corrective Service Commission of New South Wales who believed the women should be released.

Finally, on 23 April, Senator Durack announced his decision. Just before noon, his Canberra office issued a press release saying he had reviewed the application by Florice Marie Bessire and Vera Todd Hays for release on licence. He refused again to grant the application. He said he did not consider a four-year minimum period was appropriate.

The first the women heard of the decision was on the noon radio news bulletins. It was only by chance that another inmate working in the garden had a radio on that Toddie and Beezie learned of their fate. Claude Bilinsky wasn't informed directly; he had to phone the Attorney-General's office for confirmation after hearing the news second-hand.

I sped out to the prison to comfort the women. The afternoon was spent with little talk and weary tears – they were so sapped after numerous disappointments that Toddie didn't even have the energy to rant anymore. After months of waiting following the last snub just before Christmas 1981, the women had built up their hopes. They had forced themselves to stay strong, relying on the 'four-year period' referred to by Senator Durack himself on previous occasions when he had refused their release. Again it begged the question: why?

Beezie wrote home to her sister:

It's got to the stage now that we just don't care anymore. I know I shouldn't say this, but we may not live to see our beautiful United States of America ever again. I can't see us managing another year, let alone another month in this prison. Toddie's mental state is sometimes dangerously depressive and I fear what she may do with the tablets she hides. When you're asleep – you're not in here.

In fact, prison staff intentionally withheld Toddie's medication for a week after the announcement of the latest knockback by the Attorney-General. They were concerned about the sometimes excessive quantities of tablets she kept for 'emergencies'.

The other inmates in the prison were also upset by the news. The Drug Grannies were the grand old ladies of the Norma Parker Centre. They were respected and well regarded by staff and many of the inmates too.

While Toddie took yet another rejection badly, Beezie on the other hand somehow or other found renewed strength and resilience to keep going. She was the rock and she realised Toddie's survival was tethered to her own will to stay alive. The more demoralised Toddie was, the stronger Beezie became in order to support her companion and help her through the tough times. Though mentally she remained sound, physically she wasn't so robust. The demands of the gardening work were a struggle for Beezie now, and she could no longer keep up with the heavy labouring involved. When an opportunity arose to run the small prison canteen, Beezie applied to take on the role. While it wasn't True Value Hardware in La Pine, it was an organisational role that Beezie knew she would enjoy and which would be less taxing on her body.

The canteen stocked chocolates, toiletries, pens and other personal items for the inmates to purchase on their weekly buy-up using ledger credits instead of actual cash. Toddie began to help Beezie to compile orders, sell goods, stock shelves and assist with the daily reconciliation. On good days they would sell upwards of five hundred dollars' worth of their limited product line. It was a matter of pride that their paperwork was submitted to the officers on time and the books always balanced. The canteen chores became a new diversion for them both, and proved mentally challenging while they further marked time. Toddie tackled her pool responsibilities with greater commitment as a result of their work together in the canteen.

The legal eagles representing the women put their heads together, trying to devise a way – or ways – to force the Attorney-General's hand, to see reason and show compassion. Clearly the approach using American pressure had failed.

One option the lawyers considered was to seek leave in the NSW Criminal Court of Appeal; if granted a hearing, they would ask the court to impose a non-parole period. In other words, formalise Judge Staunton's post-sentence advice – of a non-parole period of not less than four years – through the courts.

A Queen's Counsel was retained to obtain the best advice. The risk as always would be that the court might impose a longer non-parole period … longer than the four years Staunton had suggested. After all, the sentencing judge's advice carried no weight in law. But there was an attraction, notwithstanding the risk, of offering the Attorney-General a chance to save political face without being backed into a corner. It was a difficult situation Durack faced given there was no non-parole period established by the court. But it wasn't as if he couldn't act.

'If we can take the decision out of Durack's hands and have the court set the non-parole period, maybe then he would be a far sight easier to deal with,' suggested Bilinsky in a note to the women.

The Drug Grannies' case had become a dilemma for the government, and it seemed the Opposition too. In an unrelated case involving convicted Italian-born drug criminal Luigi Pochi, Labor had been reluctant to become involved. They saw no votes in supporting drug criminals. Its stand was consistent with shadow Attorney-General Senator Gareth Evans's criticism in January of American support to free the Drug Grannies; being opposed to drugs – and the Drug Grannies – made for valuable political mileage.

Bilinsky met with Senator Durack on 12 May. This was Bilinsky's note for file of their conversation:

> He gave me about half an hour of his time and he tried to explain the case as he had to deal with it as best he could. He said because there was legally no non-parole period set – it was only a letter from the judge, that said he would have given four years and it was not entered in his judgment – he had to follow the advice of his department, which was that the women's imprisonment was fourteen years. He said the publicity generated in January 1982 didn't do the women any

good at all, because according to him, it polarised opinion right around Australia. People either hated the women and said throw the key away, or they showed sympathy and lodged pleas for their release. He said he had received hundreds of letters from Australians saying 'keep the women in jail', and he had to remember these people were Australians who obviously cared. On the other hand, Durack also received many letters from Australians and people overseas pleading for compassion and their release. Durack was totally unwilling to make any forecast on how much longer they could expect to stay because he said that wouldn't be right. He pointed out the women's case had been an unusual one as they had been asking for release almost from the day of their sentence. Senator Durack said it would indeed help him if the court fixed a non-parole period, although he would still have to take the advice of his department. He said he would find out from his department what their attitude would be if the women were to seek leave to appeal. You know, the more publicity their case gets, the more it comes to the attention of the people, and I suspect the more people will turn against them.

By now it seemed the Attorney-General was riding the case as a personal mission. While he claimed he deferred to his department for advice, all the evidence pointed to the contrary. With Australians due to go to the polls sometime in 1983 and the possibility of a change in government, I sensed it was time to improve my understanding of the Opposition's position on the Drug Grannies.

•

Gareth Evans, QC, was an intelligent, articulate and learned Labor senator from Victoria who had entered parliament in 1978. In a meeting with the shadow Attorney-General, and subsequent telephone conversations, I began to detect he had a better appreciation of the vexed predicament the American women faced. When I'd first discussed the matter with him in January 1982, his position was simple: the American prisoners should be treated no differently to Australian prisoners. He seemed unaware at the time that as Americans they had in fact been treated differently. He initially believed that if there was no non-parole period set and a fourteen-year head sentence imposed, so be it. But, over time, he began to become convinced of the unfairness of such an inflexible stance.

He said in one exchange with me:

> In relation to early release on licence, you are concerned about apparent disparities between the treatment of Federal and State prisoners. I share your concern in this regard. In my view the proposal for a Commonwealth Parole Board has much to recommend it ... this is certainly a matter to which I would give early consideration upon the election of a Labor Government.

I undertook to continue a dialogue with Evans and his staff to provide the shadow Attorney-General with additional information which could be useful in any future public comments Senator Evans might make.

On 5 July, the Sydney-based Queen's Counsel, whom the women had retained, offered his opinion on appeal avenues – if any – open to them. His advice was the women could *not* seek leave to appeal to the courts to set a non-parole period because in 1978, their original appeal had been withdrawn, then dismissed, and there was no longer a jurisdiction in which to hear such an application. Furthermore, though a moot point he said, while it had been ascertained the Crown would not oppose the women seeking leave to appeal, the QC was concerned the best non-parole period they would likely receive would be six and a half years. There was little prospect for success pursuing this strategy. He recommended against seeking leave to appeal.

In August, Bilinsky tried again, writing to Attorney-General Durack and suggesting the sentencing judge had erred in law. He argued persuasively for a reconsideration of the release on licence request. He got nowhere.

An appeal through the United Nations Human Rights Commission on the basis of discrimination by the Australian government was also considered – denying the women a non-parole period on the grounds of their nationality was a breach of their human rights. That idea also died a quick death for fear it had little chance of achieving a meaningful result. Indeed, it could well have further steeled Durack's determination not to be pressured into a positive decision.

Nothing was working in the women's favour when it came to the attempt to turn Durack's steadfast refusal to regard departmental advice, heed legal argument or consider diplomatic overtures as anything but an irritant. Durack had interpreted the case and sentencing as he saw fit, and, worse, he appeared to be making policy on the run.

From the outset of their incarceration, Toddie and Beezie were frustrated with the difference between their treatment as federal prisoners and that of the state prisoners. And this proved to be an ongoing aggravation. Most prisoners who maintained good behaviour at Norma Parker Centre were transferred, for example, to a pre-works release program in their final twelve months. It allowed them to attend college or to be employed during the day, as a form of preparation for re-entry into the community. But the Drug Grannies, as federal prisoners, were denied this opportunity. And to add insult to injury, because they did not have a non-parole period they were also denied the day leave offered to state prisoners (day leave enabled close friends or relatives to sign the prisoners out to spend time at their homes without formal supervision). It was a no-win situation all round.

Refusing to give up all hope, however, Bilinsky pursued another avenue through the NSW parole board. Former NSW

Corrective Services chairman Dr Tony Vinson strongly believed the women had served more than sufficient time and viewed it as unfair and unjust to keep them imprisoned any longer. But that possibility also fell over. The Drug Grannies were federal prisoners and the state parole board had no authority whatsoever to release them.

For Toddie and Beezie, the days in jail were filled with endless boredom save their outdoor and canteen chores, visits from friends and supporters, and corresponding with family and friends in the United States. I tried to make each weekly visit with them special – having a watch band repaired and returned, or buying music cassettes from time to time. I returned from the United States earlier in the year with half a suitcase of American foods such as peanut butter, cookies, BBQ sauce, ketchup, mayonnaise and hot sauce for the women. Over time, the goodies would find their way to the women during our visits and be shared with the staff and other prisoners.

Occasionally something surprising would break the monotony and lift their spirits. One winter afternoon, a tour bus pulled into the prison's parking area. The entry in the women's diaries conveys how unexpected and inspiring the event was for them both. Toddie wrote:

A tour bus stopped outside containing a bunch of people from Portland, Oregon YWCA. There were 11 women and one man that had taken a package tour deal from Oregon, to Australia. Wonder what the hell the driver thought, bringing tourists to a prison? Anyway Mr. Thompson allowed two ladies to come in. One in her early 50's with silver hair and the other of Oriental background. Lovely, lovely people. We were told by the ladies that all of Oregon was working for our release. Their stay was only about 10 minutes because of the late hour. Mr. Thompson allowed them to bring us food from Oregon: Tillamook cheese, and nut-covered toffee. What a treat for us and how wonderful it was to taste American food.

When they left, the officer told them to stand in the entrance to the jail, as our window faces their bus. All the tourists emerged from coach and waved to us and sang a beautiful spiritual song. It was beautiful. Made our day.

Another (literally) uplifting moment for Toddie and Beezie midyear came right out of thin air. As was their wont, the women watched TV in the evening – for them, it was a window from the prison out into the world. One particular night there was a story about a man in California who had strapped approximately 43 helium weather balloons to a lawn chair and took to the sky. Now there's a crazy idea. Toddie's diary recalled:

We were watching the 6.30 news and lo and behold, there's my sister Hazel's son, my nephew Larry, going up in a chair balloon. Couldn't believe my eyes. The miracle of our Lord bringing my loved ones into our room! Seems his plans were to soar over the mountains and land in the Mojave Desert. His ascent was too fast, and he climbed to 16,000 feet and had to shoot some of the balloons with his BB gun. Then he descended too fast and landed in Long Beach. The two-way CB conversation with Carol, his girlfriend, was priceless. Seems his take-off was premature and he lost his glasses. Carol was telling him to come down as he couldn't see a thing without them. He told her not to worry as he had a second pair. The interview and close-up shot was unbelievable and brought forth happy tears. BZ and I still couldn't believe it.

When I next visited Toddie and Beezie, they were in a buoyant mood recounting the TV news story. At the height of his balloon ascent, Larry was observed by two somewhat bewildered pilots flying commercial aircraft: The lawn chair landing was unceremonious – after shooting at the balloons one by one to decrease his altitude, Larry accidentally dropped his BB gun, but fortunately the descent continued until he became entangled in a power line, after which he was able to climb to safety. The legend of 'Lawn Chair Larry' was born! Discussion of the event and their mirth took them beyond the walls of the prison and that little bit closer to family in the United States. We had a good laugh over what possibilities a similar, but perhaps more elegantly executed, flight might bring for the women. It was a lift that the women sorely needed – albeit brief – to distract them from their ongoing incarceration.

•

At the end of August 1982, Attorney-General Peter Durack faced calls to resign due to the findings of the Costigan Royal Commission on the Activities of the Federated Ship Painters and Dockers Union. The commission's report contained a stinging indictment of his department and of Senator Durack himself.

Durack was able to weather the political eruption, but not the physical storm. In mid-September, he was rushed to hospital late one evening. His chest pains were diagnosed as a heart attack, and assistant minister Neil Brown, QC, was suddenly thrown into the role of acting Attorney-General.

Days later, Brown signed a letter to the women's lawyer, but over Senator Durack's signature block. It seemed the acting Attorney wanted this matter to remain the responsibility of Senator Durack ... just in case he changed his mind, yet again. It was dated 20 September 1982. It was probably the best news for the Drug Grannies in a very long time.

I have decided that an appropriate non-parole period for your clients would have been five years and I intend to deal with them as I would had the court fixed that term ... release on licence prior to the expiration of a non-parole period is granted only in exceptional circumstances and these matters do not, in my opinion, constitute such circumstances ... I do not accept your assertion that because the trial judge made a mistake in law, the prisoners are now being detained longer than if he had applied the law correctly ... consistently with my decision ... I propose to further review your client's case sometime prior to 1 February 1983, with a view to considering their possible release on licence not later than that date.

Just maybe, Neil Brown was going to be the difference the women needed as the decision-maker who controlled their fate. While the letter again offered hope, however, it did not present anything more than a date when *consideration* of their release would occur. 'Consideration of possible release' was a long way from 'granted licences to be at large'.

A copy of the letter was delivered to the women at the jail coinciding with a visit by an official from the Department of Immigration delivering the women's deportation orders, documents originally authorised for issue in February 1982. The standing orders were ready for whenever their release on licence was granted. They dared to hope ... yet again.

It was around this time as well that the New South Wales government announced the cost of keeping a prisoner in a state jail had risen to almost $25,000 a year. Not only was continued incarceration of the women unjust, it made no economic sense. The day after the women took possession of the acting Attorney-General's letter and their deportation orders, convicted hashish smuggler Lania Chedid was released on licence. Chedid was a fellow Commonwealth prisoner at Norma Parker Centre.

Her release had been expedited – it was still nine months *before* her non-parole date was even due. She had been convicted on 30 September 1981 for importing cannabis resin and was sentenced to five and a half years' prison with a two-year non-parole period.

There were celebrations within the Norma Parker Centre, especially among the other four Lebanese prisoners on similar drugs charges. And while the Drug Grannies were always happy for those being released from prison, they couldn't help but feel they'd been cheated yet again.

The women could hardly bare to consider what might happen if Senator Durack recovered and returned to his job. Would he change his mind and rescind the acting Attorney-General's letter? Did the acting Attorney-General's signature carry the same weight as Senator Durack's? Could Durack revoke or override any decision made by his temporary replacement?

These fears and the reaction to the latest and strongest sign of hope were recorded in Toddie's diary entry:

So Senator Peter Durack had a heart attack. Maybe he knows now what pressure, sensational journalism is all about. Still not writing home and telling family of the possibility we might be home sometime in February 1983. Will still believe it only when I see our release dates in black and white. However, once more, our hopes and dreams are building up to a crescendo. Damn, if they are dashed again, don't know what we will do. We are not breathing a word of this to anyone, especially family. Want so badly to write home and speak of the same, but at this point, don't dare – after the past three years of disappointment to them; besides practically destroying us. Very depressed today. Feel we will be knocked back again. Just can't shake it, and I'm at one of my lowest ebbs. Damn this country, the bureaucracy; how do they have the guts for the past three years to knock our licence back? Re-reading the diary notes today from 1981, I sound like a broken record. SHIT!!! My mood/attitude I must admit are at their worst, and with each passing day the pressure mounts. Consequently I take it out on those I love most. I excused myself from Sandi's visit; felt like I was ready to explode and I know I was very cross and sharp with him. This time it is more trying than the past three rejections of our release. One would think it would be the other way around since we have a copy of the letter stating that ours would be a five year non-parole. I still have this terrible gut feeling that something bad will happen again.

But in what felt like an auspicious sign, the women were contacted by the US Consulate, suggesting it was probably time to apply for new passports ... just in case. The passports they had used to enter Australia had now expired.

Beezie wrote: 'Got passport applications. Got to get photos taken. Consul, Mr. O'Leary said new passports will be kept with him and upon departure, regardless of day or hour, he would see that we would receive same – along with our original passports; now out of date.'

The prison planned the usual pre-Christmas events, including an open day where the number of guests each inmate could invite was relaxed. My wife and I attended and we all enjoyed a midday lunch and exchanged gifts. Laughter filled the yard within the prison's high walls. Toddie and Beezie won eleven prizes in the tombola. Toddie was convinced this was the beginning of a change in their luck.

•

A few days later, Toddie and Beezie were called to the superintendent's office. He had a folder of documents on his desk. They looked official and were imprinted with the Australian government coat of arms.

Toddie's diary records what happened:

Mr Thompson had finally received the letter from Durack about the five year non-parole date. Anyways, there were other official looking letters attached to same and all marked urgent – wanting complete report on us by the first of December from Mr. Thompson and the parole officer. We are extremely happy and showed our emotions to Mr. Thompson with a big kiss on the cheek. Finally getting something in writing, but again will not mention anything about this in our letters home. After being shot down on three other tries, we cannot have our family go through this again. Apprehension, paranoia running strong again. Can't shake this terrible gut feeling that all is not well!! If it fails this time, there's no telling what I will do.

Ever the patriot, Toddie said a silent prayer on 7 December for the soldiers who had fallen in wars past: it was Pearl Harbor Day, an event which took her back to her two years' army service during World War II. 'I can't believe it was 41 years ago. I really feel my age,' she wrote in a letter home.

She and Beezie would have a pre-Christmas visit a few days later from their steadfast Christian friends Lillian and Stan Wheatman. Having worked in prisons, Reverend Wheatman had seen and heard a lot. Police had shared with him information about Vern Todd's subsequent trips to Australia after the Drug Grannies' imprisonment.

Toddie wrote in her diary:

Stan told us the Federal Police contacted him and told him many facts of which we were never aware. My dear wonderful nephew (tongue in cheek) had seven vehicles including ours, travel from Stuttgart to Bombay at the same time as us. We were told by Vern that we would be promoting his infant Tubby Bath, both unaware of his dastardly, conniving brain. Damn. How naive can one be? The love, trust for my kin has been my undoing. Pray to God I never run into him.

A week later, Toddie and Beezie didn't stay up to see the New Year in but slept through until daybreak when the cockatoos awoke them with their squawking and screeching. It was nature's answer to the alarm clock, they said: guaranteed to awaken the heaviest sleepers – perhaps even the dead.

The new year of 1983 began slowly for the women. Uncharacteristically, the summer months thus far had not brought the customary rolling heatwaves. Instead, the weather kindly provided them with cooler-than-normal-temperatures and intermittent relief to sweltering days and sticky humidity at night.

They watched the Tournament of the Roses football jamboree between Michigan and UCLA, their hometown college, on 2 January. They cheered the final whistle with a UCLA 24–14 win.

While the women were accustomed to this waiting game and were expecting to hear whether Attorney-General Durack – who had returned to work – had decided it would be appropriate for them to be released, the uncertainty hadn't become any easier. Despite the encouraging signs they had recently received, the knowledge that Senator Durack was out of hospital and back in the chair gave them little confidence for a positive outcome. By the beginning of February, the women had heard nothing of their fate.

Unaware of these developments, both Toddie's sisters remained upbeat and hopeful. In her letter to me of 7 February, Hazel wrote, 'We keep hoping each day we will hear word of Vera and Beezie's arrival here in America. We must be patient. Perhaps as I write this they will be winging their way home.'

Toddie's other sister, Carrie, also wrote a letter on 7 February. She had recognised the women's red, white and blue outfits in a recent Christmas photo:

> Just like the girls to be wearing the red, white and blue, our beloved country's colors. They probably will be wearing the same when they return to the States – plus a yellow ribbon or two. What a glorious day this will be. We haven't ventured far from home in the event of missing that all important phone call.

The women's minds began to play games, as evidenced in Toddie's diary entries written at this time:

We are wondering if Mr. Thompson has our release papers but told to keep quiet – not to tell us or anyone as they, Corrective Services, Canberra etc. don't want the news media to be aware of anything! We feel we won't be given any notice at all and we will be taken quietly away some evening. You can see how the mind works. Grab at any given straw. Had a strange, wonderful dream last night. BZ and I were in our room when one of the officers came in with tears streaming down her face holding our release papers for Feb 7. She was so happy for us, but again the tears were of great sadness in saying goodbye. We all had a good cry. We know when the time comes, there will be a few tears with a few of the officers plus one or two girls. The most tears will be walking out that gate!! Also need to check my going home clothes, purchased for the past three supposedly release dates; hope they will still fit. Now I am feeling they will do the same to us as they did to Glen; make us wait until April the 21st, the day of sentence, before they release us, and even that isn't definite. Damn this country and their bare-faced lies.

On 3 February I made my way out to Norma Parker Centre on an all-too-familiar errand I intensely disliked, and which became more difficult each time. The Attorney-General had faxed a letter to the women's lawyer, a copy of which I carried with me. It read:

I refer to previous correspondence concerning your clients, Mesdames Bessire and Hays. I have again reviewed the question whether your clients should be released on licence under Section 19A of the *Crimes Act 1914* and have determined that it would not at present be appropriate to make a recommendation to His Excellency the Governor-General that they be so released.

The women were utterly devastated. Still, the possibility remained that a decision would be made closer to the date of sentencing: 21 April.

Hell hath no fury like a prisoner refused their due release, especially when it happens again, and again, and again. Toddie's diary entry was scathing:

> Well the damn bastards did it to us again. Shit. Sandi came out with the message this afternoon. We just can't believe it. Our poor families. Durack did it again. Believe he rules the government, overrides everyone. Will we ever get out of the boring rut we're in? I had a terrible gut feeling about this; I wasn't wrong. Where, how do we go from here?

Within twenty-four hours, the Prime Minister announced the nation would go to an election on 5 March.

Toddie and Beezie could only laugh at how politics had yet again interfered with the potential of an early release. They asked me what I thought might happen if a Labor government under Bob Hawke was voted into office; would anything change? Privately I was hopeful Senator Evans – a decent man – now seemed to fully recognise the unfairness of the women's situation and would release them. However, it was impossible to tell what might arise in the next four weeks' electioneering. What if the Drug Grannies were used as an example by the two major political parties to illustrate who could be the 'toughest on drugs'? And who knew the election's outcome so far out? It didn't bear contemplating and it was better not to raise the women's hopes.

As was convention after an election was called, the government went into caretaker mode. No major policy decisions could be enacted; no high-level appointments could be made; no major contracts could be signed; and no international political visits could be undertaken until the election result was known.

And no Drug Grannies could be released now the election writs had been issued. While the women's release was not explicitly covered by the conventions, they provided cover for Senator Durack and the government, who did not want a 'soft on drugs' backlash running during the campaign.

CHAPTER EIGHTEEN

THIS IS FOR REAL, RIGHT?

For Toddie and Beezie, the early months of 1983 felt like the slowest of their lives: there was 'objective' time that they followed on their calendar, and then there was 'lived' time which they felt, acted and experienced. It was the latter which seemed to lock them into perpetual slow motion.

February belatedly unleashed the summer's hot weather and the women wilted in the heat and humidity. They kept themselves occupied with their canteen duties, and Toddie maintained the swimming pool and encouraged other inmates to learn how to carry out the work.

Their diaries tread a fine line of cautious optimism and veiled anxiousness, as Toddie's entry showed:

Received heartbreaking letter from sister – the second to arrive after the news of our latest knockback. The anger, frustration they feel, tears me apart. Bilinsky has the feeling that it won't matter which party gets in, Liberal or Labor. He still feels that within a couple of months we should be on our way. This time our hopes are not soaring. We are tired of seeing that light flicker at the end of the tunnel only to go out for the past three years. David O'Leary, US Consul was out to visit. Like us, he is very upset and can't understand the politics in this country nor the reason for our not going home. He feels, as we do, that our release will be coming soon. Just has to be. Sandi came to visit for about an hour to say goodbye before he leaves for Europe with his ice hockey team. Will be gone for a couple of weeks, and once more that will be like a couple of years to us.

Australians awoke to the news on the morning of 6 March that they had a new prime minister – Bob Hawke – leading a Labor government. His party had been swept to power, soundly defeating the Liberal government and, to the delight of Toddie and Beezie, Senator Peter Durack no longer controlled their destiny. Each government department arranged post-election briefing binders during the campaign, ready for a new minister or the same minister or, as in 1983, for an entirely new government. The new Attorney-General, Senator Gareth Evans, and his staff were likely already poring over the incoming government brief the Attorney-General's Department had prepared.

Among the first decisions Evans would need to make would be what to do about the Drug Grannies. There were other more substantial policy issues to address, such as a suite of tax reforms, responding to two royal commissions on drugs and tax avoidance, and a range of laws requiring new legislation dear to Evans's and Labor's campaign undertakings, but they were longer-term, bigger ticket items.

There was no guarantee what the new government would do with Toddie and Beezie. However, a letter Senator Evans wrote a year earlier to Claude Bilinsky indicated that Labor might take a more sensible approach. In it he said:

I certainly do not think there should be any differentiation in the penalties given to Australian and non-Australian citizens in cases such as this and if Australian citizens would have been eligible for parole ... then there can be no justification for denying such benefit to non-Australians.

The sentencing judge had already indicated he would have set a four-year non-parole period, so that met one of Evans's theoretical criteria for release. Senator Durack had accepted that premise at one time. Later he arbitrarily imposed a new and higher bar of a five-year non-parole period. Both cases met Senator Evans's own requirement, albeit posed when in the comfort of Opposition, that there could be no justification for denying such a benefit to non-citizens.

The issue now was would Senator Evans and Labor in government be true to their word?

•

It was the last day of the working week. The intercom in the office of Sydney-based American Consul General David O'Leary buzzed. He glanced at his watch – it was 10 am. The date –18 March 1983. His secretary told him she had a caller on hold who was from Senator Gareth Evans's office to discuss the case of the Drug Grannies. Clearly the incoming Attorney-General was wasting no time. The conversation was brief and to the point. O'Leary made notes as he talked. It was possible his weekend plans could change.

The phone call coincided with Toddie's sixty-fifth birthday. She had received cards during the week from family but she could not bear to open them because depression set in – which was typical on birthdays and at Christmas.

•

David O'Leary, a near 25-year veteran US diplomat, was sworn to secrecy about the content of his telephone call with Canberra. If it leaked, it could jeopardise an important announcement the new Hawke government was soon to make.

On Monday 21 March, Senator Evans's office made an appointment with the Governor-General Sir Ninian Stephen, requesting he sign a set of documents which had been prepared and included in the minister's incoming briefs relating to the Drug Grannies. The process was short and swift, and the documents collected and returned to the minister's office within the hour.

In the days following Toddie's birthday, the women remained oblivious to the cogs of bureaucracy that were slowly beginning to turn in their case. They listened carefully every morning to the radio news bulletins, hanging on every word. On Tuesday 22 March, as usual, Beezie worked in the canteen, Toddie cleaned the pool, and some new inmates were checked into the prison. For the women it was just another boring and slow day.

On Wednesday 23 March they heard that the stoush between the former Liberal Party Treasurer John Howard and the new Liberal Party leader, Andrew Peacock, had not abated. Peacock was demanding his deputy account for claims he had made as Treasurer during the election campaign, which the Liberals had lost. Far away from Canberra, in the Australian outback, the nation's eyes were firmly focused on Prince Charles and his wife Diana, Princess of Wales, visiting remote communities. The media was captivated. A riot in an Adelaide prison after sixty prisoners went on a rampage had finally been brought under control. The Tasmanian premier, Robin Gray, rejected the new prime minister's request he cease work on the Gordon-Below-Franklin Dam, a heritage site Labor had promised to save. But there was no news about the Drug Grannies.

That morning Hayden Strang, a senior bureaucrat from the Attorney-General's Department, was flying from Canberra to Sydney. He caught the first flight just after 6 am. At about 10 am, in the company of David O'Leary and an Immigration official, Strang arrived at the Norma Parker Centre. They presented their identification at the main gate and were quickly ushered into the superintendent's office. Acting prison superintendent, Shirley Goodfellow – nicknamed 'Goodie' – was always preoccupied with three things at once, and today was no different. There had been a break-out over the weekend, more drugs had been detected in several of the prisoners' urine samples, and head office was beginning to tire of requests for the dog squad to search the jail. Still, the Norma Parker Centre was one of the best things to happen to prison reform in the state in the twentieth century, though challenges would likely occur from time to time.

Goodfellow had a sneaking suspicion why the three men were there. Strang told her he was carrying the Governor-General's orders for the release on licence of the prisoners Hays and Bessire. He asked that the prisoners be summoned from their room with as little fuss as possible. It was his formal duty to convey the decision. Strang explained to the acting superintendent the pair would become Immigration's responsibility once they left the prison. It followed, he explained, that the year-old deportation orders would then come into effect.

Superintendent Goodfellow left to go and find the prisoners. Beezie was in the canteen doing bookwork. Toddie was outside, working on the pool. As was customary, Toddie found it best in the warmer months to make as early a start as possible to beat the heat. Goodfellow sent Beezie out to summon Toddie to the canteen for this unexpected 'meeting'. She concentrated on the details written on the canteen spreadsheets and paperwork Beezie was working on while awaiting her return with Toddie.

The relationship between Goodfellow and the women was one of mutual warmth and utmost respect. The senior prison officer was a consummate professional, but she had a soft spot for the two older prisoners and appreciated their courtesy and willingness to help in the jail, mentoring other women. She was just as frustrated as the two women by the politicking surrounding their continued incarceration.

'I was just getting to that damn filter, and now you've interrupted me ... it better be important,' Toddie chided as she entered the canteen.

Drawing a deep breath while trying unsuccessfully to suppress her growing smile, Goodfellow gave the women the news they'd longed to hear for five years. 'What I'm about to say is to go no further than these canteen walls ... you understand?' she whispered. 'Least of all to the three gentlemen waiting at this very moment in my office. You're going home tonight on the first plane to the United States of America!' The two prisoners were not to let on that Goodie had let the cat out of the bag.

Neither Toddie nor Beezie flinched for a moment. They then threw their arms around each other, embracing tightly, savouring the moment they feared would never come. As instructed, they remained quiet, giddy with anticipation of what the three simple words actually meant: 'you're going home'. They were likely in shock but didn't allow it to completely disarm their sense of reality.

Beezie began to cough and then take deep breaths to recover. Toddie shook her head disbelievingly, but continued to smile, and removed her glasses which were starting to fog up.

Beezie looked at Goodfellow, her face suddenly becoming serious. She asked, 'This is for real, right? You're sure now?'

'Yes, yes ... quick, tidy up and hurry over to my office ... and remember, you know nothing,' the superintendent said before leaving to return to the visitors.

Toddie and Beezie made themselves presentable and then walked calmly to the superintendent's office. They still held a slight apprehension that they would wake up all of a sudden and find it was a dream.

The women entered the office and were ushered into an anteroom removed from the administration staff. It was the same room where I had once told them their release – assured by officials in Canberra as 'definite' – had been denied, but they were now face-to-face with Strang, O'Leary and the Immigration officer.

After a brief introduction, Strang addressed the women. 'Mrs Hays and Miss Bessire, I'm from the Attorney-General's Department in Canberra. I have with me your release papers, signed by the Governor-General acting on the advice of the Attorney-General, Senator Gareth Evans.'

By now he was smiling. Toddie and Beezie were savouring every word he uttered.

'Here are your papers. You are now free but you must understand that until arrangements can be confirmed with an airline for your passage home to the United States, the Immigration authorities will be placing you in the custody of Mrs Goodfellow,' Strang said.

Tears trickled then streamed across the women's faces as they both grasped the gravitas of the moment. Strang and O'Leary were aware of the protracted nature of the case and its sad history of appeals. Goodfellow embraced the two women. Beezie raised her eyes skywards, shook her head and amid the tears, said, 'Thank you, Lord, and bless this Labor government.' Finally Toddie released her emotions and declared, 'Oh my god! Who would have been able to predict how these minutes have been … it's just too much … but I love, I love, I love it!'

It was an intensely moving scene. Government bureaucrats rarely had the chance to convey a Governor-General's release on licence to a prisoner, let alone two at the one time.

The women shared a cup of tea and biscuits with Superintendent Goodfellow and the three officials as they celebrated the news. Word spread quickly throughout the prison; the grapevine was a fast although not always accurate communication system. This time it was both fast and accurate.

Their official business completed, the visitors departed the prison, wishing the women well. Toddie and Beezie headed back to their room to begin packing. They got no further than the veranda outside the administration building when a cheer went up from a group of inmates.

The women were escorted to their room by a throng of laughing, shouting and weeping women, all delighting in the long-awaited good fortune of Toddie and Beezie's release. As they tried to pack, inmates filed into the bedroom to wish them luck and a safe trip home. Rules forbidding prisoners to be in each other's quarters were discreetly overlooked as women moved openly in and out of the grannies' room. Some helped pack, others eyed off what they might claim if the women didn't have space to take all their possessions with them.

Beezie had earmarked their television for Ferguson Lodge, where she often volunteered, caring for paraplegic and quadriplegic patients. Clothes that didn't fit into the women's suitcases were quickly passed onto fellow inmates.

I had been back in Australia barely forty-eight hours and was fighting jet lag when I was contacted at work with the news. It was impossible to get a call through to the jail as the lines were jammed, so I made plans to drive there later in the day to join the expected media throng outside and wave the women goodbye before answering journalists' questions about their next steps. I had a standing arrangement with the women that in the event of their sudden release, if they did not have an opportunity to contact me, they would send a message as soon as they touched down in mainland USA.

Just before noon the federal government issued details of the Drug Grannies' impending freedom. News bulletins led with the story and the afternoon editions of the tabloids screamed 'Drug Grannies Go Free'.

The women remained faithful to their jail diaries and each made an entry upon hearing the wonderful news. Beezie wrote, 'It happened. We're leaving today – WOW – back to the USA.' Toddie stayed true to her desire to record events in detail:

9.30AM BZ came to pool area to tell me a fellow from Canberra was here. Mrs. Goodfellow took BZ and me to canteen to tell us we would be leaving here 7PM TONIGHT!!!! We are to act surprised when the man from Canberra tells us. We are in another state of shock, but beautiful – HOME, HOME, HOME. No more tears!

Just after 5 pm, the final muster of the day was conducted. For the very last time, Toddie and Beezie made their way down from their room to attend the prisoner roll call. Both were attired in the outfits they'd purchased several years earlier to wear home when the joyous time came.

There was an air of celebration as the women's names were called out, an excited buzz of talking, laughter and hoots.

'Vera Todd Hays,' called the officer.

'Yes, ma'am!' shouted Toddie, offering a mock salute.

'Florice Marie Bessire,' said the officer.

'Yes ma'am!' replied Beezie with a smile from ear to ear.

The gathering erupted into a loud cheer followed by more shouting and laughter. Several of the women returned to the kitchen, where they'd already prepared a bon voyage cake in honour of Toddie and Beezie. Officers remained at the prison after their shifts had finished to join in the long-awaited celebrations and to bid their farewells.

At 6 pm, with a press pack massing at the prison entrance with their cameras, microphones and helicopters beaming live TV footage back to their news bulletins, the Drug Grannies were ushered through the gates of the Norma Parker Centre for the last time. They got into a waiting Commonwealth car which was to ferry them and their luggage to Sydney International Airport terminal for their flight home to the United States.

'How's it feel to be free?' shouted one journalist.

'Beautiful, just beautiful,' replied Beezie.

They waved and blew kisses as they were driven off to the airport. Journalists spotted me by the women's car as they departed. I held an impromptu press conference, thanking the new Labor government and Attorney-General Senator Gareth Evans for the correct and swift decision to grant the women a release on licence, and indicated their next steps once home would be to adjust to being free and rid of the prison rules under which they'd been living for the past five years. The women, I said, had been incarcerated for such a long period of time due to an unfair system in which they had been dealt a very poor hand, and certain politicians had not made it any easier for them.

Qantas made arrangements to secure the women's privacy until the plane was ready to depart. They were issued boarding passes under assumed names – Mrs Simpson and Mrs Martin – and seated at the very rear of the Qantas 747 jet on their flight to San Francisco via Hawaii.

Toddie made one closing entry in her jail diary while aboard the flight:

Winging our way home on Qantas flight 003. What a helluva mess trying to leave Norma Parker. Immigration had our tickets under aliases, but it didn't do any good. All the media were waiting for us to leave!! Channel 7 and 9 helicopters out etc. Made a tape of the girls coming in and out of our room. What a joyous day for all; especially us. Don't know how we managed to get in the car – what with the news media pushing, shoving microphones in our faces etc. Tight security at airport. In back way, down tunnels, up elevators, long corridors – managed all without news media. We were snuck on the plane, last three seats in tail section, but this didn't bother us as we were treated like VIPs all the way. Immigration told stewardess and male stewards we were not to have any alcohol beverages until we reached Hawaii. Hell, as soon as smoking lights went out, unfasten seat belts, the alcohol poured. We called it 'The Champagne Flight'. Think we tried to make up for the past five years in one night. BZ went to sleep around 2AM. I was sick all night. What a way to go. Upon arriving in Hawaii, media waiting for us. Qantas took excellent care of us. Kept everyone away. The lay-over about half an hour and we were aboard first.

Toddie and Beezie had not yet had the benefit of reading *why* the new Attorney-General set them free, as outlined in his press release issued in Canberra.

First, Senator Evans acknowledged they had been discriminated against by Judge Staunton 'because they were United States citizens' when he sentenced them to fourteen years in prison and failed to impose a non-parole period. Evans went on:

> The two women have now served a sufficiently lengthy period in prison to justify a favourable response to their application for release. I have taken into account their age, their health, favourable prison and parole reports and their cooperation with West German authorities which led to the conviction of one of the principals in an international drug syndicate.

In other words, *all* of the reasons on which *all* of the previous submissions had been based and submitted for the former Attorney-General Senator Peter Durack's consideration – and that he had rejected – were now acknowledged, and accepted.

Senator Evans denied any suggestions he, or Labor, were going 'soft' on drugs. He said his decision was what any 'reasonably compassionate' attorney-general would do.

Durack sought to deflect responsibility for repeatedly choosing to keep the women imprisoned, unapologetically ignoring their requests for release on licence. On Melbourne radio on 24 March he remained remorseless and unrepentant. He told 3DB it wasn't his fault Hays and Bessire were locked up for five years. His excuse? 'I think Judge Staunton made a mistake in not fixing a non-parole period,' Durack said. He continued in *The Australian* newspaper on the same day, accusing Labor of going 'soft on drugs'.

> Just over a year ago, Senator Evans said he was disturbed by suggestions that 'unusually favourable treatment may be given to the Drug Grannies' by me. There was no basis for any such concern as I revealed by my decision last April [1982] not to release these women from prison. Senator Evans now

says that less than five years is a sufficiently lengthy period as punishment for such an horrific crime. This is barely a third of the sentence whereas a year ago, he said, at least one half should be served. Is this a new soft policy for drug offenders?

On board the flight home, the women were approached by an Australian reporter who had purchased a first-class air ticket in an attempt to secure an exclusive interview with them. Upon arrival in San Francisco, a phalanx of news reporters awaited their first steps back on mainland USA. Also on hand were Toddie's sisters – but not her two brothers – to welcome them home.

After several phone conversations with the women following their return to the United States, and six days after their arrival, my wife and I flew out to join them at the home of Beezie's sister, in the north of Washington state. We prepared to help the women relocate to La Pine and liaise with a pre-arranged *60 Minutes* crew filming their homecoming. It was an emotional greeting on our arrival as we embraced the women, free at last on their home soil.

On the first night of our reunion, Toddie and Beezie set about making dinner – roast Cornish hens and baked vegetables – and no-one else, including Beezie's sister and brother-in-law, was to lift a finger. It was, they insisted, something they wanted to own: the decision about what to eat, when to eat, with whom to eat. They were wasting no time in exercising their newfound liberty – beginning with the most basic of decisions.

Several days later we rented a self-drive moving van and loaded their effects: suitcases and boxes from their five years in jail, as well as cartons of books and household items that Beezie's sister and brother-in-law had retrieved from their home in La Pine for safekeeping during the unplanned extended absence. La Pine neighbours such as plumber Bill Tokstad set to work readying their home for immediate occupancy. He hooked up all of the water and drainage pipes, which had been disconnected since August 1977; mended a burst pipe he'd recently discovered; and helped other neighbours thoroughly clean the house. He also installed new water heater elements in the hot water service.

During the two-day drive home, Toddie and Beezie's moods fluctuated between unbridled excitement and elation to moments filled with apprehension and uncertainty about the reception they'd receive from La Pine's townsfolk. We also had to spend time planning their *60 Minutes* interview and consider where the best place would be for them to record it. They'd agreed to doing the interview in our telephone conversations before we flew to join them, but now they were home and trying to adjust to their new-found freedom, there was understandably some nervousness and apprehension. We agreed to let the visiting reporter Jana Wendt and her crew accompany the women on the last few miles of the journey to film their eventual return home. A formal interview was scheduled for a few days after they'd resettled.

Toddie and Beezie were working through a process of readjustment. On arrival in La Pine, we drove down the main street and the women immediately noticed new buildings, new business names and new houses.

While physically the town had changed, the drive through the town centre was yet another scene plucked from their dreams, the relief of being freed from prison and returning home to La Pine.

As we approached the driveway of their home, they spied yellow ribbons tied around the tall trunks of the pine trees at the entrance. Word had quickly got around that Toddie and Beezie were at last coming home. Before long, friends and neighbours began to quietly and respectfully drop by and bring the women up to date on five years' news and gossip. They couldn't have hoped for a better reception from those who cared.

'Not many people in La Pine think they were guilty, and certainly not those who knew them well,' Tokstad told an

Australian journalist in a phone interview. 'There is a feeling that the Australian government didn't really look far enough into the case.'

Over the next few days we helped Toddie and Beezie start the process of re-establishing their identities: they rented a mailbox at the local post office and applied for credit cards. We drove them to Bend to apply and take a driver's licence test. Their orange Volkswagen Fastback had remained in the garage the entire time, maintained, as was their house, by neighbours. The car was in near perfect condition. Toddie looked forward to being able to drive where and when she pleased, and was thrilled to pass her test with flying colours.

The *60 Minutes* reporter Jana Wendt – whose story aired on 1 May – described La Pine as 'a very hick town; people come straight out and tell you what they think [about the Drug Grannies]. About 60 per cent of the town said they have paid their dues and should be allowed to live out their life where they want. The rest say they are two lesbians who have been leading a scandalous life together for years.' I didn't know why observations or assumptions about the women's relationship should have had anything to do with the fact they'd clearly been betrayed by their nephew and had suffered terribly for it.

'They are very emotional ladies and very strong,' Wendt said. 'They are vitriolic about the legal system in Australia but they are still full of praise for Australians and particularly the prisoners with whom they shared the five years. I guess I shouldn't say this but I was impressed with their ignorance about what was happening [during the campervan journey], if not their innocence.'

The women's relationship was also the subject of an attack from an unnamed 'prisoner source' in a trashy Australian tabloid, the *Melbourne Truth*, who claimed on 2 April the pair had 'outraged jail inmates by openly flaunting their lesbian love'. I took little notice of the report and hoped it wasn't syndicated in the United States through the *National Enquirer* or a similar scandal sheet. These were two mature-aged if not elderly women who had been companions for more than twenty years. Was it, as some called it, a 'romantic friendship', or even a 'Boston marriage'? The nature of their relationship was none of anyone's business. It was remarkable for surviving under extreme duress, and a testament to the unwavering support and dedication they had to each other. It was accepting of the ups and downs, strengths and weaknesses they had; how complete strangers wanted to brand it was irrelevant.

By the time my wife and I were preparing to return to Australia in mid-April, I felt confident the women were on their way to resuming and reclaiming their lives. The next step was an important moment in Toddie and Beezie's readjustment. For so long I (and others) had held their hands throughout the protracted and turbulent period of their imprisonment and struggle for freedom. We'd shared ups and downs, too many disappointments, and memorable good times like birthdays, Christmases, stage performances, joke telling, and endless hours visiting in prison. Now it was time for them to put the past five years behind them.

Toddie and Beezie had learned a lot about the ill and the goodwill in humankind – the hard way. Though physically free, their minds and spirits would no doubt take longer to completely heal, but simply being home and in charge of their own destiny was a damned good start.

It also meant my life's direction would take a new turn. What began as journalistic curiosity became a passionate near four-year crusade to right what I perceived as an injustice meted out to two complete strangers. Toddie and Beezie's case was not one I was intending to champion, but they were vulnerable human beings, a long way from the home they loved and the nation they'd served. I felt they deserved better than what had been delivered after their misadventure had left them abandoned as pawns in a political chess game. I was not going to let them down. They bravely put their trust in me, and others, despite flawed attempts to secure their release from a possible 'death sentence'. I was determined to advocate for them until they walked free. With that accomplished and the pair finally settled back home, it was time to return to Australia and embrace the next phase of my life.

Returning home was an easier step for me to take than for the two women.

Toddie never set eyes on, let alone spoke to her nephew, again, and her contact with her brothers Vernon and Grover was strained and rare. She had longed for her sisters' support and love, and they continued to offer it in spades. But after the five years of her incarceration in Australia, the once remarkably tight family bond to which she once cleaved was not to be found. Beezie's sister and brother-in-law were supportive of both women and helped them in their readjustment to La Pine. The small community, however, had changed too: there were many new residents, old friends had moved away, and the Drug Grannies' infamy set tongues wagging in ways to which they'd hitherto not been subjected.

After all of my dealings with the women and their case, there was no doubt in my mind Toddie and Beezie had been completely duped and betrayed: by their nephew, by the law and justice processes, by politicians, and by the system overall. Yes, they were naive to have overlooked Vern's throwaway reference to there being 'a little grass' in the campervan when he first made the overseas holiday proposition in 1977; yes, they had been gullible to have accepted the threats that the vehicle's carnet prevented them from simply abandoning the campervan and flying home – be it from Bombay, from Hong Kong, from Sydney or wherever. Theirs was a classic case of being seduced by a too-good-to-be-true opportunity. Far too late did they discover they'd been ensnared in a global criminal enterprise. The fact a trusted family member was behind it made it all the worse.

They were innocents abroad and only now were they safely back home.

Within the Cascade Ranges in north-western Oregon and the Deschutes National Forest, the ancient caldera of the Newberry Volcano surrounds the twin Paulina and East lakes.

It was early April 1983, and the tall conifer forests surrounding the deep Paulina Lake shore gave off a heady pine fragrance. In spring, dusk was always a reliable time to be on the banks, patiently trolling lures for brown trout.

This was America the beautiful; the home of the brave and the land of the free.

Toddie and Beezie knew there was still time to catch fish and catch up on life – on their own terms and at their own pace.

EPILOGUE

It has been almost forty-five years since Toddie and Beezie left their home in La Pine for their three-month 'trip of a lifetime' at the behest of Toddie's nephew Vern Todd. As it turned out, they didn't stay long in La Pine once they were freed, for a variety of reasons including Toddie's deteriorating health, the colder Oregon weather and the changed La Pine community dynamics. Toddie's painkillers, antidepressants and sleeping pills, to which she had become addicted in prison, also had a high cost. On 17 October 1983 they sold their home and land for $USD9000 and relocated south to the sunnier and warmer climes of Yuma, Arizona, where they purchased a similar sized house in a mobile home park at the city's foothills. From there it was a 25-mile (40-kilometre) round trip to the one-stop *farmacias* and *consultorios* across the Mexican border where the women could consult with a doctor and have a script of generic pharmaceuticals dispensed for one tenth of the price in the United States. Yuma was also only a five-hour drive to Toddie's sisters' homes in Los Angeles (as opposed to the 12 hours from La Pine).

Over a drink after their return to the United States, the women admitted to me the elation they'd experienced upon release had quickly given way to the reality of their notoriety. And any reminders of their years in jail were bringing back painful memories. Now they craved anonymity and peace. Toddie said she wanted only to face the sun so the shadows would fall behind them both.

This is when I realised that, while we had become very close over those years, the figurative umbilical cord needed to be cut. It was the only way they could put Australia – and their jail ordeal – behind them and move on.

●

So where are they today?

Toddie celebrated three more birthdays and Christmases as a free woman in her beloved USA with Beezie, her family and friends before she died at the Yuma Nursing Centre on 30 April, 1986, aged 68. Her ashes are interred at the Woodlawn Cemetery in Santa Monica. Her death notice listed the American Cancer Society for donations. She was survived by all four of her siblings. Beezie was there by her side to the end.

Beezie moved to Port Angeles in Washington following Toddie's passing, to live closer to her sister and brother-in-law. I had maintained annual contact with the women and last visited Beezie with my wife and children at her new home in Washington state in 1996. She died from chronic obstructive pulmonary disease in 1998, aged eighty-two.

Vern Todd, who was never seen again by the women after fleeing from Sydney in early 1978, died in Los Angeles in 2019, reportedly suffering with Alzheimer's. A special 'wrap' party in Sydney after his passing attracted Australians who had known him in the seventies, including members of the Australian arts and film world, as well as his ex-wife and sons. He had lived overseas since 1978, evading Australian, German and US police by changing his name and identity documents. He maintained regular contact with his Australian family from the United States. Before falling ill, he owned and operated a restaurant with his second wife in Laurel Canyon in Los Angeles.

Phillip Shine (aka Bob Lange) successfully appealed his ten-year prison sentence and had his term reduced to six and a half years. Upon release from prison, he visited the German prosecutor Dr Harald Körner to personally thank him for the fair treatment he had received both at trial and in jail. He told Dr Körner he was returning to the thing he loved most: antiques.

Mr X's relationship with his wife, Mrs X, ended in the early 1980s. He was arrested three times but each time negotiated his freedom with little difficulty. He escaped first in Ibiza, then twice in Bombay: in 1979–1980, and again in early 1982. Mr X met another woman, the daughter of German diplomats, in Bonn in 1986, and they later married. He founded a tourism enterprise in 1993 which has grown to three boutique hotel properties, which he operates to this day.

Mrs X, whose mother had close connections to the Goa Freedom Movement, met her husband-to-be, Mr X, through this association. Mrs X was arrested in Germany and freed on bail in 1978. She fled to Nepal, then India and never returned for her trial. In her absence, she was convicted, with Phillip Shine, of drug smuggling. It was only after her crimes had exceeded the statute of limitations that she returned to Berlin where she lives to this day.

•

Shortly after Toddie and Beezie's release in 1983, an important issue on which the women's fate rested – the rights of Commonwealth or federal prisoners – was the subject of an address by the then chairman of the Australian Law Reform Commission (and later High Court judge), the Honourable Justice Michael Kirby. He said: 'The law governing the punishment of federal offenders needs to be reformed, and this has become obvious after the release of Vera Hays and Florice Bessire. The federal system for the early release of prisoners is the most defective one in Australia. The administrative procedures are uncertain and unfair.'

The Commonwealth law *was* eventually changed but it still remains that under section 19AG of the Crimes Act (introduced in 2004 and significantly improved in 2012), the Attorney-General is solely responsible for the release of federal offenders on parole or licence. While there is a Commonwealth Parole Office (CPO), unlike states' and territories' independent parole boards, it plays no role making actual decisions; these pronouncements can only be made by the Attorney-General (or on occasion, a senior delegate).

In December 2019, authorities in Australia seized a record-breaking haul of methamphetamine worth A$820 million hidden inside stereo speakers shipped from Thailand. One of the three convicted men (who pleaded guilty but who police considered was merely a dogsbody) was sentenced to seven years in prison with a non-parole period of four years.

The modus operandi remained the same.

The law had slightly improved.

Only the types of drugs had changed.

POSTSCRIPT

As this manuscript was being finalised for publication, a last-minute opportunity arose for me to speak to a long-time Sydney-based friend of Vern Todd's – one of only a few of Vern's old friends who did agree to speak to me. The two men had first met in Melbourne's arts circles in 1969, and the pair remained friends on and off for almost five decades – including after Vern had fled Australia. Under the alias of 'Frank Maloney', Vern relocated to Los Angeles, where he owned and operated a highly regarded Japanese restaurant in Laurel Canyon, a neighbourhood in the Santa Monica Mountains in the Hollywood Hills West district. In the 1960s, the mountainous area had become famous as the home of many of LA's top musicians and songwriters, including Frank Zappa, The Mamas and the Papas, The Byrds, Joni Mitchell and Crosby, Stills, Nash and Young.

In the course of this conversation, I learned that it apparently had never been Vern's original intention to ship the campervan with a two-tonne load of hashish secreted throughout the floor to Australia. That had simply been his Plan B. Plan A had, in fact, involved a yacht he was having built in Hong Kong. When Toddie and Beezie arrived at the end of their odyssey in Bombay, expecting to meet up with Vern and believing they had completed their journey, it was Phillip Shine (aka Bob Lange) who met them instead. He casually explained Vern could not collect the van as he was in Hong Kong seeing to a yacht he had under construction there, so he needed the women to instead accompany the van to Australia (see page 65).

In 1985 in Los Angeles, Vern (now Frank Maloney) was purchasing a new car when he serendipitously ran into his long-time Australian friend at the car yard who, as it happened, was also looking to buy a vehicle to use while chasing acting jobs in Hollywood. Now sporting a beard, Vern was easily recognisable despite having been out of touch since he fled Sydney, days before Toddie and Beezie were arrested, in 1978. With their relationship rekindled, Vern and his long-time Australian friend would occasionally board a yacht for a 48-hour voyage along the US and Mexican west coast. It was the same yacht that Vern had designed and had custom built in Hong Kong – for other purposes – but which he now had moored in the US.

Using the same approach he had adopted with the specially fitted-out campervans – with their hidden floors and converted water tanks – Vern had committed more than one hundred thousand dollars to shipbuilders designing and constructing the ocean-going yacht with large below-deck secret containers and storage cavities: sufficient space to hold several tonnes of cannabis or hashish. His Plan A was to sail the new yacht from Hong Kong to Bombay, load it up with the campervan's two tonnes of hash, and then sail on to Australia. Toddie and Beezie, as they had steadfastly maintained, had never planned to travel beyond their agreed 'trip of a lifetime' final destination of Bombay, however the yacht's construction was behind schedule. In the end, Vern hastily decided to execute a Plan B.

The rest is history.

APPENDIX 1

The Vern Todd–Phillip Shine syndicate was set up, according to West German authorities, in about 1972, although its activities didn't appear on their radar until 1977. Their standard operation was concealing consignments of hashish, originating from Pakistan and Afghanistan, then exporting the drugs around the globe. The syndicate's headquarters was based in Berlin. It had contacts throughout West Germany as well as other European destinations, and many other countries including Sweden, Australia, New Zealand and the USA.

Three members later identified as belonging to the syndicate were arrested in West Germany in 1974 and convicted of importing hash into Frankfurt. In that instance, they used six-inch-square dice in which the compressed resin was secreted. The dice were consigned as 'artefacts' from India, said to have been manufactured by crippled children in a Bombay orphanage. The dice were constructed from white plaster of Paris and it was only misfortune that one of the dice fell while being transferred from a plane at Rhein-Main Airport. The impact cracked open the plaster, drawing drug detector dogs to the secreted hashish. Narcotics detectives in West Germany discovered more packages and suitcases laden with hashish being sent to Germany from Pakistan, and also found other shipments from Bombay destined for Sweden via West Germany.

It was at this time that Mr X formally appeared on German police radar. His waist-length hair and dark skin attracted inevitable attention, especially from women. He met Mrs X in Berlin and after marrying they divided their time between Germany and the Spanish island of Ibiza until the early 1980s, 'tuning in, dropping out, living it up' (as he told the *Times of India*). He purchased his hashish to ship globally from the famous Khan clan in Peshawar.

The organisation diversified and began shipping LSD between the USA, Germany and Canada, although it was never confirmed whether Todd, Shine or Mr X had a direct hand in that enterprise.

The West Germans pinpointed three types of vehicles that the syndicate most commonly used: Renault R4 vans, and two styles of Mercedes-Benz campervan. Sometimes the vans were sold overseas after their stash was successfully unloaded, and then used for conventional purposes. The syndicate's bodywork specialists were located in Stuttgart, Berlin and Dusseldorf, although often when time was tight, unsuspecting body-shop operators were approached to fashion the special hiding places. In those instances, the excuse given was the need to store light-sensitive movie film for safari expeditions into India and Africa. It was usually Mr X or Shine who organised the work to be carried out under the guise of heading a TV documentary company.

When the West Germans sniffed out the syndicate in 1977, they suspected a large operation but didn't realise the magnitude and sophistication of what they were to find. Bank accounts, mostly in Mr X's name, held in South-East Asia and Europe showed the syndicate's conservative value was US$40 million. However, Todd was also included in bank documents, as was his signature. In addition to the headquarters in Berlin, the syndicate also owned a mansion and other properties on Ibiza.

At one stage in the West German investigations, prosecutor Dr Harald Körner travelled to Ibiza following the arrest of several of the syndicate's conspirators. Six members of the syndicate were being held in a local jail after warrants were issued in West Germany. When Körner arrived, he was to discover the power of the organisation against which he was operating. He took with him the extradition warrants for the six and presented these to Spanish justice authorities upon his arrival. When he arrived at the jail, he was told an inexplicable error by a Spanish Justice Ministry official had allowed three of the six to go free. Lawyers hired by the three men had argued with the official that the West German warrants being circulated by Interpol did not in fact apply to their clients, and the official accepted this explanation. One of the three men was Mr X.

Upon interviewing the three remaining syndicate members, Körner was told they hadn't enough money to bribe the authorities in Ibiza and so remained in jail. Körner successfully fought for the extradition of the remaining trio to West Germany where they were tried and imprisoned.

When Shine was finally arrested in Paris, Körner returned with investigators to Ibiza, where they searched Mr and Mrs X's mansion and took evidence, such as bank books, telex messages, flight schedules, phone books and photographs from the numerous albums containing snapshots of important faces and identities who comprised the syndicate.

Soon Körner accumulated fifty bulging files on the syndicate which included its letters, documents, legal papers, briefing notes and evidence to be used in court. From this compilation Körner was able to track and map almost every move the members had made in the previous five years. The syndicate's password when dealing with business partners and prospective merchants was a torn document: half of a magazine article in a letter or proffered at a meeting signalled it was safe to deal with the person.

Mr X's cover on Ibiza was to perform the role of a real estate agent. He conducted his enterprise complete with a shopfront known as Immorbiliaria Ibiza. The regular arrival of strangers to his mansion by private helicopter was therefore not considered unusual, given the nature of his business and the lifestyle of many of the rich island inhabitants.

The syndicate also employed its own counter-surveillance, and members could never be certain they weren't under their own organisation's watchful eye. This ensured total faith and dedication to Mr X, Todd and Shine, and also guaranteed that, in return, members could rely on steady incomes and a pleasant lifestyle. The mansion was the centre of attention for the syndicate when it wasn't actively organising shipments and surveilling its 'delivery' vans and cars throughout Europe, Asia and Australia. Big parties were common, held either by the pool or out on the water aboard Mr X's yacht. Underneath the mansion, German investigators discovered a storage cellar, piled high with hashish which was kept there until ready for shipment. They identified funds to pay for the syndicate's travel and operations passing through complex transactions in bank accounts traced to India, USA, Germany and Switzerland, before finally finding their way to Hong Kong and Singapore.

Photographs discovered by Körner's investigators showed Mr X's wife and their two-year-old daughter; Mr X with both long and short hair; as well as associates (whose names would later appear on charge sheets in Australia arising from their drug importations) Manfred Möller, Phillip Shine and Helmet Hanks.

Syndicate members would fly to South-East Asia and make telegraphic transfers of the funds to Europe to pay for the vans and the bodywork. While the members fulfilled a variety of roles – as accountants, legal advisers, bodywork specialists, secretaries, planners and couriers – Todd, Mr X and Shine regularly recruited unlikely looking 'mules' to act for them. Besides being brazen enough to inveigle the likes of Vera Todd Hays and Florice Bessire, they employed other unwitting tourists to travel abroad with hashish secreted in suitcases. Young students travelling as newlyweds on honeymoon was another favourite ruse. So apparently naive and blissfully in love, the couples often convinced customs officials of their bona fides when they might have otherwise been considered suspicious.

Körner, in fact, uncovered an almost identical case to that of the Drug Grannies set up by Todd, Mr X and Shine. Another elderly US couple successfully transported a van loaded with hashish, following almost the same route as Hays and Bessire, and eventually arrived in Australia. They returned to the USA undetected – at the time – although West German authorities maintain the American couple would have been apprehended if ever they had set foot on West German soil.

Once the couriers were recruited and provided with the necessary documents, Todd, Shine or Mr X would act as overseers throughout the operation, tracking from a distance to ensure their plans were executed smoothly. They flew from country to country just as they had with the Drug Grannies, although never physically handling the loads being transported. Rarely did Todd, Shine or Mr X personally approach the couriers; the Drug Grannies were the notable exception. Vern's relationship with his aunt, as well as the size of the importation, likely influenced their change in operations. It was their normal practice to employ other, lesser members of the syndicate to maintain physical contact with the couriers.

Australia was a lucrative export market. It was through Vern Todd and Phillip Shine that Mr X was to export much of his hash shipments to Sydney and Melbourne. Once the Drug Grannies were arrested, and Shine was on trial in Frankfurt, the connection throughout the world began to fall into place for Körner.

The cooperation and support he attracted from police in Australia, India, Spain, France, Switzerland, Singapore and Canada was crucial to filling in many of the questions still unsolved from his intelligence gathering. Financial institutions in many of those countries, including on Ibiza, helped him to piece together the complex financial structure of the syndicate although even as late as 1983, Körner still hadn't tracked down all of the syndicate's funds.

Körner told me, when I travelled to Frankfurt in 1982, it was unlikely he would press for extradition of the Drug Grannies once/if they were released from Australia and returned to the USA. It might be more accurate to say Körner realised American authorities would probably have refused any request on the basis of the women's earlier testimony and the severe penalty they had already paid. A new condition of an existing US–West German extradition treaty had set a high bar to reach before US authorities would agree to sending one of their citizens overseas for trial.

Körner was careful not to criticise the Australian judicial authorities, although he observed that had the women been tried in West Germany and cooperated with the authorities to the same extent, they would probably have been dealt with much less severely. He said their ill health and their roles as mere 'pawns' in the syndicate would also have been in their favour. He was, however, unconvinced the women were entirely unaware of their part in the 'holiday of a lifetime' but agreed there was never any evidence to suggest they were actively involved in any of the syndicate's operations.

The trial of Phillip Shine was a protracted and at times highly controversial affair. Securing the conviction was a success for Körner. Shine was a major cog in the Todd–Shine syndicate. He was a well-known supplier of drugs in Sydney in the late 1960s and early 1970s and associated with many of Sydney's entertainment and music industry identities. He was in great demand for the high quality of drugs he supplied. He was involved with overseas shipments of drugs in a small way at first, using the postal system until he was caught and warned by narcotics agents. It is not known why charges were never laid.

Shine's young German lawyer, Hans Euler, was a friendly but unconventional legal representative whose penchant for cannabis he did not hide. He was surprised to learn of the fourteen-year sentence handed down to the women. He believed there were far more dangerous criminals – murderers and terrorists, for example – against whom the law and the state should be acting, instead of chasing cannabis smugglers.

Naturally, Euler was bitter about the way the women's testimony against his client was secured and he hoped Shine's appeal would rule their statements as inadmissible on the basis they were 'bought'. He was, however, fearful of what might happen if the charges were dismissed and the extradition of Shine was sought by Australian authorities.

The Attorney-General's Department in Canberra maintained in 1983 it would seek Shine's extradition, although no formal treaty existed between the two countries. Shine could possibly have faced further charges of conspiring to import drugs into Australia and the prospect of a 25-year sentence had the department followed through.

'If Phillip would have to spend any more time in jail in Australia after he has already served time in West Germany, he would commit suicide I am sure before sacrificing himself to any more jail,' said Euler.

One of the more remarkable aspects of the entire enterprise is that neither Vern Todd nor Mr X ever faced a court let alone served any prison time in relation to their roles in the syndicate's operations. On one occasion when Mr X was detained on an international warrant in Bombay in 1982, he complained to the authorities about the police watch house's unhygienic conditions. He offered to pay for his own accommodation in a hotel as well as the salaries of the guards required to watch over him. He disappeared within an hour of his transfer.

There was some suspicion in Australia that Mr X and Todd were involved in another remarkable shipment of hashish, this time in steel containers that had been welded to the hulls of Australia-bound vessels leaving Bombay harbour. On 17 February 1982, two Australians and an American appeared in a Bombay court charged with attempting to smuggle drugs out of India. A Customs official told the court the three were members of an international drug syndicate and might flee if granted bail. And that is precisely what happened. The two Australians jumped bail, never to be seen again.

APPENDIX 2

The following court cases and police investigations occurred during the period of the Drug Grannies' odyssey and their incarceration covering 1977 to 1983. These examples offer insight into how the Australian justice system operated at the time. They are listed to allow readers to consider for themselves the appropriateness of Hays's and Bessire's sentences.

The Oscar-worthy case of Michael Dzialowski
On 3 January 1978, a Renault R4 sedan arrived in Adelaide after having been shipped on board the *Vivsha Bivhuti* from Bombay. Its owner, it was later revealed in court, had driven it from Frankfurt to Bombay and arrived in Australia to take delivery of it for an 'Australian holiday'. The man driving it was 33-year-old student Michael Dzialowski, whose brother-in-law was a resident of Sydney. Dzialowski travelled on an Israeli passport. He came from a well-respected Jewish family residing in Germany. When Dzialowski appeared in the Port Adelaide Magistrate's Court on 24 January, he was charged with possessing and importing a prohibited drug on 3 January after Narcotics Bureau agents followed the car through South Australia and arrested Dzialowski in Waikerie on 9 January.

The prosecutor, JP Colton of the Crown Law Solicitor's Department, gave evidence that Dzialowski had told Narcotics

Bureau agents he was to be given $10,000 upon delivery of the van to Sydney. The load of cannabis resin was secreted in a compartment behind the front seat, measuring 1.2 metres (47 inches) by 70 centimetres (28 inches) by 15 centimetres (6 inches). The 95-kilogram stash of hashish was in thick blocks, wrapped in light-coloured adhesive tape and sealed inside plastic bags. Some of the blocks in Dzialowski's $3 million shipment were carefully cut into small wedge-shaped pieces to take up every available inch of space in the specially framed compartment. They were identical to the hashish packages found in the Drug Grannies' campervan.

When the case first went to court on 24 January, Dzialowski's name, address and details of the charge were suppressed by order of the magistrate so as not to endanger bureau investigations of the Drug Grannies and several others. Dzialowski's performance in court was deserving of an Oscar. Peter Waye appearing for Dzialowski told the court his client had lost his speech because of the shock of finding the drugs in his car.

'His emotional condition is quite genuine,' Waye told the court. During proceedings, Dzialowski passed notes to his lawyer.

'He has had speech difficulties since he was a child and the shock of drugs in his car caused him to lose the power of speech,' said Waye. 'He can speak and write some English and was able to be interrogated by police.' In applying for bail, Waye said his client required urgent psychiatric treatment to regain his speech and offered to find accommodation for him. The prosecutor, mindful of the fact that more than one hundred drug offenders on bail had absconded since 1974, protested strongly. The magistrate decided on allowing bail of $5000 and two sureties of $5000 each in cash.

Considering Dzialowski knew few people in Adelaide and was unlikely to make friends quickly, the bail provisions were appropriate. The case was adjourned and finally, on 12 August 1978, a jury convicted Dzialowski in the Supreme Court of

Adelaide of possessing and importing the hashish. Dzialowski slowly crumpled in the dock after the verdict and fainted. He remained in a state of collapse in the dock for almost twenty minutes with two prison officers in attendance while his counsel made submissions on mitigation of penalty. Shortly after the court was adjourned, Dzialowski again collapsed and prison officers called an ambulance when no pulse could be found.

On 30 September, Dzialowski was sentenced to seven years' prison, but after psychiatric evidence was offered, a seven-and-a-half-month non-parole period was set. In April 1979 Dzialowski was extradited to Israel.

The case of Helmut Hanke

Almost three weeks after Dzialowski's arrest, Helmut Detlef Hanke, a 36-year-old advertising agent/salesman of Bad Homburg, appeared in court in Sydney charged with importing cannabis resin in a Renault R4 car which Narcotics Bureau agents alleged arrived from Bombay by ship in Melbourne on 9 January. Hanke, it was alleged in Central Court, had taken delivery of the motor vehicle in Melbourne after staying with an associate in Sydney, and then began driving the vehicle to its destination in Woollahra.

The prosecutor Greg Smith told the court:

When apprehended, Hanke had an airline ticket to Frankfurt and was due to leave 20 January.

In the last six months we have found a substantial number of German residents involved in the importation of cannabis resin. In the situation where overseas people are involved they have a tendency to flee on bail. Our experience of this matter when people are on even $30,000 bail, they will flee and leave private property worth much more behind. The onus is very heavily passed onto the shoulders of the defendant in these matters to have a reasonable excuse showing no involvement.

Hanke had been arrested in Sydney allegedly trying to flee the country. He told the court he could not understand the charges as his English was not good enough. Hanke allegedly admitted to the Narcotics Bureau agents the Renault was his vehicle and that he had made shipping arrangements for it from Bombay to Melbourne, but he claimed he did not know the cannabis resin was in the car.

Bail was subsequently refused and the case adjourned to the Special Federal Court for further hearing. A German interpreter was ordered for the next hearing on 23 January. When the case finally came to trial, in the Melbourne County Court where the vehicle had been imported, a jury acquitted Hanke of having knowingly imported the eighty kilograms of hashish valued at about $2 million.

Returning to West Germany, wearing a beard to avoid detection and carrying false documents, Hanke was arrested at Frankfurt Airport, and under West German law, which ignored the prospect of double jeopardy, he was charged with conspiracy to export drugs and sentenced to four years' imprisonment. He faced a ten-year term but owing to his testimony against the organisation, his sentence was reduced.

The case of Möller and Püppelmann

On 1 May 1978, Manfred Möller, aged thirty, and Werner Püppelmann, aged thirty-two, both West German nationals, were charged with importing and possessing cannabis resin found in a short-wheelbase Mercedes-Benz shipped from Bombay to Sydney. They appeared before the District Court in Sydney. Their lawyer argued that information provided by the Narcotics Bureau agents attested to an importation of forty kilograms of hashish – about $1 million worth, and yet only two or three kilograms were actually ever produced as evidence. It was a technical argument, but sufficient to win an important point in the accused's defence. Both men pleaded guilty to the new charges which were laid as a result of the lawyer's argument and Möller was sentenced to three and a half years' imprisonment with an eighteen-month non-parole period, while Werner Püppelmann was acquitted and returned to West Germany almost immediately. Upon arrival home, Püppelmann was arrested to face further drug charges.

The case of Donald Tait

Donald Roy Tait was a professional drug smuggler whose Cessna aircraft crash-landed in the Northern Territory near Katherine in January 1978, carrying a $3.5-million load of marijuana. Tait was sentenced to six years and eight months' jail, with a non-parole period that would see him released by 1981. The *Daily Telegraph* opined in its editorial of 4 May:

> Donald Roy Tait, pirate and professional drug smuggler has for his crimes been sent to prison for six years and eight months. With remission this man who knew exactly the risk he was taking could be back in circulation in less than three years. Yet two grandmothers from Oregon, while no less guilty than Tait and who showed themselves to be both gullible and amateurish by allowing themselves to be set up by professionals, receive sentences of 14 years' jail. As the details published show, there seems to be very little consistency and certainly no uniformity in the penalties meted out to drug offenders. Somehow a balance must be achieved which will deter the amateur drug smugglers and at the same time deter and heavily punish the professionals who know very well the risks they are running for the sake of huge profits.

The Sydney *Sun* on the same day in its editorial echoed the *Telegraph*'s call:

> One of the expectations which must flow from efforts to break illegal drug trade is that offenders will be severely punished.

Yet Donald Tait, a professional drug runner has only to serve two years and nine months in jail before being eligible for parole. He could be flying again while the two drug running Grannies – gullible amateurs – still have 11 years to serve with no parole so far being mentioned. That kind of inconsistency tends to bring our legal system into disrepute. Some measure of uniformity in punishment is needed if the public is to continue to support official efforts to beat drug crime.

On appeal by the Crown, Tait's sentence was increased to eight years and eight months and a non-parole period of four years and four months was imposed. Unknown to most people and only recently uncovered, Tait had been funded by the Vern Todd organisation on several previous trips, and this one was another Todd-backed job.

The case of the Olympic star

On 9 October 1978, Murray Stewart Riley, Olympic bronze medallist and eighteen-year veteran of the police force, was sentenced to ten years' imprisonment for his role in the importation of 4.6 tonnes of cannabis, valued at up to $50 million, on board a yacht.

The charge Riley and his associates faced resulted from months of painstaking detective work by the New South Wales Crime Intelligence Unit, the Drug Squad, and the Federal Narcotics Bureau, which received a tip-off from a disgruntled criminal figure in the Sydney underworld. The planning for the drug run of the yacht *Anoa* began four months before the yacht sailed from New Zealand bound for South-East Asia in February 1978. But the endeavour eventually came unstuck, leading to the arrest and court appearances of Riley and others.

In September 1978, Riley pleaded guilty to conspiring to import cannabis into Australia and appeared in the same NSW District Court as the two Drug Grannies, but his case was heard before Judge Torrington. To say Riley was treated with remarkable empathy by the court is an understatement. The police prosecutor who presented Riley's antecedents merely emphasised his Queen's commendation for bravery in 1956, his Olympic medal, and several other medals for Australia in sporting events.

The sergeant stated: 'The prisoner is very health conscious. He is fastidious about his diet and has been a keen jogger for many years.' More startling was the prosecutor's statement that Riley was in fact only a 'transport agent' for the 4.6-tonne shipment. This was Riley's uncorroborated statement and nothing more, yet it was being endorsed by the prosecution.

Unfortunately, both the judge and the prosecutor seemed entirely unaware of Riley's antecedents and the numerous references in royal commissions and police intelligence reports detailing his insidious background in organised crime.

When Judge Torrington came to pass sentence, he commented: 'Weighing these matters, particularly the plea of guilty, together with his earlier achievements in life, including the sporting achievements, I have come to the conclusion that I should order a minimum period of imprisonment.'

Riley ended up with a ten-year sentence for his role in the *Anoa* drug shipment, with parole possible after five years.

As the *Sydney Morning Herald*'s chief reporter, Evan Whitton, commented in a story about Riley a few years later: 'Riley's was a light sentence compared with the 14 years awarded by another New South Wales court to two American grandmothers for a lesser amount of cannabis smuggling.'

In September 1980, Riley was sentenced to a further five-year prison sentence for conspiring to defraud American Express, and two years for forging a passport application, both sentences to be served concurrently. Riley died in 2020, aged ninety-four, on the Gold Coast.

The case of Lawrence Lamond

One of Riley's associates, Lawrence Roy Lamond, appeared in the NSW District Court on 1 December 1978, charged with possession of a prohibited import, cannabis, in the form of Buddha sticks. In evidence, police detailed how Lamond had been engaged to drive a large truck to the *Anoa* and take delivery on the night of 9 June 1978 of 2.73 tonnes of cannabis. After evidence was placed before the court and Lamond's defence was presented by his barrister, the sentence was delivered, again by Judge Torrington, on 4 December 1978.

Said the judge in his sentencing:

> I had the impression, and the strong impression at the time, that I was not convinced that you were correct when you said you believe that these men were smuggling incense. 2.73 tonnes of it filled a large pantechnicon ... I have never heard of smoking incense yet, and I do not think for one minute you really believed that was incense ... one has only to look, not at the size by weight of 2.73 tonnes, but the pictures of the large pantechnicon and your utility laden with drugs to see what a huge enterprise it was ... the sentence in some respect will be a compromise in that one has to bear in mind the need to deter others ... I sentence you to be imprisoned with hard labour for six years. I specify a non-parole period of two years and ten months.

The case of Kenneth Derley

The next case to raise the ire of those critical of the Drug Grannies' sentence was that of another Murray Riley associate who was believed to be his right-hand man in the *Anoa* operation. Kenneth Robert Derley, described as a car salesman but with a record for burglary, theft, malicious injury, wounding, and numerous drink-driving offences, appeared before Judge Torrington in the NSW District Court charged with conspiring to import 4.6 tonnes of cannabis.

Kevin Murray, representing Derley, succeeded in making the point that his client's intellectual ability would not have enabled him to conspire to any great extent in planning the shipment –

'that he was a labourer and the whole scheme was probably beyond his ability'.

Derley's probation report submitted in court attested to the accused's difficulty 'in adjusting to the requirements of society so far as honesty and self-control were concerned'. When Judge Torrington sentenced Derley, he commented in his judgement:

> The crime is probably one of the largest drug crimes in the history of the Australian drug scene ... it is one of the worst possible crimes that could have been committed in smuggling drugs into Australia ... it is clear Riley engaged you and you were acting under his direction in a lesser capacity ... you were on parole at the time of committing this offence ... after considering your age ... I have come to the conclusion that I should give you the opportunity to have parole ... the crime is so great I have weighed very carefully as to whether there can be any other sentence other than that of 10 years. However your part in it is subsidiary ... I sentence you to be imprisoned with hard labour for eight and a half years. I order that there be a minimum sentence of three years and ten months.

The case of the false Buddha sticks

In March 1979, police seized hash valued at $1.5 million when they stopped a car and then raided a home in the Sydney suburb of Lane Cove. The accused – two businessmen, one an American – appeared before the notorious and later convicted criminal and discredited Chief Stipendiary Magistrate Murray Farquhar. This was how the *Sun-Herald* reported that case on 1 July 1979:

> The Sydney police force is still buzzing about the last major drug case handled by now retired Chief Stipendiary Magistrate, Murray Farquhar. The day before he retired, Mr. Farquhar released on a bond, an American, Roy Bowers

Cessna, involved in a drug seizure originally described as being valued at $1.5 million. Cessna was found in possession of more than 140 parcels of Buddha sticks ... when the case came to court, the figure of $1.5 million was removed from the charge sheet because an analyst's report showed the content of the crucial ingredient to be less than 3 per cent, a fact which reduced the street value. Under the law, the maximum charge would have been 10 years upon conviction. Had it been over the 3 per cent, the maximum was 15 years. Cessna was charged along with Timothy Milner who claimed in evidence that Cessna was unaware that the Buddha sticks were in the trunks found in the car in which he was travelling. Milner, who admitted that he wanted to sell the Buddha sticks was given a sentence of 18 months. Considering the quantity involved, the two men appear to have got off lightly compared to other penalties for similar offences.

The case of Romanus Fidler

On 2 June 1979 an American involved in an elaborate marijuana-smuggling syndicate which used specially fashioned suitcases to transport their loads from Bangkok as part of the Moylan mob, appeared before Judge Hicks in the NSW District Court. Raymond Romanus Fidler, thirty-four, and travelling on an American passport, was sentenced to five and a half years' imprisonment for conspiring to import cannabis. A non-parole period was imposed, enabling Fidler the opportunity to be released by March 1981. He barely served twenty months for his crime.

The case of Tusch and Hemberger

And finally, only nine weeks before the Drug Grannies were released on licence after more than five years' imprisonment, West German tourists Eberhard Erwen Tusch, 25, and his 29-year-old girlfriend Winfred Anton Hemberger were arrested in Melbourne.

They were importing a Mercedes-Benz campervan.

It was full of hashish. Sound familiar?

They told the Supreme Court in Melbourne during preliminary hearings they had been approached by a man in India who offered them $10,000 to bring the van to Australia.

There's one born every minute.

ACKNOWLEDGEMENTS

This book, documenting the case of the 'Drug Grannies', which led me into a fight for justice during my twenties, required a lot of support to bring to fruition almost forty-five years later. My thanks go to all those who helped along the way.

It was finally brought to light by my publisher – Sophie Hamley. She recognised that not only was this an incredible tale of family, deceit and betrayal, but an important marker in Australian history, given the issues it covers including Australia's attitude to drugs (and specifically cannabis in this case), the role of the law (with deep-seated corruption seemingly tolerated in policing, the judiciary and even parts of the legal fraternity) and politics.

In addition to Sophie, who has been an absolute rock with her patience and good humour, the rest of the Hachette team – Louise Adler, Emma Rafferty, Chrysoula Aiello, Meaghan Amor, Emma Dorph, Ailie Springall, Sharon Mo, Jenny Topham, Giovanna Nunziato, Lidija Tembeleski and Chloe Honnef – has been incredibly helpful and professional.

An important special mention is also due to my very approachable, unfailingly helpful and reliable media lawyer Michael Easton (www.michaeleaston.net.au/) for his guidance and counsel along a path which I had never before ventured.

The idea to dig out the old documents, manuscripts, photos, newspapers, cassettes and videotapes from 1977–1983 – part of an original project Lance Reynolds supported – came from film producer Bill Leimbach. He'd approached me in early 2021 to ask if I was the journalist who had once been involved in campaigning for the Drug Grannies, and whether I would talk to him about it. He'd been unaware of the story until a colleague had recently mentioned it over coffee.

COVID lockdowns and decluttering imperatives helped motivate me to delve into old trunks, and the story came to see the light of day again. Bill's scriptwriter, Sarah Smith, and fellow producer Brian Thomson offered constructive feedback and encouragement on the manuscript in its development.

The former narcotics agent Michele Khoury I have known since the time I first met Toddie and Beezie in 1979. Michele, or 'Miche', was still involved in narcotics investigations as an intelligence analyst after the disbanding of the Federal Bureau of Narcotics when we first spoke, and she struck me as an empathetic and genuine woman who recognised the Drug Grannies were betrayed – by everyone. She recognised they were mere pawns in a much bigger game. She has supported my telling this story and has been an excellent fact-checker while bringing a genuine insider's insights based on her undercover deployments leading to the arrest and conviction of Toddie and Beezie.

US editors, publishers, photographers and PR executives have been cooperative approving the use of materials originally created and/or published by their predecessors and I thank them: Steve Boyer, formerly a *Bend Bulletin* photographer; Gerry O'Brien, *Bend Bulletin* editor; Dean Guernsey, *Bend Bulletin* photographer; Therese Bottomly, Editor, *The Oregonian*; Valerie Nelson, *LA Times*; Erin Calhoun, Showtime Networks; and Larry McCallister, Paramount Pictures.

Toddie and Beezie's family, friends, neighbours and others who are no longer alive were all stitches in my tapestry of research. The La Pine residents who knew the women in the 1970s and who spoke to me recently – Nancy Carter, Carol

Brewer and Brian Earls – were most generous with their time, as were Beezie's relatives Alma Wright, the late Bob Wright, Michael Wright and Suzan Powell.

In Europe, researchers, translators and legal professionals all played a role – right from the early 1980s – getting to the bottom of the Todd–Shine global drug network as its activities were investigated by police and the participants prosecuted in the courts. Thank you to Günter Schlothauer, Peter Brendle, Elke Kößling, Dr. Harald Hans Körner, Phillip Shine and his lawyer Hans Euler.

It was good to renew acquaintances with former Norma Parker Centre deputy superintendent Shirley Goodfellow after many years. Shirley confirmed the stories from the women's prison diaries, and with her husband, Keith, graciously invited me into their home during my research. Likewise, the former Attorney-General who released the women, Professor the Hon Gareth Evans AC QC, was generous with his time and his recollections of one of the first decisions he made when Labor came to power under Prime Minister Bob Hawke in March 1983.

Research, picture selection advice and publishing insights from Jennifer Heward, Andrew Parsons, Dario Postai and Simon Rosentool were exceptionally valuable, as was digitisation assistance from PhotoAccess (photoaccess.org.au) and its highly capable staff of Wouter Van de Voorde, Greg Stoodley and Caitlin Seymour-King.

Journalists and media operatives I would like to thank and with whom I have either worked or in some way engaged in writing this book include Caroline Jones, Louise Milligan, Michelle Rayner, James Vyver, Nick McKenzie, John Sylvester, Natalie Zizic, Trudy Biernat, Anastasia Symeonides, Adam Weiner and the Australian Federal Police's Gabrielle Knowles.

Former law enforcement and narcotics agents who helped me put missing parts of the puzzle together and without whom this would not have been as complete a story include Bernard

(Bernie) Delaney, John Shobbrook (and his especially prescient book *Operation Jungle* about his time as a federal narc, from UQP) and narcotics intelligence analyst John Howard.

My long-time old-timer ice hockey buddy Don deserves special mention. He has heard this story told and retold for decades now, especially when new members of our team have joined us on road trips; and post-game debriefing invariably leads to storytelling around the locker room. He has urged me for at least ten years now to 'write the book' about the Drug Grannies because 'no-one else knows the inside story like you'. So, Don, here is the book.

My grandmother and mother taught me from a young age to always ask questions, especially 'why?' and 'why not?', so I credit them for my passion for good journalism and even better stories.

To my children and their families, your input, suggestions and being a cheer squad for this homework assignment confirmed for me how important it is that this story is told.

Finally, everything has been made possible due to the constant support and assistance, at every level, by my wonderful wife, who lived much of this story with me as it transpired.

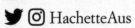

AUSTRALIA

If you would like to find out more about
Hachette Australia, our authors, upcoming events
and new releases you can visit our website or our
social media channels:

hachette.com.au

HachetteAustralia

HachetteAus